TEACHER EDITION
Contents

SECTION 3: TOMATOES

STUDENT EDITION

ACKNOWLEDGMENTS

Garden Genetics is the result of collaborative effort between Cornell scientists, science educators, and high school and middle school science teachers. Without all their input, the project would never have come to fruition.

The cucumber chapters and activities are based on plant breeding laboratory exercises developed by Cornell University Professor Emeritus Henry Munger, using the Marketmore cucumber varieties that he bred. These activities had further scientific input from Cornell scientists Rebecca Smyth and Martha Mutschler. Tim Setter, Vern Gracen, T. Clint Nesbitt, and Dan Ardia provided scientific input and review of the corn chapters. Theresa Fulton and Yolanda Cruz were involved with the scientific design and review of the tomato chapters.

Science education specialists Linda Tompkins, Nancy Trautmann, and Leanne Avery all provided important pedagogical insights and help to design chapter and activity formats. Activities 5 and 6 were designed in partnership with Ithaca High School teacher Nicole Benenati. Teachers at Cornell Institute for Biotechnology (CIBT) and Amherst College Genomics workshops reviewed the activities. The chapters and activities were piloted in the classrooms of Pete Saracino, Thea Martin, Ellen Garcia, Nicole Benenati, Karen Taylor, Teresa Gable, John Fiori, Mary Galliher, and Margaret Brazwell.

The pen and ink drawings that appear in *Garden Genetics* were drawn by Gillian Dorfman. The book was produced by NSTA Press and included participation by director Claire Reinburg, project editor Andrew Cocke, production director Catherine Lorrain, and art director Will Thomas, Jr.

The book was developed while the first author was a fellow in the Cornell Science Interns Partnership Program, with support from the National Science Foundation Graduate Teaching Fellows in K–12 Education Program (DUE #0231913; PI: M. Krasny, co-PI:N. Trautmann) and the College of Agriculture and Life Sciences at Cornell University.

Finally, we thank our families for their support in spite of corn plants growing under the bathroom sink and for their tolerance of the extra hours we put in to bring the project to completion.

INTRODUCTION TO GARDEN GENETICS
Teacher Edition

Why Garden Genetics?

Garden Genetics uses a series of inquiry activities and experiments to teach both traditional and cutting-edge genetics. Throughout the text and activities, connections are made between genetics, evolution, ecology, and plant biology. The activities are targeted for use in grade 9–12 biology classes with students of all levels. Many of the activities are also suitable for middle school science classes. *Garden Genetics* is designed to supplement and enhance the content normally taught in biology classes.

Why *Garden Genetics*? Presenting science in a way that is meaningful to students can be challenging. What better way than to present science in the context of familiar foods? The readings and activities in *Garden Genetics* focus on cucumbers, corn, and tomatoes. They also address issues students are hearing about in the media—like the environmental and social impacts of genetically engineered food plants.

How does *Garden Genetics* present genetic concepts in ways that are new and exciting to students? To learn about Punnett's squares, students taste variations in bitterness of cucumber seedlings and trace these differences back to the parental generations. Students then go on to design and conduct experiments investigating the surprising role that bitterness plays in protecting cucumber plants from insect predation. To learn about the genetics of plant breeding, students re-enact a trial in which farmers sued seed companies to compensate for one billion dollars of U.S. corn crop losses caused by genetic uniformity. Other examples of student activities include creating geographic maps of the origin of food plants and genetic maps of economically important traits like tomato color.

Garden Genetics is designed to be used flexibly in different classroom settings. Each chapter can be used as a separate, stand-alone unit. Alternatively, because each chapter explicitly emphasizes connections to subjects in other chapters, teachers can use multiple chapters or the whole book. In this way, students will gain a more complete understanding of genetics and its connections to other biological disciplines (evolution, ecology, and plant science). The activities utilize a variety of formats, from guided worksheets to open-ended inquiry. The experiments involve working with young plants and thus are relatively short in duration. Suggestions for more in-depth inquiry are included in various chapters.

The activities in *Garden Genetics* were developed by Dr. Elizabeth Rice working hand-in-hand with high school and middle school science teachers. At the time, Dr. Rice was completing her PhD on genetic conservation of corn. She was also a National Science Foundation Graduate Teaching Fellow in K–12 Education (GK–12 Fellow) at Cornell University (see *http://csip.cornell.edu* for other curricula developed by the Cornell GK–12 Fellows). She was assisted in writing this manual by Dr. Marianne Krasny, a Cornell professor of natural resources and director of the Cornell GK–12 program, and Dr. Margaret Smith, a Cornell professor of plant breeding and genetics.

Content

Garden Genetics not only includes innovative content at the cutting edge of biology, but also emphasizes the thinking, problem-solving, and inquiry-based skills increasingly demanded in biology classes today. Its chapters can be divided into three sections focusing on cucumbers, corn, and tomatoes.

Section 1: Cucumbers

Chapter 1, *"It Skips a Generation": Traits, Genes, and Crosses*, begins with Mendelian genetics and applies an understanding of genetics to hybrid cucumbers. In the first activity, students taste cucumber cotyledons and use Punnett's squares to deduce the bitterness of parental generations. In Chapter 2, *Bitterness and Non-Bitterness in Cucumbers: A Story of Mutation*, students explore the history of the bitter gene in cucumbers, which was found in a genebank and traded internationally between cucumber breeders. The students then explore transcription, translation, and the DNA basis for different types of mutations. The activity uses one of the modern tools of genomics—sequences from the GenBank public database—to explore mutation of cucumber genes. In Chapter 3, *Survival Strategies*, students learn about generalist and specialist strategies of insect predation on plants. Students design and implement experiments exploring the relationship of cucumber bitter genes to a predator, the cucumber beetle. Contrary to student expectations, the beetles choose to eat the bitter plants. As students wrestle with this seemingly incongruous finding, they learn valuable lessons about ecology, evolution, and the process of science.

Section 2: Corn

In Chapter 4, *Domestication: Evolving Toward Home*, students follow the fascinating discoveries of scientists studying the origins of corn to learn about domestication—a particular form of evolution. In the associated activity, students use archeological and genetic evidence to explore the timescale of evolution. By examining photos of archeological samples, students discover that corn has had both periods of rapid change consistent with the theory of punctuated equilibrium, as well as slow cumulative changes associated with gradualism. Chapter 5, *The Risks of Improvement: Genetic Uniformity and an Epidemic*, explores the important role of genetic diversity in crops. Using hybrid corn as an example, the text discusses artificial selection and the genetic narrowing that accompanies improvement in traits like yield, as well as explores the ecological and evolutionary consequences of genetic uniformity in crops. In the activity, students re-enact a class-action lawsuit from the 1970s in which farmers sued corn seed companies because of an epidemic caused by lack of genetic diversity.

The series of chapters on corn continues with an exploration of the DNA basis for genetically engineered Bt corn, as well as a discussion of unintended consequences and regulatory issues associated with genetically engineered corn (Chapter 6, *Genetic Engineering*). In the Chapter 6 activity, students hold a congressional hearing and write a short informed opinion paper about the basis of the testimony they have heard. A discussion of corn would not be complete without exploring sweet corn and its genetic basis (Chapter 7, *Sweet Genes in Corn*). In this chapter, students embark on a mouth-watering exploration of the biochemical pathways that lead to conversion of sugars into starches in sweet corn and then design their own experiment to test the effect of seed reserves on germination and seedling growth using starchy, sweet, and super-sweet corn seeds.

Section 3: Tomatoes

Building on the lessons from bitter cucumbers and sweet corn, students turn to tasty tomatoes in the last two chapters. Chapter 8, *Centers of Diversity*, discusses genetic diversity in relation to geographic centers of origin of crop plants. Students use graphs and world maps to understand which biomes have been the most important sources for annual and perennial plants. In the final chapter (Chapter 9, *Quantitative Traits*) students learn about quantitative trait loci (QTL) studies to examine tomato fruit size. In the activity, students use recently published data to create a genetic chromosome map of regions associated with red color in tomato. They then explore the connection between DNA and blockage of biochemical pathways by comparing their QTL map to the genetic locations of color mutations (such as those found in tangerine tomatoes).

Together the chapters present a unique way of looking at food and agriculture—one that applies textbook concepts in an exciting, innovative, and interesting context. We hope you and your students will enjoy this exploration of genetics, evolution, ecology, and plant biology—along with tasty vegetables and healthy learning!

How to Use This Book

For your convenience, this teacher edition is bound with the full student edition. The teacher edition includes specific teacher notes before each activity, giving tips, warnings, and optional directions for using the activities to spur further inquiry in the classroom. The teacher edition provides the answers to the activity questions (in italics), along with special items to note as the students carry out each activity.

SC_i_**LINKS**®
THE WORLD'S A CLICK AWAY

How can you avoid searching hundreds of science websites to locate the best sources of information on a given topic? SciLinks, created and maintained by the National Science Teachers Association (NSTA), has the answer.

In a SciLinked text, such as this one, you'll find a logo and keyword near a concept, a URL (_www.scilinks.org_), and a keyword code. Simply go to the SciLinks website, type in the code, and receive an annotated listing of as many as 15 web pages—all of which have gone through an extensive review process conducted by a team of science educators. SciLinks is your best source of pertinent, trustworthy internet links on subjects from astronomy to zoology.

Need more information? Take a tour—_www.scilinks.org/tour/_

SECTION I
Cucumbers

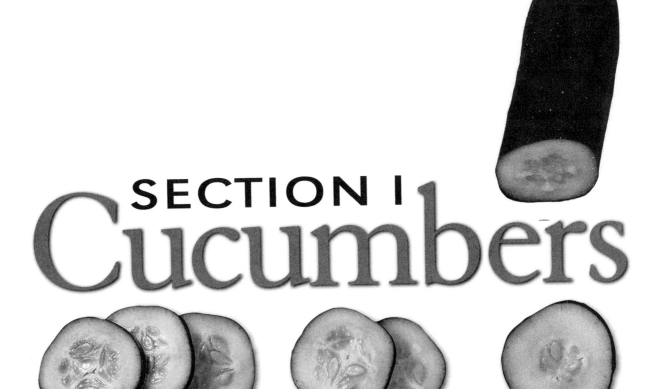

"IT SKIPS A GENERATION"

Traits, Genes, and Crosses

Long before they understood why the strategy worked, farmers knew how to crossbreed plants to obtain more desirable traits. Even today, a farmer who knows nothing about genetics can tell you that when a blue type of corn crosses with a yellow one, the offspring are blue. However, the farmer might add, if you cross a corn plant with small ears with a large-eared one, the offspring will have ears that are intermediate in size. Without any knowledge of genetics, the farmer has just told you a great deal about how the genes for blue color and for ear size work.

Gregor Mendel, an Austrian monk often described as the "father of genetics," worked with pea plants in the 1860s to understand how traits are passed from one generation to the next. Mendel made his discoveries by making crosses between **true-breeding** pea plant populations with different characteristics and keeping careful track of the characteristics of their offspring. Sometimes, when he transferred pollen from one tall plant to another tall plant (like in the cross shown in the F1 generation of Figure 1.1), some of the offspring were tall but some also were short. Where was this shortness coming from, if not from the parental populations?

"It skips a generation"—the shortness was coming from the grandparental populations. Shortness, the **recessive trait**, was masked by the tall **dominant trait** in the "**hybrid**" or F1 generation. In essence, the shortness was hidden because of sexual recombination. Each offspring receives one copy of a gene from its mother and one from its father. In this way, gene combinations are shuffled with every generation and new types may appear.

Many of the early discoveries in genetics occurred in plants. Plants have a few special characteristics that make them ideal for studying genetics. From one known cross, many genetically similar "siblings" are produced. Pea pods, like the ones Mendel worked with, produce about five peas, and a cucumber has hundreds of seeds. Furthermore,

A tall plant population that has all tall offspring (when crossed with itself or another tall population) is **true-breeding**.

A **recessive trait** is not expressed unless two copies of a gene are present. A single copy of a recessive gene is "hidden" by the presence of a **dominant trait**.

SciLINKS.
THE WORLD'S A CLICK AWAY

Topic: Gregor Mendel
Go to: *www.sciLINKS.org*
Code: GG01

Topic: Dominant and Recessive Traits
Code: GG02

Figure 1.1. Crossing Generations. When plant breeders make crosses between plants, they talk about the parental (P), hybrid (F1), and segregating (F2) generations.

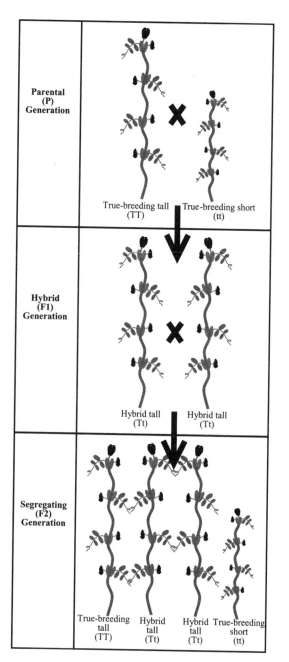

some plants (but not all) have the remarkable capability of being able to fertilize their own flowers. This means that the same plant can be both the male and female parent of a seed. Therefore, scientists can easily and naturally create whole populations of genetically identical individuals.

The cross in Figure 1.1 resulted from two true-breeding individuals. The F1 generation would have contained 5–10 seeds that were genetically identical to one another for the alleles that determine height (all had the Tt alleles). To make the F2 generation, Mendel had two options: He could self-pollinate the plants, or he could cross two different individuals of the F1 generation. Regardless of which method he used, in the F2 generation, the individuals would not all be genetically identical!

HYBRID CORN AND SEGREGATION OF TRAITS

Why do seed companies like Dekalb and Pioneer make corn seed, when farmers already have seed they can plant?

The key lies in a concept called hybrid vigor. It's a phenomenon that scientists still don't fully understand, and accounts for most of the increased harvest from farmers' fields since the 1920s. The process works like this: A corn breeder takes two very different, true-breeding types of corn as parents. When the corn breeder makes a cross between the right two corn types, the F1 generation, called the **hybrid** generation, can have a 30% gain in yield compared to the parents. To a farmer, this translates into 30% more money in his or her pocket.

So why would a farmer ever have to buy expensive, new seed again? The corn plant makes seed for the next generation. However, what happens in the F2 generation? Traits begin to segregate, meaning that at all the plant's genes, AA, aa, and Aa genotypes are possible, instead of the uniform Aa in the hybrid generation. As segregation happens, the yield advantage disappears. This can mean 30% less money in the farmer's pocket—a powerful incentive to keep buying hybrid seed.

From the company's perspective, if people are willing to keep buying seed, the company will keep producing new varieties. Thus, the segregation of traits contains the key to an entire seed industry!

Mendelian and quantitative traits

Bitterness in cucumbers is a Mendelian trait, meaning that it is controlled by a single gene—just like the traits that Mendel studied in peas (round versus wrinkled, or yellow versus green). Mendelian traits are also sometimes called **single-gene traits**, or traits under simple genetic control. With a single-gene trait, inheritance and behavior are fairly easy to understand.

Many traits, like yield, flowering time, plant height, and color, are more complex and are controlled by multiple genes. These complex traits are called **quantitative traits**. Table 1.1 has examples of both Mendelian and quantitative traits. Note that some traits like plant height can be both Mendelian and quantitative. For example, plant height in normal plants is influenced by many genes. However, in plants with dwarfing genes, plant height behaves as a Mendelian trait. In essence, a single dwarfing gene overrules the otherwise quantitative trait of plant height. Table 1.1 also shows the abbreviations that scientists often give single gene mutations, like "dw1" for a dwarfing gene or "y" for a yellow gene.

A **Mendelian** or **single-gene trait** is controlled by a single gene.

Quantitative traits are controlled by many genes.

SCi LINKS.
THE WORLD'S A CLICK AWAY

Topic: Mendel's Laws
Go to: *www.sciLINKS.org*
Code: GG03

Topic: Explore Mendelian Genetics
Code: GG04

Table 1.1. Mendelian and quantitative traits.

	Mendelian (single-gene)	**Quantitative** (multi-gene)
Cucumber	Spiny—controls the production of small spines on the fruit, producing a prickly cucumber.	
	Bushy—controls whether the plant grows as a bush or as a vine.	
Tomato		Fruit size—About 12 genes control fruit size by impacting characteristics like cell division in the fruit and growth hormones.
Corn	Dwarf (dw1)—controls the production of gibberellin, a plant hormone responsible for vertical growth.	Plant height—More than 20 genes are important in plant height in corn.
	Yellow (y)—controls whether a kernel is yellow or white.	Kernel color—Many genes modify exactly what shade of yellow a corn kernel will be, from canary yellow to a pale cream.
		Yield—The most important trait of all is influenced by dozens of genes that affect things like number of rows on an ear, number of kernels, kernel size, kernel density, and plant tolerance of competition in a field.

Questions for further thought

<u>Evolution</u>: What evolutionary advantage might reshuffling genes, caused by sexual reproduction, give to a new generation of plants?

> *Reshuffling genes leads to genetic flexibility (i.e., new gene combinations that allow populations to respond to changing environmental conditions).*

What disadvantages could it have?

> *Reshuffling could lead to the loss of good genetic combinations or beneficial alleles.*

<u>Genetics</u>: When a blue type of corn crosses with a yellow type of corn, the offspring are blue. What type of trait is involved?

> *A dominant trait (likely at a single [Mendelian] locus [site]).*

When a corn plant with large ears crosses with a small-eared plant, the offspring will have intermediately sized ears. What type of trait is involved?

> *A quantitative trait.*
> *(Though given the information above and in their textbook, students could correctly answer incomplete dominance. Incomplete dominance is actually still a single gene or Mendelian trait.)*

If a true-breeding spiny cucumber plant crossed with a non-spiny cucumber always had spiny offspring, how many copies of the spiny allele would it have?

> *Assuming that it is a diploid cucumber, it would have two copies of the dominant spiny allele. Any true-breeding diploid individual has two copies of whatever allele is in question—it is homozygous. Remember that the notion of true-breeding predates our understanding of DNA and the genetic basis for traits by many years.*

How do geneticists and plant breeders know if a plant is true-breeding?

> *This is a deceptively simple question. The short answer is that plant breeders keep very careful records of how crosses were made, and the phenotypes of the offspring. A plant breeder would cross the plant to itself (or to a near relative if self-fertilization isn't possible) and observe the next generation!*
>
> *But there's a problem... most agricultural species like peas, corn, and cucumbers live only a few months and reproduce only once. Therefore, how could you know that a plant is true-breeding until after you've planted it or its progeny?*
>
> *The key lies in the fact that when talking about crosses in plant genetics, we are dealing with populations of (nearly or completely) genetically identical plants, not just individuals. Often a population is derived from a single cross in a previous generation. Think of an ear of corn. From one cross of known parents, 500 genetically similar offspring are produced.*

Furthermore, many (not all) plants are self-fertile, meaning that their pollen can fertilize their own ovules. Self-fertilization quickly leads to two identical copies of an allele at a locus (homozygosity)—the genetic basis for "true-breeding" plants. Because an ear of corn or a pea pod produces more than one offspring, a plant breeder can: (1) make crosses to determine if the population is "true-breeding" and (2) simultaneously reserve some seed from the population for future crosses.

Chapter 1 Teacher Notes

Overview and Concepts

Overview

Chapter: Building from Mendel's crosses with peas, students review plant breeding populations and crosses. Emphasis is placed on recessive and dominant traits as well as Mendelian and quantitative traits. Questions focus on genetics and evolution.

Activity: Students taste the bitter or non-bitter phenotypes of a population of cucumber seedlings. Using Punnett's squares and logic, they deduce the genotypes of their unknown population as well as of its parents. Students make a hypothesis about the behavior of the cucumber bitterness gene and use statistics to evaluate their hypothesis.

Concepts covered

Dominant and recessive traits, crosses, hybrids, segregation of traits, Mendelian (single-gene) and quantitative (multi-gene) traits, Punnett's squares, statistics

Prior knowledge required

The text and activities of *Garden Genetics* are intended to apply and supplement textbook concepts. Students should have familiarity with the following:

- **Genes and alleles: Genes** are the unit of inheritance. They are segments of DNA that code for proteins. **Alleles** are different versions of a gene. We have two alleles for each gene, one from each parent.
- **Crosses and sexual recombination: Sexual recombination** takes one set of alleles from one parent and combines them with another set of alleles from a second parent. Long before farmers understood why it worked, they used sexual recombination to make **crosses** between plants with different characteristics. Remember Mendel used crosses to understand inheritance in his peas.
  - **Punnett's square:** A chart showing the possible gene combinations for the offspring of a cross. To the left is a Punnett's square for a cross between two tall hybrid pea plant parents (like Mendel used).
  - **Genotype:** A **genotype** is a representation of the genetic make-up of an individual. The parents in the cross on the left have the genotypes Tt.

**Teacher Figure
Punnett's square**

Alleles tall parent contributes

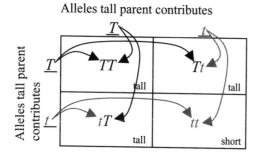

- **Phenotype:** A **phenotype** is a physical description of a trait. The parents in the cross on page 8 both have tall phenotypes. The offspring have three tall phenotypes and one short phenotype.

Activity notes

Preparation prior to the activity

- Order seeds several weeks in advance of planting date. Seed companies can be slow to deliver.
- Plan on 10 to 14 days between planting seeds and time of activity.

Time frame

- Day 1: Students taste plants.
- Day 2: Students finish worksheets and do statistical exercise.

Materials

Seed sources

Seed Company	Bitter Variety	Non-Bitter Variety	Website	Phone	Fax
Yankee Gardener	Marketmore 76 (#HSV 2029, $1.29)	Marketmore 97 (#HSV 2030, $1.69)	*www.yankeegardener.com/ seeds/hartseed4.html*	(203) 776-2091	(203) 776-1089
Peaceful Valley Farm Supply	Marketmore 76 (#SNV8048, $1.99)	Marketmore 80 (#SNV9014, $1.99)	*www.groworganic.com*	(888) 784-1722	
Specialty Seeds	Marketmore 76 ($1.49)	Marketmore 97 ($1.69)	*www.specialtyseeds.com*	(860) 721-9617	

Ideally, you want to use seed from similar genetic backgrounds so you're comparing the effects of the gene of interest, instead of effects of many other genes. Marketmore 76 and 80 are nearly identical genetically, except for the bitter gene. The non-bitter variety Marketmore 97 is also similar to Marketmore 80. Other bitter varieties: Poinsett 97 and Tablegreen 65. Tablegreen 72 is non-bitter.

Seed preparation for planting

- Instead of investing the time in making crosses and tending 2 generations of cucumber plants, you can simulate your own "segregating" population by mixing the bitter and non-bitter seeds. Mix seeds in a ratio of 3 bitter to 1 non-bitter. (The bitter gene is dominant to the non-bitter one.)
- Save a few seeds of each type as taste controls.
- Mix at least 20% more seeds than the class will need, to reflect the role of probability in segregation ratios. Therefore, if a class needs to plant 40 seeds, mix a minimum of 12 non-bitter + 36 bitter seeds for a total of 48 seeds. The students will then choose 40 seeds from the cup and plant them. Eight will not be planted at all.

Planting seeds

- Students should plant enough individuals of their "unknown" population to get segregation ratios close to 3:1. Minimum 20 plants for a class. Ratios will be closer to 3:1 with more plants.
- At the same time the students plant their "unknown," you or they should plant at least 2 bitter and 2 non-bitter taste "controls" per class.

Safety notes

- This lab violates all normal prohibitions against students eating in the laboratory by asking students to taste the leaves of young cucumber plants.
    - If possible, the tasting portion of the activity should be conducted somewhere other than the laboratory (the cafeteria, a home economics classroom, the hallway, etc.).
    - If students must do the tasting portion in the lab, please emphasize that this is the exception to the rule that one should NEVER put anything in a laboratory into one's mouth.
    - The tasting should be optional. If a student doesn't want to taste, someone else in his or her group can do it.
    - All students should wash their hands after handling the plants and again after the activity.
- Cucumber leaves and stems, especially those of young cucumbers, are edible. They sometimes appear in recipes, though they are usually cooked. Students should not consume large quantities of leaves, because of their potential emetic properties (induce vomiting). We piloted this activity with more than 250 students and no student had a problem with tasting cucumber leaves. For further information see _http://allallergy.net/fapaidfind. cfm?cdeoc=469._

- As many of the compounds present in cucumber fruits (also squash, zucchini, and melon) are present in cucumber leaves, **students who are allergic to cucumbers, squash, melon, and zucchini should NOT taste the cucumbers**. Someone else in their group can taste for them.

Lab notes

- This activity provides an excellent opportunity to remind students of the importance of math skills in biology. Mendel's insights came from the fact that he viewed his results in the form of ratios. His colleagues, many whom were doing similar experiments, all viewed their results as decimals, and therefore could not see the patterns that Mendel did. One cannot do science without the useful tool of mathematics.
- It's easiest to do this lab in pairs (or small groups). Students can consult about taste.
- Students should work in pencil, in case they need to change answers and hypotheses.
- You may want to skip the statistics section (Part IV) if it is too complicated for your students. The conclusions section (Part V) is designed to be relevant without Part IV.
- Disposal:
    - The plants can be used for Activity 3 as well. If you are not planning to reuse the plants, they can be thrown away. Alternately, students may enjoy the process of watching them grow for a longer period of time. Cucumbers in a warm greenhouse environment will produce seed in about three months. You can have students make crosses between bitter and non-bitter plants using a paintbrush or a bee glued onto a stick.
    - The planting containers and soil can be reused. The container should be washed out with soap and water. Ideally, to prevent accumulation of soil-borne diseases, soil should be autoclaved or baked in an oven between 180 and 200 degrees. The soil (not the just the oven) should be above 180 degrees for at least 30 minutes. (Higher temperatures can produce toxins.) Alternately, the soil can be sterilized in the microwave—90 seconds per kilogram (2.2 pounds) on full power.

Taking it further

You can also create other "unknown" genetic scenarios and have students deduce the genotypes of the parents, given the output.

Cross	Offspring	Simulate with
Bb x bb	Bb, Bb, bb, bb	2 bitter seeds : 2 non-bitter seeds
BB x anything	B?, B?, B?, B?	All bitter seeds

Further reading

Genetic action of the bitter gene in cucumbers

Robinson, R., A. Jaworksi, P. M. Gorski, and S. Shannon. 1988. Interaction of cucurbitacin genes. *Cucurbit Genetics Cooperative* 11: 23.

A-maize-ing photos of corn mutant plants

Neuffer, G., E. H. Coe, and S. R. Wessler. 1997. *Mutants of maize.* Woodbury, NY: Cold Spring Harbor Laboratory Press.

Activity 1.

Edible Punnett's Squares—Segregation Ratios You Can Taste

In the student edition, this activity begins on page 7.

Objective
To discover whether the bitter gene in cucumber plants is dominant or recessive.

Background
Cucumber plants, as well as their close relatives the squashes and melons, make a unique protein called cucurbitacin. Cucurbitacin tastes bitter to humans. Bitterness in cucumbers is caused by a single gene that has a recessive and a dominant allele. Your task in this assignment is to use your knowledge of genetics, particularly your understanding of crosses and Punnett's squares, to figure out how this bitter trait behaves. (Is bitterness dominant or recessive?) This is how scientists traditionally have learned about genes. They use populations of cucumbers or other organisms, make crosses, and use statistics to test their hypotheses about how genes behave.

Topic: Punnett Squares
Go to: *www.sciLINKS.org*
Code: GG05

Materials
- A population of "unknown" plants at cotyledon stage—about 10 days old
- Populations of bitter and non-bitter plants to act as taste controls—about 10 days old
- Plant tags
- Pencil
- Calculator (optional), for Part IV statistical analysis

Safety Notes
- Under normal circumstances, you should never taste anything in a biology laboratory. However, this laboratory makes an exception by asking you to taste a tiny piece of a cucumber plant's leaf.
- Students who are allergic to cucumbers, squash, melon, or zucchini should NOT taste the plants.
- If you are allergic or not comfortable tasting the plants, please ask someone else in your group to do it for you.
- You should wash your hands after handling the plants.
- You should wash your hands AGAIN at the end of the activity.

Activity

Part I. Your unknown population

1. Taste* the controls your teacher has set out. Tear a tiny piece off the edge of one of the cotyledons (see Figure 1.2). Chew the leaf between your front teeth, biting into it many times, and letting the flavor wash over your tongue. Can you tell the difference between bitter and non-bitter? Do you and your partner agree?

    The difference between bitter and non-bitter should be very clear to most people if they truly bite into the leaf. We have not heard of people lacking the ability to taste this bitterness.

Figure 1.2. Tasting the cotyledons of a cucumber seedling.

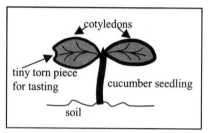

cotyledons

tiny torn piece for tasting

cucumber seedling

soil

*Students who are allergic to cucumbers, squash, zucchini, or melon should not taste the plants.

Many of the compounds present in cucumber fruits (also squash, zucchini, and melon) are present in cucumber leaves. Students who are allergic to one of the above should NOT taste the cucumbers. Someone else in their group can taste for them. See teacher notes for more information.

2. Taste your own plants. Are they bitter? Non-bitter?

3. Once you have decided whether each of your plants is bitter or non-bitter, label that plant with a tag and place the tag in the soil next to the plant.

4. Taste your partner's plants. Are they bitter? Non-bitter?

    4a. Do your answers agree? Why or why not?
    Even though the differences between bitter and non-bitter plants are distinct, partners may not agree. Make sure students are really biting into the leaf. It is very bitter, so some students want to avoid this. They can re-taste controls, re-taste their own plants, taste each other's plants, and/or draw others into the discussion in order to resolve differences. It is a good idea to make sure students re-taste all non-bitter plants. Sometimes they don't chew the leaf enough to get a strong taste.

    4b. What can you do to improve your measurement?
    This is a real-world problem for scientists. Their major strategy is to replicate measurements. In this case, plants could be tasted multiple times and results could be averaged. Another strategy could be to create a tasting panel of "expert" tasters and accept the judgment of this panel for all plants.

    In all cases, the more data a student or scientist has, the less important any one data point is. Therefore, if one data point is wrong (and this happens!) it doesn't invalidate the results.

5. Collect the totals for the class. (Sample below)

Sample calculation	Bitter	Non-bitter	Total
Number of plants	40	15	55
Percentage	40/55 = 0.727 = 72.7%	15/55 = 0.272 = 27.2%	55/55 = 1.0 = 100%
Ratio	40/15 = 2.7 ≈ 3	15/15 = 1	*3:1*

To find the percentage, divide the number of plants in the bitter and non-bitter categories by the total number of plants. To find the ratio, divide the larger of the bitter or non-bitter number of plants by the smaller number of plants. Your results will probably not be perfect, whole numbers.

6. To figure out the genotypes of the parental generations, you need to know which genotypes go with which phenotype.

   6a. What is a phenotype? What are the phenotypes of your plants?
   A phenotype is the physical manifestation of the trait. Usually, the phenotype is how a plant looks or behaves. In this case, it is how the plant TASTES. Your phenotypes are bitter and non-bitter.

   6b. What is a genotype?
   A genotype is the genetic structure underlying the trait. Usually, we assign letters to represent the gene, so genotypes for these plants might be: AA, Aa, or aa.

7. Which phenotype is there more of?
   Bitter

At this point we don't know which allele is dominant. But you can make a hypothesis (an educated guess) using your data. In Part IV you will test whether or not the data support this hypothesis. Right now, there isn't a "right" answer, but there are two logical ones.

8. Make a hypothesis about which trait (bitter or non-bitter) is dominant. This will be the hypothesis you test in this activity. Support your hypothesis.
   Any logical reasoning for a hypothesis should be an acceptable answer. The students will test the hypothesis with the rest of the activity.

   Most students will choose "bitterness is a dominant trait" as their hypothesis. Most will give the abundance of the bitter phenotype as their reason. In general, as in this case, the dominant trait will be more abundant.

(However, in the world beyond bitter cucumber plants, there are many exceptions to this explanation because dominance and abundance are two independent concepts. Dominance relies on gene action. Abundance is a function of gene frequency. For example, human achondroplasia (a type of dwarfism) is a dominant gene that is at very low frequencies in human populations. As a result, very few people are dwarves even though the trait is dominant.)

9. Using your hypothesis from the last step, what symbol do you choose to represent the bitter allele? (Remember that dominant alleles are usually given a capital letter. Recessive alleles are usually given the same letter, but lowercase.)
   B (Another capital letter is acceptable.)

10. What symbol do you choose to represent the non-bitter allele?
    b (lowercase of letter in question 9.)

11. To summarize, fill in the table according to your hypothesis from step 8.

	Bitter	Non-bitter
Number		
Possible Genotypes	BB, Bb	bb

You may want to check students' work at this point. If they proceed with a "wrong" hypothesis, for example that non-bitterness is dominant, their results ultimately won't make sense. This is certainly the way it happens in laboratory science. Once they get to the end and see that their guesses are not consistent with the data they'll have to double back and redo these sections.

If students are seeing the material for the first time, or you're working together as a class, you may want agreement at this point. If students are advanced or working independently, you may want to let them proceed with "incorrect" assumptions.

Part II. Parents and grandparents

Figure 1.3. Pedigree representing the crosses leading to the unknown population.

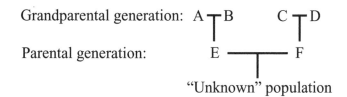

Grandparental generation: A ⊤ B   C ⊤ D

Parental generation: E ———⊤——— F

"Unknown" population

The pedigree in Figure 1.3 is a drawing that represents the crosses leading to your unknown population. Each of the letters represents a population. These are crosses between POPULATIONS, not just individuals. However, since each of the starting populations (A, B, C, and D) was genetically identical, you can think about it the same way as for individuals.

> *You may want to remind students how crosses are made in cucumbers. (The plants would be bee-pollinated in nature. However, crosses can be done with a paintbrush in the lab, greenhouse, or classroom.) Because the result of a single cross leads to a cucumber full of seeds, all with the same parentage, it is easy to maintain breeding "populations."*

12. Describe what is happening in the pedigree.

   12a. What is crossed with what to give your unknown population?
   Parent E × Parent F

   12b. Which cross led to population E?
   Grandparent A × Grandparent B

   12c. Which cross led to population F?
   Grandparent C × Grandparent D

13. Complete the table by writing in the possible genotypes.

Population	Phenotype		Possible genotype
	% Bitter	% Non-bitter	
Grandparent Population A	100%		*Bb, BB*
Grandparent Population B		100%	*bb*
Grandparent Population C	100%		*Bb, BB*
Grandparent Population D		100%	*bb*
Parent Population E	100%		*Bb, BB*
Parent Population F	100%		*Bb, BB*

Part III. The crosses of the different generations

14. In Punnett's Square 1, what population is on the left of the square? _Grandparent A_
> 14a. What is the phenotype of this population? _bitter_
> 14b. What are the possible genotypes of this population? _Bb and BB_

15. In Punnett's Square 1, what population is on the top of the square? _Grandparent B_
> 15a. What is the phenotype of this population? _non-bitter_
> 15b. What are the possible genotypes of this population? _bb_

16. In Punnett's Square 1, what population is in the middle of the square? _Parent E_
> 16a. What is the phenotype of this population? _bitter_
> 16b. What are the possible genotypes of this population? _Bb and BB_
> 16c. In which other Punnett's square does this population occur again? _Square 3_

17. In Punnett's Square 3, what population is in the middle of the square? _Our unknown_
> 17a. What are the phenotypes of this population? _bitter and non-bitter_
> 17b. What are the possible genotypes of this population? _bb, Bb, and BB_
> 17c. Where did the parents for this population come from? _Squares 1 and 2_

18. Now you have all the information you need to test the hypothesis you made earlier about how the bitter gene works. Use the Punnett's squares on page 19 to work backwards to understand all the crosses that led to your population.
    - Begin with what you know for sure. Which phenotype has only one possible genotype? _bb_
    - Do you always know BOTH alleles for a dominant genotype? _No_
    - Do you know one of the two alleles? _Yes, the B._

Figure 1.4. Punnett's squares for activity, Teacher Edition.

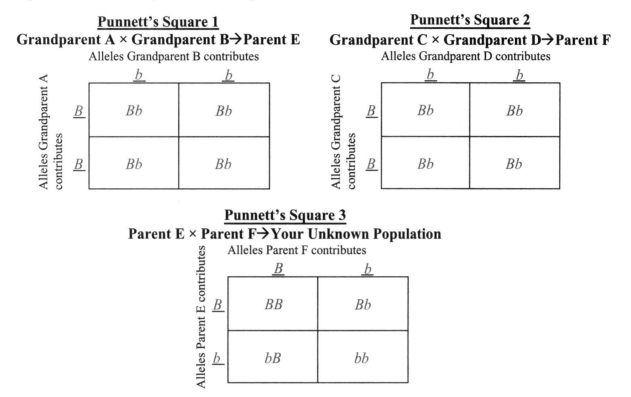

Part IV. Testing your hypothesis

Teacher note: Part V may still be relevant for those who skip this statistical section.

Back at the beginning of this lab, you took a guess about whether the bitter or non-bitter trait was dominant. Now you have to evaluate whether or not that was the best guess. **Statistics** are the way scientists test whether or not their data fit their hypotheses or models. No data ever fit a model perfectly, because **random chance** also plays a role in results of an experiment.

For example, if you flip a coin, you have a 50% chance that it comes up heads. If you flip the coin twice, are you guaranteed that you'll have 1 head and 1 tail? Of course not. The second coin flip still has a 50% chance of coming up heads. Instead, we say there is a 50% chance that you will flip a head each time you flip a coin. In much the same way, you might pick a bitter or a non-bitter seed out of a bag. Each time you have a certain probability of planting a bitter seed, depending on the percent of bitter seeds in the bag. The populations you taste are only a sample of the total plants. Similar to the situation with flipping a coin, you would expect the proportion of bitter plants in your sample to be close to but not exactly the same as the true proportion of bitter plants in the population.

Statistics are the way scientists test whether or not their data fit their hypotheses.

Given a certain set of parental genotypes, there is a probability (could be 0, 25, 50, 75, 100% chance) that offspring will have a certain genotype. You need to test if the difference between what you see and what you expect can be explained by random chance. If the difference is too large to be explained by random chance, there is probably something wrong with your hypothesis.

To determine whether or not the differences are real or due to chance, scientists use a test called a **chi-squared (χ^2) test**. This test takes the difference between the number you would *expect* and the number you *observe*, and then squares the difference to eliminate the positive or negative sign. Then you sum all the squares (in this case of the bitter and the non-bitter plants) and compare the sum to a table of probabilities.

19. Here is the data you need:

		Bitter	Non-bitter	Total
1.	Number of plants sampled			
2.	Ratio expected (from Punnett's squares)	*3*	*1*	*4*
3.	Percentage expected (express the ratio as a percent)	*75%*	*25%*	
4.	Expected number of plants (line 3 × total plants)	*Total × 0.75*	*Total × 0.25*	
5.	Observed – expected number of plants (line 1 – line 4)	*observed – expected*	*observed – expected*	
6.	(Observed – expected) squared (square line 5)	*(observed – expected)²*	*(observed – expected)²*	
7.	(Observed – expected) 2 ÷ expected (line 6 ÷ line 4)	*(observed – expected)² ÷ expected*	*(observed -expected)² ÷ expected*	*Add line 7 (bitter + non-bitter)*

The mathematical representation of what you just did in the table is:

$$\chi^2 = \frac{(\text{observed bitter} - \text{expected bitter})^2}{\text{expected bitter}} + \frac{(\text{observed non-bitter} - \text{expected non-bitter})^2}{\text{expected non-bitter}}$$

Next you compare your chi-squared total value from line 7 to the critical value in a chi-square table. In the chi-square table on page 21, the top row of numbers indicates probabilities. You have one degree of freedom (df) for this test (number of phenotypes -1). Then you scan across the 1 df row until you find the number closest to, but smaller than, your number. In genetics, you are looking for an insignificant difference. You want your observed values to be close to your expected values.

20. What value do you find?

df	Probability (p)										
	0.95	0.90	0.80	0.70	0.50	0.30	0.20	0.10	0.05	0.01	0.001
1	0.004	0.02	0.06	0.15	0.46	1.07	1.64	2.71	3.84	6.64	10.83
2	0.10	0.21	0.45	0.71	1.39	2.41	3.22	4.60	5.99	9.21	13.82
3	0.35	0.58	1.01	1.42	2.37	3.66	4.64	6.25	7.82	11.34	16.27
4	0.71	1.06	1.65	2.20	3.36	4.88	5.99	7.78	9.49	13.28	18.47
5	1.14	1.61	2.34	3.00	4.35	6.06	7.29	9.24	11.07	15.09	20.52
6	1.63	2.20	3.07	3.83	5.35	7.23	8.56	10.64	12.59	16.81	22.46
7	2.17	2.83	3.82	4.67	6.35	8.38	9.80	12.02	14.07	18.48	24.32
8	2.73	3.49	4.59	5.53	7.34	9.52	11.03	13.36	15.51	20.09	26.12
9	3.32	4.17	5.38	6.39	8.34	10.66	12.24	14.68	16.92	21.67	27.88
10	3.94	4.86	6.18	7.27	9.34	11.78	13.44	15.99	18.31	23.21	29.59
	Not significant								Significant		

In this case, with one degree of freedom, we will use the critical cut-off value of 3.84 (5% chance that the data can be explained by random chance alone). If your value is below this, then you can conclude that the difference between observed and expected values can be explained by random chance and that your data fit your hypothesis. If the value is greater than the critical cut-off value, the difference is greater than can be explained by random chance and something is likely wrong with your hypothesis or with your experiment.

Most scientists use a threshold of 5% as an acceptable degree of uncertainty. This means that they're 95% sure that their data fit their hypothesis. Note that it's not 100% certain. Very little in science is 100% certain.

21. If the hypothesis you made in Part II about how the bitter gene behaves is not correct, you need to go back and try a new hypothesis. If your model looks good, you've solved the genetic problem.

Part V. Conclusions

22. How does the bitter gene behave? (Is it dominant or recessive?)

    The bitter gene is dominant.

23. What were the genotypes of the parents of your unknown population?

    The parents were both Bb.

24. What were the genotypes of the grandparents?

    The grandparents were BB and bb. This is just like Mendel's experiments. He initially crossed two plants that were true-breeding for two different characteristics. In this case the grandparents (also called the "parental generation," or P, in the plant breeding world) were bitter plants that only had bitter offspring, and non-bitter plants that only had non-bitter offspring. This cross gave the hybrid generation (F1), in which plants had one bitter allele and one non-bitter allele. These were crossed (probably selfed, or crossed to themselves) to give the F2 or segregating generation. The unknown population is a segregating generation for a classic, Mendelian, dominant trait.

25. What were the genotypes of your unknown population?

    BB, Bb, bb

26. What would the genotypes of the offspring be if two individuals out of your unknown population were to mate? Use a Punnett's square.

    Students will use one of the following:
    BB × BB → all BB
    BB × Bb → ½ BB, ½ Bb
    BB × bb → all Bb
    Bb × Bb → ¼ BB, ½ Bb, ¼ bb
    Bb × bb → ½ Bb, ½ bb
    bb × bb → all bb

Optional Directions for Filling in the Punnett's Squares

We have found that most students do not need these directions. However, if you prefer to give students more guidance, these instructions go through filling in the squares step-by-step.

1. Begin with what you know for sure. Which phenotype has only one possible genotype?
   The recessive bb.

   Fill in the Punnett's square for all the generations you have tasted. For offspring, fill in the whole genotype in a box. For parents, the two alleles are split and go on the outside of the box. Look at the text for examples, if needed.

2. Look back at your ratio in number 5 of Part I (page 15). This should give you a clue about how many squares of your unknown population should be bitter and non-bitter.
   The ratio should be about 1 non-bitter to 3 bitter. Therefore, one of the unknown squares should be bb.

3. Now, pick one square where you know some of the genotypes. If you know the genotype of the offspring, what does that tell you about the genotypes of the parents?
   Use the unknown population as an example. If you know that there are non-bitter offspring (bb), then you know that the recessive allele must be somewhere in BOTH parents, even if it doesn't show up in the phenotype.

   If you know the genotypes of the parents, what does that tell you about the genotypes of the offspring?
   This comment is to remind students to carry alleles through into the centers of their squares. You may have to remind them that populations E and F are in the squares twice (once as offspring and once as parents).

4. At this point, you will still have some holes left in your square. Think about what you know about the populations. Were they all bitter? Were they all non-bitter? Remember, to taste a dominant phenotype there must be at least one dominant allele present.
   Here is where students add the dominant alleles. If their hypothesis is that the bitter allele is dominant, a bitter phenotype must have at least one B allele. Carry it through the Punnett's square.

5. At this point, you may still have some holes left in your square. You have all the tools to figure them out. If there are holes related to the parent, think about the offspring. Were they all bitter? All non-bitter? Then which alleles must the parents have had?
   This is how the students should be able to deduce, for example, that Parent

E was all bitter, therefore, Grandparent A must have had two B alleles. Otherwise, the offspring (from the cross with the non-bitter Grandparent B) could not have all been bitter.

BITTERNESS AND NON-BITTERNESS IN CUCUMBERS

A Story of Mutation

If you had lived in Europe in the early part of the 20th century, when you bought a cucumber in the market, you would have found a small notch cut out of its top. The notch caused problems for the cucumber. Bacteria and fungi had a quick route past the cucumber's protective skin. Thus a notched cucumber spoiled more quickly than one without a notch. Why then did cucumbers have notches cut in them?

Professional tasters cut the notches into the cucumbers (Figure 2.1). The leaves, stems, and flowers of cucumber plants are usually bitter. Sometimes, especially under the warm, moist conditions found in greenhouses, the cucumbers can become bitter too. If the top of the cucumber was not bitter—meaning the bitter protein had not made it into the top of the fruit—the rest of the cucumber was not bitter either. Therefore, cucumber growers employed professional tasters to test each cucumber before it was sold. Not surprisingly, the tasting crew was an expensive part of cucumber production.

Figure 2.1. Cucumber with notch cut for tasting.

Bitter cucumber gene history

The bitterness of cucumbers is caused by a protein called cucurbitacin, which also makes some people burp. The protein is found in the stems and leaves of many cucumber plants. Sometimes the protein can be found in the cucumber itself. This is why some people remove the skin and seeds of cucumbers before eating them.

In the 1930s, a Dutch cucumber breeder decided to make a cucumber variety that was not bitter. Before he could make such a variety, he had to find a non-bitter cucumber plant. Traditionally, a plant breeder can only use variation she or he finds in nature. This

SCiLINKS.
THE WORLD'S A CLICK AWAY

Topic: Genetic Mutations
Go to: *www.sciLINKS.org*
Code: GG06

Topic: Seed Banks
Code: GG07

cucumber breeder contacted other cucumber breeders around the world and asked for a few seeds of their varieties. He also collected different cucumber types from **genebanks**, which are special facilities designed to preserve genetic diversity and protect seeds for future use. He then grew the different varieties in a greenhouse, under uniform, controlled conditions. Eventually, he had a crew taste thousands of cucumber plants. In an old United States variety called "Longfellow," he found the mutant, non-bitter gene.

The Longfellow variety was old and it was not patented or protected. Today, when a plant breeder creates a variety, she or he often applies for a **patent**. (Historically, plant breeders applied for a "plant variety protection" or PVP, but today breeders are more likely to use a patent.) A patent for a plant variety works just like a patent for a chemical or a machine. It lasts for 20 years and keeps other people from profiting from the "invention." The non-bitter gene was incorporated into a new Dutch variety.

Genebanks are special facilities designed to preserve genetic diversity and protect seeds for future use.

Patents are used to protect new varieties of plants. A patent means that someone must pay the plant breeder for the use of his or her "invention."

PATENTING GENES

In recent years, many companies, researchers, and plant breeders have been applying for patents. In the United States, a patent costs about $40,000 and gives 20 years of protection for a gene, a variety, or a genetic process. Between 1985 and 2002, 914 patents were issued for plants. The vast majority of these have been issued for field corn (565 patents) and soybean (327 patents). Potato, tomato, cotton, rice, wheat, and alfalfa have all received fewer than five patents each.

Why are there so many patents for corn and soybean? They are two of the most important crops in the United States, and they have the biggest seed industries. If a company invests in producing a variety, the company wants to find a way to protect its investment. A patent is one way to do so.

Patents for plants and genes have been very controversial. To patent anything—whether it's a gene or a toothbrush—it must be novel, meaning it is something new. Is a gene novel if it already exists in nature? Is it novel if you identify it and can change it, through genetic engineering?

SCiLINKS.
THE WORLD'S A CLICK AWAY

Topic: Mutations
Go to: www.sciLINKS.org
Code: GG08

Topic: Transcription
Code: GG09

For years, cucumber breeders in the United States tried to gain access to the Dutch non-bitter trait (they didn't know where it had come from originally). The Dutch breeders saw no reason to share it. However, in the 1950s, the Dutch had a problem with a disease outbreak in cucumbers. A plant breeder at Michigan State University had already found a gene that gave cucumbers resistance to survive the disease. So the Dutch and American breeders made a trade—the non-bitter gene for the disease resistance gene. Since then, the non-bitter gene has been bred into many commercial varieties, which are often called "burpless" or "sweet." However, there are still many cucumber varieties available with the bitter gene. Why would plant breeders keep the bitter gene around? The gene has some positive effects on the plant's health and doesn't usually cause problems because the bitterness rarely finds its way into the fruit.

From DNA to bitterness

Bitterness in cucumbers is a trait controlled by a single gene. But what exactly is this bitter gene in cucumbers, and how does it work? The gene, as you know, is just a section of DNA that contains the genetic code for making a protein. In this case, the protein is cucurbitacin, the compound that makes cucumbers bitter.

What then is the non-bitter gene? The non-bitter gene is a mutated version of the original, which results in the plant being unable to make cucurbitacin. The gene no longer encodes the protein, and thus the plant has no way to make it.

Most **mutations** are negative for the plant's well-being. Like the non-bitter allele in cucumbers, mutations often result in the plant losing its ability to make a protein. The plant needs most of the proteins that it makes. For example, if a mutation occurs in a gene involved in producing chlorophyll—a compound that is essential to the plant's survival—the mutation is fatal. A plant cannot survive without chlorophyll. However, a cucumber plant can survive without cucurbitacin.

A bitter gene in a cucumber plant serves an important, but not essential, function. Bitterness makes cucumbers less palatable to insects and other herbivores. Therefore, a cucumber plant without bitterness might be at a disadvantage relative to other cucumber plants. On the other hand, non-bitter cucumber plants might have some less obvious competitive advantages in a field of other cucumber plants.

A mutation is simply a genetic change.

Point mutations change only one base in the genetic code.

Mutation

A mutant isn't a monster. The word *mutation* comes from the Latin word meaning to change. That's all a mutation is—a change in the genetic code. The changes can be large or small. The smallest is a point mutation, which changes only one base in the DNA. Point mutations can be caused by mistakes in copying DNA in the cells.

Sometimes such a point mutation has no effect at all—it doesn't even change the amino acid encoded. How is that possible? Remember that the genetic code has more than one way to encode each amino acid. The code is read in codons—sets of three bases that together code for a specific amino acid.

The codons of DNA are the template for all the proteins a body needs to make. However, a cell has a problem. The DNA can't leave the nucleus (Figure 2.2). Proteins are made outside of the nucleus, at the **ribosomes**. How are the instructions transferred from the DNA in the nucleus to the ribosomes? The DNA template is **transcribed** by a molecule called a **messenger RNA** (mRNA). The mRNAs then leave the nucleus and go to the ribosomes where they are "translated" into proteins.

Figure 2.3 shows the genetic code. What does cga encode? Using the table, you can see cga encodes the amino acid arginine (sometimes abbreviated with an r). A mutation that changed the c to an a would make the codon aga instead. However, aga still encodes arginine. So the mutation caused no change. This is called a **silent** mutation.

Figure 2.2. Transcription and translation.

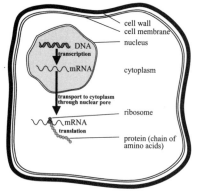

Figure 2.3. The genetic code.

The **nucleus** of a cell is where the DNA is found.

Proteins are assembled at the **ribosomes**.

The DNA bases are **transcribed** (copied) by a molecule called **messenger RNA (mRNA)**.

Second letter

First letter	u	c	a	g	Third letter
u	uuu uuc } Phe(f) uua uug } Leu(l)	ucu ucc uca ucg } Ser(s)	uau uac } Tyr(y) uaa Stop uag Stop	ugu ugc } Cys(c) uga Stop ugg Trp(w)	u c a g
c	cuu cuc cua cug } Leu(l)	ccu ccc cca ccg } Pro(p)	cau cac } His(h) caa cag } Gln(q)	cgu cgc cga cgg } Arg(r)	u c a g
a	auu auc aua } Ile(i) aug Met(m)	acu acc aca acg } Thr(t)	aau aac } Asn(n) aaa aag } Lys(k)	agu agc } Ser(s) aga agg } Arg(r)	u c a g
g	guu guc gua gug } Val(v)	gcu gcc gca gcg } Ala(a)	gau gac } Asp(d) gaa gag } Glu(e)	ggu ggc gga ggg } Gly(g)	u c a g

A mutation that causes no change in the resulting protein is a **silent** mutation.

Not all point mutations are silent. Let's return to our cga codon for arginine (r). If instead, the c changes to a u, we have an entirely different situation. Then uga is a stop codon. This means the end of the protein. The amino acid sequence will stop. Therefore, the protein will be very different from what it would have been without the mutation. This is called a **non-sense** mutation.

There is another type of point mutation. A **mis-sense** mutation is one that changes the function of a protein. The result is usually a protein with a slightly different shape or function, but one that still can function within the body. These mutations are one of the most important sources of variation for evolution to work upon.

Mutations that involve single changes in a codon, whether silent, non-sense, or mis-sense, are all point mutations. In contrast to these small mutations, **frame-shift** mutations are usually insertions and deletions of DNA ranging in length from one to thousands of base pairs. Because the codons are read in sets of three bases, adding or removing even one base can lead to major changes in the encoded protein. Consider the three-letter words in Figure 2.4:

Figure 2.4. Insertion and deletion.

A set of 3-letter words, like the codons of DNA:	THE CAT ATE THE FAT RAT
Suppose a deletion causes the removal of the C: Then an insertion causes the addition of an N:	THE ATA TET HEF ATR AT THE ANT ATE THE FAT RAT

In this case, the insertion counteracts the deletion and restores the reading frame with only minor differences. However, the insertion alone would have produced equally radical changes: THE CAN TAT ETH EFA TRA T. It's amazing what a difference one little base can make!

Frame-shift mutations can affect proteins in the same way that point mutations do. Very rarely are they silent. Sometimes, they cause alterations in the function of a protein (mis-sense mutation). Often, they introduce stop codons and are non-sense mutations.

A **non-sense** mutation is one that results in a stop codon and the premature end of a protein.

A **mis-sense** mutation changes the function of a protein.

A **frame-shift** mutation is caused by an insertion or a deletion of DNA and results in a different sequence of codons.

Questions for further thought

<u>Experimental Design:</u> Why did the cucumber breeder need to grow the plants in a greenhouse, under controlled, uniform conditions?

> *Uniformity and control were needed so the breeders knew they were seeing the effects of a gene, not of environmental conditions (a confounding variable).*

<u>Evolution:</u> Why might a cucumber be bitter?

> *Bitterness is a defense compound. Plants use these compounds to deter insect predators.*

What advantage could a bitter cucumber have over a non-bitter one?

> *The bitterness would make it less palatable to a predator.*

<u>Genetic Diversity:</u> Why do we still keep the old, bitter cucumber varieties even though there are now non-bitter ones?

> *They could contain important genetic diversity that we might need in the future for reasons we can't predict now. Furthermore, under most conditions, bitterness in cucumbers is not a problem—the bitterness rarely gets into the fruit. Plus, the bitterness can help the plant defend itself against some predators (though not ALL predators, as the activity in Chapter 3 shows).*

<u>Translation:</u> Why does Figure 2.3 have a base named u? Isn't DNA made up of a, c, g, and t?

> *The codons are mRNA not DNA. RNA uses a u instead of a t.*

Chapter 2 Teacher Notes

Overview and Concepts

Overview

The introduction explores the history of the bitter gene, which was found in a genebank and traded between cucumber breeders. The box explains patenting of genes and plant varieties. The chapter continues and explores the links of transcription and translation leading from DNA to proteins. Finally the chapter focuses on the DNA basis for different types of mutations. Questions explore experimental design, genetics, and evolution.

The activity uses genomics and genetic databases to understand mutation and its effect on both DNA and proteins. The mutation lessons are then applied to explore the genetic basis of bitter and non-bitter alleles in cucumber plants.

Concepts covered

Mutation, DNA, transcription, translation, proteins, codons, genebanks, patents, genomics, genetic databases

Prior knowledge required

The text and activities of *Garden Genetics* are intended to apply and supplement textbook concepts. Students should have familiarity with the following:

- **Genes and alleles: Genes** are the unit of inheritance. They are segments of DNA that code for proteins. **Alleles** are different versions of a gene. We have two for each gene, one from each parent.
- **DNA (deoxyribonucleic acid):** A double strand of base pairs (A, C, G, and T) that stores and transmits genetic information from one generation to the next.
- **RNA (ribonucleic acid):** A single strand of base pairs (A, C, G, and U) that acts as an intermediary between the DNA and the **ribosomes** where protein synthesis occurs.
- **Protein:** One or more amino acids encoded by DNA. The chain of amino acids then folds into a three-dimensional structure. Many of the important components of an organism are made up of **proteins** (structures like muscles, as well as enzymes and defense compounds).
- **Transcription:** The process by which DNA is copied into a complementary strand of RNA.
- **Translation:** The process in which RNA is decoded into a protein.

- **Genotype:** A **genotype** is a representation of the genetic make-up of an individual.
- **Phenotype:** A **phenotype** is the physical expression of a genetic trait. A phenotype can be structural, physiological, behavioral, or biochemical—it is not just an organism's physical appearance. (Though that is certainly the easiest type of phenotype to identify!)

Activity notes

Preparation prior to the activity

- None required, though it might be useful to acquaint yourself with the National Center for Biotechnology Information (NCBI) website (*www.ncbi.nlm.nih.gov/About/index.html*).

Time frame

- One to two class periods. If used as reinforcement of concepts already covered, the activity can be done during a class period. Depending on the ability levels of the students, they may even have time to do the reading in class or to discuss the activity.

Data Sources

- This activity makes use of GenBank and the public databases used by researchers. To extend the activity, you could show students the database and ask them to find their protein and sequence on the computer.
- The specific database records used in this worksheet can currently be found on GenBank using the permanent protein accession number, AAQ72288, and permanent DNA accession number, AY365247.1. (Note: You want the "CDS" sequence not the "source" sequence. The "source" sequence contains extra bases before and after the gene, as a relic of the sequencing technique. The "CDS" is the sequence from the atg start codon to the tag stop codon.)
- NCBI has a very nice page of tutorials and educational materials. The tutorial for the Entrez part of GenBank (the part we use for this exercise) is available at *www.ncbi.nlm.nih.gov/Entrez/tutor.html*.
- Cucumber sequences have relatively low representation on the database (a reflection of their priority in the grand scheme of research). The Entrez section of GenBank contains links to 3-D protein structures, though there are only two available (at this point) for cucumber, and neither is suitable for this exercise. For the two cucumber examples with 3-D structure, see: *www.ncbi.nlm.nih.gov/ Structure/mmdb/mmdbsrv.cgi?form=6&db=t&Dopt=s&uid=5765*

and *www.ncbi.nlm.nih.gov/Structure/mmdb/mmdbsrv.cgi?form=6 &db=t&Dopt=s&uid=5141*. They require the use of a free viewer called "Cn3D" in order to see the 3-D shapes of the proteins.

Further reading

A-maize-ing photos of corn mutant plants
Neuffer, G., E. H. Coe, and S. R. Wessler. 1997. *Mutants of maize.* Woodbury, NY: Cold Spring Harbor Laboratory Press.

Korean target-leaf spot study
Kim, M. S., Y. C. Kim, and B. H. Cho. 2004. Gene expression analysis in cucumber leaves primed by root colonization with *Pseudomonas chlororaphis* O6 upon challenge-inoculation with *Corynespora cassicola. Plant Biology* 6:105–108.

Patenting genes—the case of a yellow bean
Pratt, T. 2001. Patent on small yellow bean provokes cry of biopiracy. *New York Times* March 20.
Tolan, S. 2001. A bean of a different color. *NPR News and American RadioWorks.* Available online at *www.americanradioworks.org/ features/food_politics/beans/index.html.*

Patents and PVPs
Lesser, W., and M. Mutschler. 2002. Lessons from the patenting of plants. In *Intellectual property rights in animal breeding and genetics*, eds. M. Rothschild and S. Newman, 103–118. Cambridge, MA: CABI Publishing.

Activity 2.
Proteins, Codons, and Mutations
In the student edition, this activity begins on page 25.

Objective
Use protein and genetic sequence data to evaluate the effect of different kinds of mutations. Understand how mutation could have created a non-bitter gene in cucumbers.

Background
There are two approaches to learning about a gene. The **genetic approach** is the traditional one—a researcher finds a mutant individual and makes crosses to understand how the mutant gene or genes behave. In essence, the genetic approach studies genes by looking at their effects. This is how cucurbitacin, the bitter gene, has been studied in cucumbers.

The other way to learn about genes is to look directly at the DNA sequence—the line-up of a, c, t, and g bases. This is often part of a **genomic approach**. **Genome** means all the genes in an individual, whether it's a fish, a human, or a cucumber plant. The genomic approach looks at the sequence of many genes, often all at the same time. There have been a series of genome projects with the goal of sequencing all the genes in an individual person, mouse, bacteria, or rice plant. To do this, scientists use chemistry and instruments to read off the base pairs from one individual's DNA.

To obtain DNA for the genomic approach, scientists create **DNA libraries**. A DNA library can be obtained in one of two ways. To make a **genomic library**, all of an organism's DNA is sequenced (Figure 2.5). Reading the entire DNA sequence shows the number and location of genes, but gives no information about what they do. This approach also sequences a lot of "junk" DNA, or DNA that is not part of genes. (The chances are good that this DNA isn't "junk" at all, but we don't yet fully understand its function.) Reading this complete sequence is a good way to learn about the structure of genes, their regulation, and how they relate to one another.

Where do scientists get the DNA sequence to study cucumber plants using the genomic approach? The cucumber genome has not been sequenced. Instead, scientists use **cDNA libraries** (Figure 2.5). This method copies all the messenger RNA (mRNA) active in a cell into **cDNA** (copy DNA). Remember, **mRNAs** are the precursors to proteins. This is a more efficient way to understand the effects of genes, because mRNAs come only from the genes in a cell that are "turned on." Reading the mRNA tells you just what you want to know. Which genes are turned on in response to cold? Which genes are activated when the plant is infected by a disease?

Sidebar:

A **genetic approach** uses mutant individuals and crosses to understand how genes behave.

A **genomic approach** looks at the sequences of many genes at the same time. A **genome** is all the genes in an organism.

A genomic approach often relies on **DNA libraries**.

A **genomic library** is the sequence of all the DNA in an individual's genome.

A **cDNA library** is the sequence of the active genes in a cell. **cDNAs** are copies of the **mRNAs** in a cell.

Figure 2.5. cDNA and genomic sequence.

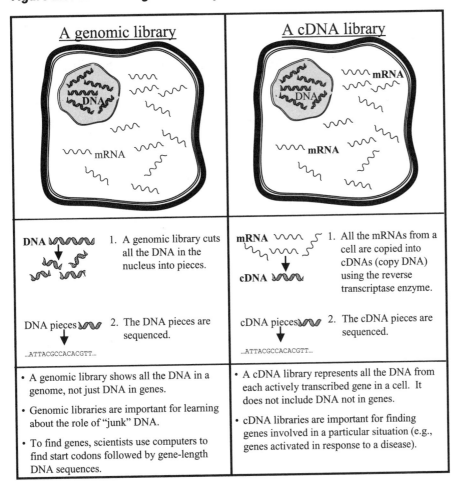

A genomic library	A cDNA library
DNA [DNA illustration] ↓ [fragments]	1. A genomic library cuts all the DNA in the nucleus into pieces.	**mRNA** [mRNA illustration] ↓ **cDNA** [cDNA illustration]	1. All the mRNAs from a cell are copied into cDNAs (copy DNA) using the reverse transcriptase enzyme.
DNA pieces [illustration] ↓ ...ATTACGCCACACGTT...	2. The DNA pieces are sequenced.	**cDNA pieces** [illustration] ↓ ...ATTACGCCACACGTT...	2. The cDNA pieces are sequenced.
• A genomic library shows all the DNA in a genome, not just DNA in genes. • Genomic libraries are important for learning about the role of "junk" DNA. • To find genes, scientists use computers to find start codons followed by gene-length DNA sequences.		• A cDNA library represents all the DNA from each actively transcribed gene in a cell. It does not include DNA not in genes. • cDNA libraries are important for finding genes involved in a particular situation (e.g., genes activated in response to a disease).	

Whether genetic sequence comes from a genomic or cDNA libary, any genetic sequence can be compared to any other genetic sequence. So knowing about the genes a plant uses for defense against a disease can teach you about the genes used by another species of plant in defense against a different disease. When scientists discover a gene, a genetic sequence, or a protein, they record it in a public database along with as much other information as possible. What does the gene or protein do? How was it discovered? What organism (plant, animal, bacteria, or fungus) did it come from?

Why do scientists bother to use these databases? Discovering a genetic sequence is time consuming and expensive. Therefore it makes sense to share information as it is gathered. With genomics, the more information that is available, the stronger the science. Today's powerful computers can easily compare millions of genetic sequences and find similarities between them. Increasingly, genetics is done in front of a computer using databases, instead of in a lab, a greenhouse, or a field!

Activity

Part I. DNA sequence

Though scientists know a lot about cucurbitacin and how it behaves, they still don't know the actual sequence of the gene that encodes it or exactly where it is located on a cucumber's chromosomes. Cucurbitacin has been studied with the genetic approach. It has not been studied with the genomic approach.

To think in detail about mutation, and how it might cause non-bitter cucumbers, we will study another example from cucumbers where the genetic sequence is known.

Some Korean researchers wanted to understand how cucumber plants respond to a disease called "target leaf spot." They compared the mRNAs from infected leaves with the mRNAs from uninfected leaves. When a cucumber leaf is infected, the gene shown in Figure 2.7 is activated. The protein made from this gene plays a role in plant defense against the disease.

Figure 2.6. The DNA sequence was created from a cucumber mRNA.

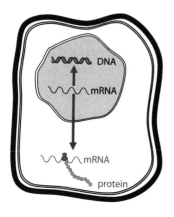

1. Where does the template for the amino acid sequence come from? In what part of the cell is the template located?
   The template comes from DNA in the nucleus.

2. How do organisms move information from the DNA sequence inside the nucleus to create proteins outside the nucleus?
   The template DNA is copied by mRNAs that move out of the nucleus to a ribosome. At a ribosome, each three-letter mRNA code is fitted with a tRNA that carries the corresponding amino acid. You may want to discuss that the sequence in Figure 2.7 is actually from a cDNA (copied from mRNA) and therefore contains no exons (non-coding regions of DNA that are cut out of mRNAs before they are translated). Therefore the genomic DNA sequence for the same gene might be longer than what is shown in Figure 2.7.

Topic: DNA
Go to: www.sciLINKS.org
Code: GG10

Note: GenBank uses lowercase letters in their DNA and protein sequences (see Figures 2.7 and 2.11). For consistency, we will use lowercase letters as well.

GenBank is a database for genetic sequence data (*www.ncbi.nlm. nih.gov/gquery/gquery.fcgi*). Figure 2.7 shows the sequence of Gen-Bank entry AY365247.1. It has 855 base pairs. The numbers on the side tell you how many base pairs there are, and the letters are shown in sets. The DNA begins with base number 1 (a). Line 1 has 60 bases, ending with an a. Line 2 starts with base number 61 (t). Line 3 begins with base number 121 (a), and so on.

Figure 2.7. Cucumber DNA sequence from GenBank.

```
1   atgggtcaag  cccttggttg  cattcaagtc  gaccagtcaa  ctgtagctat  cagagaaaca
61  tttgggagat  ttgacgatgt  gcttcaacct  ggttgccatt  gtctaccatg  gtgccttggg
121 agccagatag  ctggtcatct  ttctttacgt  ctccagcagc  ttgatgttcg  atgtgagaca
181 aagacaaagg  acaatgtttt  tgtcactgtc  gttgcctcta  ttcaataccg  agccctagca
241 gacaaggctt  cagatgcttt  ttataagctt  agtaatacaa  gagaacagat  ccaggcatat
301 gtttttgatg  ttattagggc  aagtgttcca  aagttggacc  tagattctac  ttttgaacag
361 aagaatgata  ttgcaaaggc  ggtcgaagac  gagctggaga  aggccatgtc  ggcttatgga
421 tacgagatag  ttcaaactct  aattgtggac  attgagccag  atgagcatgt  aaagcgagca
481 atgaatgaaa  taaatgcagc  tgcaagactg  agagttgctg  caactgagaa  agctgaggca
541 gagaagatat  tgcagattaa  gagagctgaa  ggagatgccg  aatccaagta  tctggccggg
601 cttggtattg  cacggcagcg  tcaagccatt  gtcgatgggc  tcagagacag  tgtactagca
661 tttgctgaaa  acgtccctgg  aacgacatct  aaggatgtca  tggacatggt  tcttgtgact
721 caatacttcg  acacgatgaa  ggagattgga  gcgtcatcaa  agtctaattc  tgtgttcatc
781 ccacatggac  ctggtgcagt  taaagatatt  gcttcacaga  tcagggatgg  tcttctccaa
841 gcaagccaaa  cttag
```

3. Is the sequence above DNA or RNA? How can you tell?

   The above sequence is a DNA equivalent (notice the ts instead of us) of the mRNA sequenced.

   Teacher note: To obtain the sequence above, researchers start with mRNA. From this, they create double-stranded cDNA (copy DNA). To make translation easier, they choose to show the strand that corresponds to the mRNA, instead of its complement (the paired strand), from which the mRNA would be transcribed. For the database, it doesn't matter which strand they show, since the computers automatically search both strands.

   To avoid confusion, we'll convert the above sequence back into an mRNA sequence (Figure 2.9).

Figure 2.8. The cucumber mRNA.

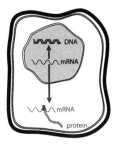

Figure 2.9. Converted cucumber mRNA sequence.

```
1   augggucaag  cccuugguug  cauucaaguc  gaccagucaa  cuguagcuau  cagagaaaca
61  uuugggagau  uugacgaugu  gcuucaaccu  gguugccauu  gucuaccaug  gugccuuggg
121 agccagauag  cuggucaucu  uucuuuacgu  cuccagcagc  uugauguucg  augugagaca
181 aagacaaagg  acaauguuuu  ugucacuguc  guugccucua  uucaauaccg  agcccuagca
241 gacaaggcuu  cagaugcuuu  uuauaagcuu  aguaauacaa  gagaacagau  ccaggcauau
301 guuuuugaug  uuauuagggc  aaguguucca  aaguuggacc  uagauucuac  uuuugaacag
361 aagaaugaua  uugcaaaggc  ggucgaagac  gagcuggaga  aggccauguc  ggcuuaugga
421 uacgagauag  uucaaacucu  aauuguggac  auugagccag  augagcaugu  aaagcgagca
481 augaaugaaa  uaaaugcagc  ugcaagacug  agaguugcug  caacugagaa  agcugaggca
541 gagaagauau  ugcagauuaa  gagagcugaa  ggagaugccg  aauccaagua  ucuggccggg
601 cuugguauug  cacggcagcg  ucaagccauu  gucgaugggc  ucagagacag  uguacuagca
661 uuugcugaaa  acgucccugg  aacgacaucu  aaggauguca  uggacauggu  ucuugugacu
721 caauacuucg  acacgaugaa  ggagauugga  gcgucaucaa  agucuaauuc  uguguucauc
781 ccacauggac  cuggugcagu  uaaagauauu  gcuucacaga  ucagggaugg  ucuucuccaa
841 gcaagccaaa  cuuag
```

Even most professional geneticists don't know the genetic code by heart. They use a table like Figure 2.3 (p. 28) to remember how the codons (sets of three bases) are translated into amino acids.

4. What are the first eight codons and amino acids of our gene? (Use Figure 2.3 to fill in the table in question 5.)

5. Using Figure 2.3, determine how many different ways there are to code for each amino acid. Give a number and list the codes.

Amino acid	Codon	Amino acid name	Number of ways it can be coded	List the different codes
1	aug	methionine	1	aug
2	ggu	glycine	4	ggu, ggc, gga, ggg
3	caa	glutamine	2	caa, cag
4	gcc	alanine	4	gcu, gcc, gca, gcg
5	cuu	leucine	6	uua, uug, cuu, cuc, cua, cug
6	ggu	glycine	4	ggu, ggc, gga, ggg
7	ugc	cysteine	2	ugu, ugc
8	auu	isoleucine	3	auu, auc, aua

6. What might be one of the advantages of having more than one way to code for the same amino acid?

More than one way to code for an amino acid, also known as degeneracy, lends flexibility to the code. It means that mutations can occur without always causing changes in amino acid sequence.

Figure 2.10. The cucumber protein.

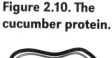
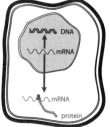

Part II. Protein sequence

The DNA sequence you decoded in Part I is linked in the database to the protein sequence, shown below.

Figure 2.11. Cucumber protein sequence from GenBank database.

```
  1 mgqalgciqv dqstvairet fgrfddvlqp gchclpwclg sqiaghlslr lqqldvrcet
 61 ktkdnvfvtv vasiqyrala dkasdafykl sntreqiqay vfdvirasvp kldldstfeq
121 kndiakaved elekamsayg yeivqtlivd iepdehvkra mneinaaarl rvaatekaea
181 ekilqikrae gdaeskylag lgiarqrqai vdglrdsvla faenvpgtts kdvmdmvlvt
241 qyfdtmkeig assksnsvfi phgpgavkdi asqirdgllq asqt
```

What does that alphabet soup mean? Each letter represents an amino acid. Proteins can be long and complex; this one has 284 amino acids. The numbers on the side tell you how many amino acids are involved and they are shown in sets of ten. Scientists use a one-letter abbreviation for each amino acid as shown in Table 2.1.

Table 2.1. Codes for the 20 amino acids common in living organisms.

1-letter abbreviation	Amino Acid	1-letter abbreviation	Amino Acid	1-letter abbreviation	Amino Acid	1-letter abbreviation	Amino Acid
a	alanine	g	glycine	m	methionine	s	serine
c	cysteine	h	histidine	n	asparagine	t	threonine
d	aspartic acid	i	isoleucine	p	proline	v	valine
e	glutamic acid	k	lysine	q	glutamine	w	tryptophan
f	phenylalanine	l	leucine	r	arginine	y	tyrosine

7. Use Table 2.1 to decode the first 10 amino acids in the sequence: mgqalgciqv.

   m=methionine, g=glycine, q=glutamine, a=alanine, l=leucine,
   g=glycine, c=cysteine, i=isoleucine, q=glutamine, v=valine

8. The DNA sequence for this protein has 855 bases in it. The protein itself has 284 amino acids. How are the two numbers related?

   $$\frac{855\ bases}{3\ bases/amino\ acid} = 285\ codons\ (that's\ 284\ plus\ the\ stop\ codon!)$$

9. Why are there 284 amino acids in the protein and not 285? (Hint: Look at the last codon.)

   Because tag (in DNA terms) is the same as uag (in RNA terms)—which is the stop codon. It is not part of the protein.

The 10 amino acids you just decoded are all strung together in a line. Each amino acid has its own chemical structure, and together, they have chemical interactions that cause the string to fold up into a unique 3-D structure. During the folding process, many amino acids are folded into the center of the protein or made chemically inactive because of bonds to other amino acids. A few remain in active sites—these are the sites that can bind to proteins and are where chemistry occurs.

Part III. Mutation

So, now we've seen that proteins come from amino acids, and amino acids come from genetic code. Let's see what happens if there are mutations in the genetic code.

Scenario 1

10. Let's start with the first glycine from our protein, encoded "ggu." What is its abbreviation? *g*

11. What are the different ways to code for glycine? *ggu, ggc, gga, ggg*

12. What sequence occurs if a one-base mutation changes the last letter to an a? *gga*

13. What does that codon encode? *glycine—no change*

14. Describe the mutation:
      14a. How does it affect the DNA? (point or frame-shift mutation)
      point
      14b. How does it affect the protein? (silent, non-sense, or mis-sense?) *silent; also know as synonymous*

15. What would that mean for our protein? *no change*

Scenario 2

16. Let's start with a cysteine from our protein. What is its abbreviation? *c*

17. What are the different ways to code for cysteine? *ugu, ugc*

18. What sequence occurs if a one-base mutation changes the last letter to an a? *uga*

19. What does that codon encode? *stop*

20. Describe the mutation:
      20a. How does it affect the DNA? (point or frame-shift mutation)
      point
      20b. How does it affect the protein? (silent, non-sense, or mis-sense) *non-sense*

21. What would that mean for our protein?
      The protein will end where the cysteine would have been and will not be functional (though it might have some other function).

Scenario 3

22. Let's return to the first 15 bases of the sequence in Figure 2.7: atg ggt caa gcc ctt. What is the sequence of the amino acids it encodes?
      m=methionine, g=glycine, q=glutamine, a=alanine, l=leucine

23. A mutation causes a deletion of the first g to give: atg gtc aag ccc ttg. Circle where the change occurred.
      At the beginning of the second codon, there were formerly three g's. Now there are only two.

24. Now, what is the sequence of the amino acids it encodes?
    m=methionine, v=valine, k=lysine, p=proline, l=leucine

25. Describe the mutation:
    25a. How does it affect the DNA? (point or frame-shift mutation)
        frame-shift
    25b. How does it affect the protein? (silent, non-sense, or mis-sense) *mis-sense*

26. What would that mean for our protein?
    It would be a different protein. It would fold differently and might have a different function. Amazing what a difference removing one little base can make.

Scenario 4

27. Let's return to the first 15 bases of the sequence in Figure 2.7 again—atg ggt caa gcc ctt. What is the sequence of the amino acids it encodes?
    m = methionine, g = glycine, q = glutamine, a = alanine, l = leucine

28. A mutation causes an insertion of two t's to give: atg ggt cat tag ccc. Circle where the change occurred.
    The third codon is now cat, not caa.

29. Now, what is the sequence of the amino acids it encodes?
    m = methionine, g = glycine, h = histadine, STOP, (ccc = proline = p)

30. Describe the mutation:
    30a. How does it affect the DNA? (point or frame-shift mutation)
        frame-shift
    30b. How does it affect the protein? (silent, non-sense, or mis-sense) *non-sense*

31. What would that mean for our protein?
    The protein will end after the third amino acid and will not be functional (though it may have some other function).

Part IV. Mutation of the bitterness gene

We don't know the sequence for cucurbitacin (the bitterness gene) in cucumbers. But we do know of cucumber plants with a mutant gene that cannot make cucurbitacin.

32. What type of mutation would lead to a dysfunctional copy of the bitterness gene? Be specific.

There are several acceptable answers. Any mutation that leads to a stop codon (non-sense) or that leads to major changes in the protein sequence (frame-shift mutation) could cause the loss of function.

33. How could you design an experiment to find the sequence for the bitter gene? Assume you have all the same tools as the Korean researchers investigating target leaf spot disease in cucumbers.

    What would you compare?
    Students' answers will vary, but they want to compare a bitter plant (leaf, etc.) with a non-bitter one. They would look for different mRNAs (or cDNAs).

    Once you found a difference, what would you do?
    Sequence it!

The end result: a "candidate" gene for bitterness in cucumber plants. You wouldn't be sure that the gene caused bitterness until you put it into a non-bitter plant (using genetic engineering) and turned that plant bitter.

Why are some genes sequenced and others not sequenced? There are vast numbers of important genes in the world, and genetic sequencing and genomic approaches are still relatively new. The first genes to be sequenced are ones that have important consequences for major global problems. For example, scientists have sequenced genes that influence diseases like breast cancer in humans. In food plants, sequencing has focused on genes that improve yield and genes that are critical for food plants' response to diseases. Bitterness in cucumbers is not an important enough problem for scientists to have invested time and money in sequencing the bitter gene. Scientists can already solve any "bitterness problems" they have in their cucumbers with old-fashioned crosses and genes they've known about for a long time. They can use the genetic rather than genomic approach to bitterness in cucumbers.

SURVIVAL STRATEGIES

How does a plant defend itself? It can't run away or turn and fight like many animals can. Instead, plants employ a variety of **chemical and physical defenses.** Chemical defenses are compounds in or on the plant like the "poison" of poison ivy. Plant structures like a thistle's spines or a tree's bark are physical defenses. Both chemical and physical defenses are encoded in a plant's genes and have been selected over evolutionary time because they give the plant some sort of advantage.

Plant chemical defense strategies

Plants are part of complex ecosystems. They must defend themselves from predators. They also must compete with other plants for light, soil, nutrients, and water. Over time, plants have evolved many strategies for defense and competition. Sometimes, the same strategy is effective for both.

Consider the strategy of a walnut tree. Its genes encode proteins called tannins. Tannins are familiar natural acids—they make the bitter taste in black tea. Because the walnut tree and its nutshells taste so unpleasant, many **herbivores** simply aren't interested in them—an effective plant chemical defense strategy.

Interestingly, this strategy also reduces competition with other plants. When the walnut tree drops its leaves and nuts, they decay into the soil, releasing acidic tannins and making the soil inhospitable for other plants to grow. So while a walnut tree can't move away from predators, its chemical defenses force herbivores to go elsewhere. And while a tree can't move away from another plant that competes for the same sunlight, water, and nutrients, it can create an environment where it is difficult for that competitor to survive.

Herbivores, predators, and prey

How do the walnut tree's tannins help it, from an evolutionary perspective? Think about the walnut's strategy from an herbivore's point of view. Presented with a forest full of trees, why would you choose to

Figure 3.1. A thistle's spines are part of its physical defenses.

Chemical and **physical defenses** are the way plants defend themselves. The "poison" of poison ivy is a **chemical defense.** Cactus spines are a **physical defense.**

Herbivores are organisms that eat plants. Herbivory is a form of predation, but herbivores rarely kill their prey (plants).

Topic: Plant Adaptations
Go to: *www.sciLINKS.org*
Code: GG11

Generalist herbivores can eat many different plants.
Specialist herbivores specialize in one or a few plants that are usually unpalatable to generalists.

eat the bitter one, if you could choose one that tasted better and from which you could digest more nutrients? On the other hand, if many other herbivores are eating the non-bitter trees, you might get more food (and therefore have a better chance of passing your genes on to the next generation) if you ate the bitter trees that no one else wanted.

Thus, insect herbivores have evolved many different strategies. Some, like mites, grasshoppers, and locusts, are **generalists** and feed on a variety of plants. Plant chemical defenses, such as capsaicin that makes hot peppers hot (Figure 3.2), and tannins that make tea and walnuts bitter, are usually effective against generalist herbivores.

Other herbivores have evolved to specialize on particular species of plants or particular compounds produced by these plants. These herbivores are called specialists. For many specialists, chemical defense compounds like capsaicin or tannins are actually attractants. Specialists have evolved the ability to recognize these compounds and to either digest them or sequester them inside their bodies. An insect with bitter tannins in its body will taste bitter to its own predators. Most specialists retain their ability to eat other plants, though they prefer their specific plant. A few specialists go to the extreme of specialization and will eat only their specific plant—without it, they will starve.

Figure 3.2. Generalist predators are usually deterred by capsaicin, the compound that makes hot peppers hot.

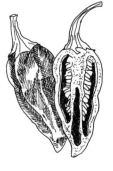

Figure 3.3. A cucumber plant food web.

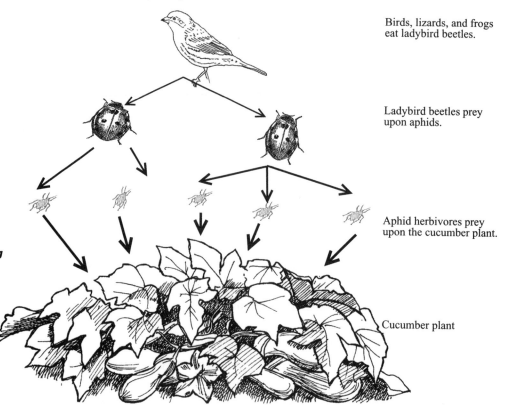

Birds, lizards, and frogs eat ladybird beetles.

Ladybird beetles prey upon aphids.

Aphid herbivores prey upon the cucumber plant.

Cucumber plant

44

The opposite of predator is prey, of course. However, in real-life food webs many organisms are both predator and prey (Figure 3.3). Consider the case of a cucumber plant. The cucumber plant is prey for aphids. The aphid, therefore, is the predator (also known as an herbivore, or plant predator). Aphids are major pests on agricultural crops. Ladybird beetles, also known as ladybugs, are predators of aphids. Often farmers use ladybird beetles to protect crops. By keeping aphid populations under control, these beetles can reduce the need for pesticides. The ladybugs in turn may be eaten by birds, lizards, and frogs. Thus, aphids and ladybugs are both predator and prey in agricultural ecosystems.

Questions for further thought

<u>Evolution</u>: What might be one evolutionary advantage and one disadvantage to being a specialist?

> *One of the great advantages to being a specialist is that you have access to an under-utilized food resource. However, if you've specialized in being able to find, neutralize, and utilize this resource and it becomes unavailable (due to a competitor, hurricane, or drought for example) you have few, if any, other food resources. In essence, your fate is intertwined with that of your host plant.*

<u>Ecology</u>: Can an organism be both a generalist and a specialist? Explain your answer.

> *Entomologists describe the differences between generalists and specialists as a continuum. Some organisms are clearly generalists or clearly specialists. There are specialists that are completely dependent on one and only one species of plant. However, most "specialist" herbivores can consume other food sources. Though they have evolved the biological mechanisms to handle plant defense compounds, most have not lost their ability to find, consume, and digest other plants.*
>
> *The spotted cucumber beetles in this chapter's activity are attracted by cucurbitacin in cucumbers. However, they retain their ability to eat many other plants. (In fact, they are major pests in corn.) Therefore they are intermediate between generalists and specialists. The striped cucumber beetles are clearly specialists. They are also attracted by cucurbitacin, and they do not eat other plants.*

Figure 3.4. Do cucumber plants have physical defenses?

<u>Ecology and evolution</u>: What are the defense mechanisms of cucumber plants? (Hint: Look at Figure 3.4 and think about cucumber plants you may have touched or tasted.)

> *As you can see in Figure 3.4, cucumber plants have small spines on them (physical defense). Some are also sticky (both physical and chemical). Many have a bitter compound, called cucurbitacin, used in plant defense (chemical).*

Chapter 3 Teacher Notes

Overview and Concepts

Overview

This chapter focuses on ecological principles of plant defenses and insect adaptations to these defenses. Insects either are generalists, often deterred by plant chemical defense compounds, or they are specialists that are attracted to the defense compound. Questions focus on ecology and evolution.

Activity: Using a process of guided inquiry, students will design their own experiment to test the effects of a bitter gene in cucumbers on a population of cucumber beetles.

Concepts covered

Ecology, predation, food webs, generalist and specialist, herbivores, defense strategies, genetic effects, experimental design

Prior knowledge required

The text and activities of *Garden Genetics* are intended to apply and supplement textbook concepts. Students should have familiarity with the following:

- Understanding of bitter gene and identification of bitter and non-bitter plants (Chapter 2).
- Predation: One organism consuming (preying upon) another.
- Chemical defense: Because plants can't move away from a predator, many use chemical compounds to defend themselves.
- Experimental design: Hypothesis formation and testing, data collection and interpretation.

Activity notes

Preparation prior to activity

- Several days in advance: Make or obtain insect cages. Directions on page 62.
- 10–14 days before activity: Plant seeds. Germination proceeds faster if the soil is warm. Often classrooms are too cold for quick germination. Teachers have had good luck placing the seeds and soil in an aquarium loosely covered with plastic wrap, with a light/heat source nearby—this simulates the warmth of a greenhouse.

- About a week in advance: Scout out whether or not you can find spotted and/or striped cucumber beetles in the field or a garden. (Both kinds can be found on the leaves of squash, cucumbers, pumpkins, and melons. Spotted cucumber beetles can also be found in fields of corn and beans. Both types of beetles can be kept alive on leaves from squash, cucumber, pumpkin, or melon. Spotted cucumber beetles can also survive on corn, beans, and other annual crop plants.)
- **If beetles can be found in the field:** One to three days before the activity, collect beetles and leaves of the plants where you find them (as a food source). Put the beetles in the insect cage. Put the leaves in water inside the cage.
- **If beetles cannot be found in the field:** Three days before activity, spotted cucumber beetles, also known as Southern corn rootworm, can be ordered from Lee French for 28 cents apiece (French Agricultural Research, Inc., RR2, Box 294, Lamberton, MN 56152, PH (507) 752-7274, FAX (607) 752-6132). They will be delivered via an overnight courier and will arrive with several days' food supply. Be sure to discuss whether there will be a "minimum order charge" and how much shipping will cost. They are shipped in a cooler and cage that you will be asked to return.

Time frame
- Day 1: Design experiment, put plants in the insect cages with the beetles.
- Day 2: Take observations, analyze data, and draw conclusions.

Materials
- Striped and/or spotted cucumber beetles
- Insect cage(s). Note: Beetles instinctively fly up to escape. Make sure that there are no potential entrances and exits near the top. We had terrible results with a "cage" that was a fish tank with screen duct-taped around the top. The beetles all slipped under the tape. However, we had good results with a cage that had a fixed top and a side entrance. The same aquarium, turned on its side, will work much better.
- Bitter and non-bitter cucumber plants in the cotyledon stage. Details on where to find seeds and how to grow can be found in Chapter 1 teacher notes.
- Optional: young corn plants about 10 days old

Safety notes

- It is possible that some cucumber beetles will escape from the cages. They are not harmful to most indoor plants (like house-plants), because they prefer fleshy annuals like corn and beans. The beetles naturally occur in fields and gardens in most of the United States and are short-lived, so you won't be introducing a harmful predator into your school environment.
- We DO NOT suggest using another smaller generalist insect predator like aphids or spider mites (which will prefer non-bitter cucumbers over bitter ones) because they will escape and eat nearly any type of plant.
- Obviously, students should not eat the beetles.
- We recommend that this activity be done without asking students to taste the cucumber plants to determine bitterness. You, the teacher, can tell the students which plants are bitter and which are not. The teacher notes for Activity 1 contain information about tasting and allergenicity.
- Students who are allergic to cucumbers, squash, melon, and zucchini should NOT taste or handle the cucumbers.
- All students should wash their hands after the activity.

Lab notes

- Students will need to understand concepts of generalists and specialists for the activity. If students do the activity before reading the background information on generalists and specialists, most hypothesize that the beetles will eat the non-bitter plants. If students do the activity after reading the background, about half hypothesize that the beetles will eat the bitter plants.
- The beetles can be kept alive for several days in the cage, with fresh leaves as a source of food and water. However, if the beetles are hungry, and young cucumber plants are nearby, the insects will find a way to escape. Keeping an ample supply of food within the cage, making sure the cage has no openings near the top, and making sure no other cucurbits are nearby should be enough to stop escapism. Beetles instinctively fly up to escape. Beetles have been known to escape under screen duct-taped onto a fish tank if the taped opening was at the top. (See notes on cages under "materials.")
- Disposal:
    - The plants can be used for Activity 1 *prior* to this activity. After this activity, very little of these plants will remain—therefore following this activity with Activity 1 is not possible. Some of the plants will survive, and students may enjoy the process of watching them grow for a

longer period of time. Cucumbers in a warm greenhouse environment will produce seed in about three months. You can have students make crosses between bitter and non-bitter plants using a paintbrush or a bee on a stick.

- If you are finished with the plants, they can simply be thrown away.
- The container and soil can be reused. The container should be washed out with soap and water. Ideally, to prevent acquiring soil-borne diseases, soil should be autoclaved or baked in an oven between 180 and 200 degrees. The soil (not just the oven) should be above 180 degrees for at least 30 minutes. (Higher temperatures can produce toxins.) Alternately, the soil can be sterilized in the microwave—90 seconds per kilogram (2.2 pounds) on full power.

Background information on the plants and insects

- This experiment works best with plants in the cotyledon stage because bitterness (caused by cucurbitacin levels) is most pronounced and uniform when plants are young.
- Striped cucumber beetles (*Acalymma vittatum*) are specialists that eat only cucurbits (squash, melons, pumpkins, and cucumbers). Spotted cucumber beetles (*Diabrotica undecimpunctata howardi* or *unidecimpunctata*) are generalists that eat many plants, including corn and beans. Both types of beetles are attracted by cucurbitacin and the beetles will avoid the non-bitter plants if there are bitter plants to eat.
- Both spotted and striped cucumber beetles sequester cucurbitacin in their own bodies and use it for self-defense. Cucurbitacin makes cucumber beetles unpalatable to their own predators (hence their highly visible coloring, as a warning signal). Additionally, cucurbitacin is such a lure to cucumber beetles that some insect-control products use it as a chemical attractant to draw spotted cucumber beetles to insecticide.

Additional experiments with the beetles

1. Students can also design experiments to test if each type of beetle is a generalist or a specialist. The only additional materials the students will need are seedlings of some other plant like bean or corn seedling. The striped cucumber beetles will eat only bitter cucumber plants. The spotted cucumber beetles will eat bitter cucumber plants and corn. Both beetle types will avoid the non-bitter cucumber plants, as long as there are enough edible alternatives.

2. Are the striped and spotted cucumber beetles using the same strategy (i.e., are they both generalists? Both specialists?)? This experiment must be set up with two cages, one for each type of beetle. If both types of beetles are in the same cage it is nearly impossible to distinguish the different feeding habits of each beetle.

3. NOT RECOMMENDED: Will a complete generalist prefer the non-bitter cucumber plants over the bitter ones? Though this makes for a nice lesson about how a compound can be an attractant to one predator and a deterrent to another, generalist herbivores are, unfortunately, generalists. Therefore, they will eat just about anything. There is always a risk of escape from even the best insect cages. Letting them loose in a classroom, school, or greenhouse is a bad idea. Researchers at Cornell have run this experiment in biology classes using spider mites (which inevitably escape and cause problems). Other generalist predators like aphids, grasshoppers, or locusts would also likely prefer the non-bitter cucumber plants. However, releasing a plague of locusts in your school is a very bad idea!

Further reading

The continuum between generalists and specialists
Fox, L. R., and P. A. Morrow. 1981. Specialization: species property or local phenomenon? *Science* 211: 887–93.

Relationships between cucumber beetles and cucurbitacin
Metcalf, R. A. 1986. Coevolutionary adaptations of rootworm beetles (Coleoptera: Chrysomelidae) to cucurbitacins. *Journal of Chemical Ecology* 12: 1109–1124.

Activity 3.

Insect Predation and Plant Genes

In the student edition, this activity begins on page 41.

Topic: Predator/Prey
Go to: www.sciLINKS.org
Code: GG13

Objective

Design and conduct an experiment to learn about the biology of cucumber beetles.

Background

There are two species of cucumber beetles—striped and spotted (see Figure 3.5). Both have similar bodies and both feed on cucumber plants. Your task is to discover more about their ecology and food preferences. Are these beetles generalists that feed on many different species of plants? Are they specialists that focus only on cucumbers? Are they intermediate between a generalist and a specialist, with some of the characteristics of each? Do they eat only certain types of cucumbers? Do the two species have the same food preferences?

Figure 3.5. Striped and spotted cucumber beetles.

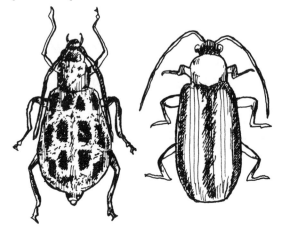

One of the cucumber plant's defenses is a bitter compound called cucurbitacin. This protein is produced in the stems, leaves, and fruit (yes, cucumbers are fruit) of cucumber plants. Though it's not harmful to humans, cucurbitacin makes the plants taste bitter. What effect does this compound have on the beetles? If the beetles are generalists, the cucurbitacin will likely deter them. If the beetles are specialists, the bitterness might actually attract them.

Materials

- Seedlings: bitter cucumbers, non-bitter cucumbers, corn
  See teacher notes about timing; see Chapter 1 for seed sources.
- Soil and containers
- Water source
- Area with light to grow plants
- Striped and/or spotted cucumber beetles
  See teacher notes about where to find or order cucumber beetles. Cucumber beetles are common species found in agricultural fields and will not cause problems for house plants. Experimenting with them in the classroom will not cause an outbreak of beetles.
- Insect cage
  See cage-building directions at end of this chapter.
- Rulers

Safety Notes

- This activity uses cucumber beetles. They are insects that naturally occur in most parts of the United States. If they escape from their cage, they will not cause harm to houseplants.
- Do not eat the cucumber beetles.
- Students who are allergic to cucumbers, squash, melon, or zucchini should NOT handle the plants.
- If you are allergic or not comfortable handling the plants, please ask someone else in your group to do it for you.
- You should wash your hands after handling the plants.
- You should wash your hands AGAIN at the end of the activity.

Activity

Part I. Design your experiment

1. Your objective is to investigate the effect of bitter and non-bitter cucumber genes on cucumber beetles. Formulate a hypothesis. A hypothesis is a possible explanation or an educated guess about what you will find. It is a starting point for your experiment.

    1) Cucumber beetles will prefer non-bitter cucumbers. OR
    2) The cucumber beetles are specialists within the cucumber species. They will prefer bitter cucumbers.

    Most students, if they have not read the chapter, will intuitively guess that the beetles will prefer the non-bitter cucumbers. However, if they've read and thought about the chapter, they will often guess (correctly) that the beetles are specialists and prefer the bitter cucumbers. If you wish the results to be a surprise, you may wish to do the activity before students read the chapter.

    This is a good time to discuss that in science, finding evidence that does not support your hypothesis is just as powerful as finding evidence that does support it. Some of the most interesting discoveries in science have been made this way! The key is to set up an experiment so that results will give you a clear answer and to be open-minded if things do not go as expected.

2. How will you plan your experiment to investigate your hypothesis?
    The results are both dramatic and unexpected. The bitter plants will be completely dead 24 hours later. The beetles often chew directly across the stem, killing the seedling completely. There will not be much left of the bitter cucumber plants to measure, but we like to leave this as a surprise and then help the students revise their experimental plans accordingly.

    2a. What do you plan to do?
    Students will have different plans for how to investigate their hypotheses given the materials you have. For example, with one insect cage, students could put all the beetles in one cage. Then the experiment might involve putting 10 labeled bitter and non-bitter cucumber seedlings in a cage for 24 hours with 30 spotted cucumber beetles. The students would also leave 10 labeled bitter and non-bitter cucumber seedlings under similar conditions outside the cage as controls.

    If the beetles eat both types of cucumber plants, they are unaffected by cucurbitacin (the product of the bitter gene). If beetles eat just the non-bitter plants they are deterred by the cucurbitacin defense. If beetles eat just the bitter plants, they are likely specialists that have evolved the ability to metabolize cucurbitacin and they are attracted to the bitter plants and not to the non-bitter ones.

2b. What supplies will you need? How will you get any that
are not already available in the classroom?
*Obviously, you can constrain students' projects by constraining their
materials. In general, students usually stick to the materials you
provide with this experiment: insect cage(s), beetles, and cucumber
seedlings. They also need a system for labeling plants as bitter or
non-bitter before they go into the cage.*

2c. How do you plan to schedule the project?
*Results will be obvious within 24 hours. If students are keen
observers, they'll see differences within 20 minutes. You may wish
to constrain their time scale to 24 hours, so they don't plan an
experiment that will take three weeks.*

2d. How will you measure your results?
*Typically students will come up with a way to measure damaged surface
area. One of the best methods students came up with used a clear grid
(graph paper photocopied onto overhead sheets) to estimate the area
affected by counting squares. Students will have to think about how to
count plants that are completely dead or gone the following day.*

*This is a good opportunity to discuss what students will do with
their data. What will they do when they have measurements for more
than one plant in a category? Should they take averages? How will
they keep a list of measurements that correspond to the LABELED
plants? (Of course, this means they must label!) Make sure they
think about what to do with the numbers once they have them! (Are
they going to graph? Average? Present a table?)*

*You may want to insert a lesson about repeatability and
"operator error." If two different people in a group take the same
measurement, will the measurement be the same? Probably not,
since students rarely are explicit about precisely what they will
measure. (For example, is height measured from the soil to the
highest point on the plant? To the highest leaf? To the base of the
highest leaf? What if there's a tiny leaf starting above it, then which
leaf do you use?) Students have no trouble deciding how to handle
these small problems, but they are rarely explicit about it!*

3. Evaluate your experiment.
*This would be a prime opportunity for students to peer review each other's
questions or discuss them in small groups. You could have student groups
pair off and present their projects to each other. Then they can reconvene
with their own group to improve their own project. Depending on how
much time you want to devote to this, you could have groups present a
"research proposal" to the class and have the class critique. Students
will be more helpful to one another in their critiques if they focus on the
questions below.*

3a. Does your experiment test the effect of cucumber bitter and non-bitter genes on cucumber beetles?

For example, an experiment that first put non-bitter seedlings into the cage for 24 hours, and then put bitter seedlings into the same cage with the same beetles for the next 24 hours, would be confounded by the beetles' hunger levels. Beetles that are very hungry will eat non-bitter cucumber plants. Satiated beetles will not. Really, students want to give beetles a choice between bitter and non-bitter plants to see which they prefer.

3b. Does your experiment frame a clear question?

In the example above, the question is confounded by the beetles' hunger levels.

3c. Does your hypothesis propose a possible answer to the clearly stated question?

Students should double-check that their hypothesis answers the question. It seems obvious, but some students struggle with this concept.

3d. Is the proposed experiment feasible given the time and materials at hand?

This is an opportunity to make sure that students have a time frame in mind that is compatible with the time and materials you have available. If they require four insect cages while you have only one, they need to adjust their plans. If they're planning to be observing the beetles outside of class time, make sure they think about whose permission they would need to do so. If they're planning on taking three weeks to run their experiment, they should adjust their plans.

Common problems: Students don't think about how to measure results. Students also often have trouble with the idea of replication and with using more than one plant of each type.

3e. What are your controls?

Students frequently forget about controls. If you have an extra cage, the best control is to set bitter and non-bitter seedlings inside a cage that does not have beetles in it. However, if you don't have an extra cage, students can set cucumber seedlings outside the insect cage (where they experience nearly identical environmental conditions).

Part II. Data and results

4. Initial description of your plants. Do they look the same? Are they the same size, shape, and color?

Students likely need an initial set of measurements to compare to. They will have controls to compare to as well, so they can run a successful experiment without doing this step. However, the way to show that the control and experimental populations are comparable is to measure them.

Some students have photographed the plants, which creates a nice record and enables students to backtrack if they decide they want to measure something else later. (Students can take measurements off a digital photo if they include a scale in the photo.) However, photos should be seen as a complement to and not a substitute for measurements! Taking data and dealing with organization and mathematics are important aspects of this experiment.

Teacher note: When students put their seedlings in the cage with the beetles, have the students pay close attention to the way in which the beetles feed. If possible, put a leaf from a bitter plant (without telling the students which kind of leaf) into a clear box with a magnifier on the lid, so they can watch the insect feed up close. The beetles position themselves on the undersides of the leaf and on the stem and scrape away at the soft tissue with their mandibles. It's great to watch! Often the beetles kill the seedling by eating through the stem.

5. Use this space to record your raw data:

   Students may want to create a data sheet that has a space for each labeled plant and the measurements they plan to take on it. For example, if students were measuring height and damaged leaf area, their data sheet might look like the sample sheet below and on the next page.

   NOTE: "Before" and "after" measurements should correspond to the same plant. Many students will write down a list of numbers without any idea which number pertains to which plant.

	Before experiment				After 24 hours			
	control		with insects		control		with insects	
	bitter	non-bitter	bitter	non-bitter	bitter	non-bitter	bitter	non-bitter
plant	ht (cm)	ht (cm)	ht (cm)	ht (cm)	ht (cm)	ht (cm)	ht (cm)	ht (cm)
1								
2								
3								
4								
5								
6								
7								
8								
9								
10								
avg								

plant	Before experiment				After 24 hours			
	control		with insects		control		with insects	
	bitter	non-bitter	bitter	non-bitter	bitter	non-bitter	bitter	non-bitter
	damaged leaf area (cm²)	damaged leaf area (cm²)	damaged leaf area (cm²)	damaged leaf area (cm²)	damaged leaf area (cm²)	damaged leaf area (cm²)	damaged leaf area (cm²)	damaged leaf area (cm²)
1								
2								
3								
4								
5								
6								
7								
8								
9								
10								
avg								

6. Make a table here to summarize your data. Include calculations such as averages for amounts of predation.

If students have made a data sheet, this step is simply a matter of tallying the columns. Some students will want to do this on a computer, others will be happy doing it by hand. To ensure that they take individual measurements, ask them to show their averaging calculations.

For example, if students were measuring height and damaged leaf area their data after predation might look like this:

plant	Before experiment				After 24 hours			
	control		with insects		control		with insects	
	bitter	non-bitter	bitter	non-bitter	bitter	non-bitter	bitter	non-bitter
	ht (cm)	ht (cm)	ht (cm)	ht (cm)	damaged leaf area (cm²)	damaged leaf area (cm²)	damaged leaf area (cm²)	damaged leaf area (cm²)
1	4.0	4.6	1.0	5.0	0.00	0.00	1.00	0.50
2	4.6	5.1	0.0	4.2	0.00	0.10	1.50	0.20
3	5.1	4.7	4.1	4.1	0.00	0.00	1.75	0.00
4	4.7	4.8	2.5	4.5	0.10	0.00	1.30	0.75
5	5.0	4.1	1.8	5.0	0.00	0.13	1.80	0.40
6	4.8	4.5	2.9	4.8	0.00	0.00	1.10	0.10
7	5.2	5.1	0.0	4.2	0.11	0.10	1.67	0.15
8	4.1	4.3	0.0	4.9	0.00	0.00	1.25	0.30
9	4.3	4.6	1.8	4.8	0.20	0.00	1.70	0.60
10	4.5	4.0	0.0	5.0	0.00	0.00	1.50	0.20
avg	4.63	4.58	1.41	4.65	0.04	0.03	1.46	0.32

7. Graph your data.

For example, if students were measuring plant height and damaged surface area, their graphs might look like this:

Figure 3.6. Sample student data.

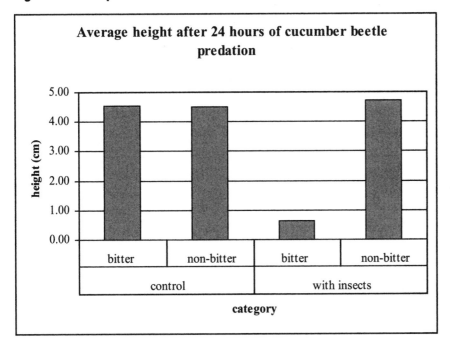

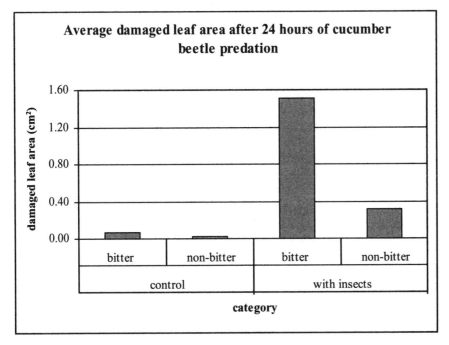

Part III. Conclusions

8. What conclusions can you reach? (What did you learn from your experiment? Was your hypothesis correct? Can you think of any other possible explanations for your results?)

   This is a good place to emphasize that it is easy to draw conclusions… but in science those conclusions must be based on data.

9. Did you have any unexpected results? What were they and why do you think they happened?

   It's also important to encourage students to come up with well-thought-out explanations for why results were not as expected (e.g., might results be due to the biology of the organisms, to some fault with the procedures, or to multiple factors?) If students attribute unexpected results to "experimental error," make sure they are specific about what they think went wrong and why.

   The way that the beetles attack the plants may lead to some surprises for students in the way they were planning to measure results.

10. How could you improve your experimental design? (Are there ways your experiment could be improved to better answer the initial question? Did you come up with questions you can't answer using your data?)

    Encourage students to think creatively and critically here! Was it a good experiment? Would more plants, more beetles, or more cages have made it better? How hungry were the beetles? Would they have behaved differently if they were more/less hungry? Were the measurements students took helpful? What else could they have measured?

    This is also a good time to point out that scientists often run an experiment more than once, especially when they are fine-tuning their investigative technique. (Were they measuring the right thing? Is there a better measurement technique? Should the plants be a different age? Would hungrier beetles give the same result?)

    This is also a good time to process and get feedback about the challenges of dealing with data. Did they collect the data they needed? How did they decide what to do with it? Did the conclusions from the data show the same conclusions they could see for themselves? (If not, were they taking the right data?) What would happen if they had ten times as much data? (The results might be clearer, because any one anomalous plant couldn't throw the average off. However, more data can make things more complicated. With more data it is CRITICAL to have a good plan for what to do with it!)

11. Based on what you know about generalists and specialists, are there other questions you would like to investigate with the techniques you developed in this experiment?

    For example, a generalist will eat other plants, in addition to cucumbers. Students could present cucumber beetles with bitter and non-bitter cucumber plants as well as corn seedlings and see which they would prefer to eat. If they eat the corn, in addition to the cucumber plants, (as the spotted cucumber beetles would) they have some generalist characteristics. If they ignore the corn and eat only cucumbers (as the striped cucumber beetles would), they are true specialists.

    Another example: Do striped and spotted cucumber beetles use the same ecological strategy? Are they both specialists? Are they both generalists? If students had two insect cages, they could put striped beetles in one and spotted beetles in the other and present both sets of beetles with bitter and non-bitter cucumber plants. (Both types would prefer the bitter.) Or they could present both types of beetles with both corn and cucumber plants. (See paragraph above for possible results).

Part IV. Applying what you've learned

12. What does your experiment tell you about bitterness in cucumbers?

    In general, cucumber bitterness, caused by the protein cucurbitacin, acts as a part of a plant's defense. Specialist herbivores, like cucumber beetles, have evolved to find chemicals like cucurbitacin an attractant. A generalist predator like a mite or a grasshopper will avoid bitter plants.

13. What does your experiment tell you about the behavior of cucumber beetles? Are they generalists or specialists?

    Striped cucumber beetles are clearly specialists as they prefer the bitter cucumber plants.

    Spotted cucumber beetles are less clearly specialists on the generalist-specialist continuum. They have some characteristics of generalists and some characteristics of specialists. They are specialists in the sense that they too find cucurbitacin an attractant and prefer bitter cucumber plants over non-bitter cucumber plants. However, they are generalists in the sense that they will eat corn as well as cucumbers.

    Remember, there is a continuum of insect strategies ranging from absolute specialization to complete generalism. Spotted cucumber beetles fall somewhere in the middle of the spectrum. Striped cucumber beetles are much more clearly specialists.

Cage Building Directions

Materials for one frame:

- 8 lengths of scrap wood to make ends (approximately 25 to 45 cm in length)
- 4 lengths of scrap wood to connect ends together (approximately 25 to 60 cm in length)
- Fiberglass screen to wrap the frame (available at hardware stores)
- 2 m knitted ribbing tube (available at fabric stores, commonly used to make collars and cuffs on knit clothing)
- Screws or nails to connect wood together
- Drill with screw attachment or hammer
- Staples and staple gun to attach screen and ribbing
- Approximately 2 cm wide strips of cardboard

1. <u>Build a frame</u>. We have had success with small (25 cm) cubes or much larger (45 × 45 × 60 cm) frames. First build the ends using scrap wood. Then connect the two ends together (Figure 3.7).

Figure 3.7. Build cage ends. Connect ends together.

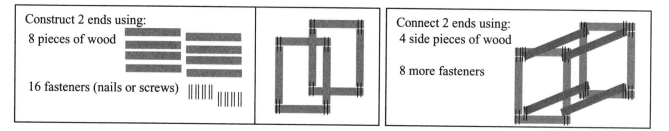

2. <u>Screen the frame</u>. Using fiberglass screen available from a hardware store, wrap the frame, stapling it securely. Place the beginning and end on one of the side pieces of wood. Cover all edges with a piece of cardboard and staple again (Figure 3.8).

Figure 3.8. Screen the frame and add sleeves to ends.

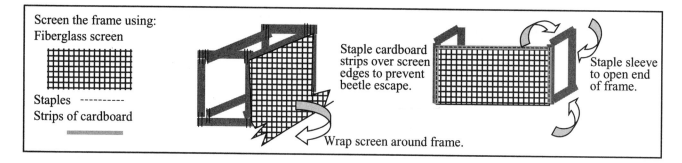

3. <u>Attach the sleeves to the end.</u> Cut the 2 m fabric ribbing tube in half to make 2 tubes, each 1 m in length. Staple each tube around one of the open ends of the frame. Tie excess fabric loosely into a knot to close the frame (Figure 3.8).

4. <u>Double-check for holes and gaps.</u> Double-check the frame to make sure there are no holes and gaps where small insects could escape. If you find any, cover them and rotate the cage so the potential escape holes are not at the top of the cage. The beetles will fly up to escape.

SECTION 2
Corn

DOMESTICATION

Evolving Toward Home

How did dogs become our companions? Once they were wolves, roaming in packs. What did that first wolf that left the pack to join a human group look like? People probably found the wolf-dogs useful for keeping the true wolves away from human camps and helpful for hunting. Humans saw the value of these animals and began to feed them. People and their dogs have been inseparable ever since.

It's easy to see the evolution from wild wolf to docile dog as **domestication**. The wolf lives in the wild and feeds itself. The dog lives with humans and is fed by them. Imagine a Chihuahua trying to survive on its own in the wild! The dog has joined the circle of a human home. The word *domestication* comes from the Latin word *domus,* meaning home. Domestication is literally the process of bringing an organism, animal or plant, into the home. A domesticated plant is one that is dependent on humans for its survival. In turn, we humans couldn't survive very long without our domesticated plants.

A **domesticated** plant or animal is dependent on humans for its survival.

*Sci*LINKS.
THE WORLD'S A CLICK AWAY

Topic: Crop Pollination
Go to: www.sciLINKS.org
Code: GG14

The changes of domestication

What makes a domesticated plant? Something about the wild plant has to change. Think about a field of wild grasses. When you walk through a field of wild grass, you come home with different kinds of seeds or grain stuck to your legs. When you touch some heads of grain, they explode or shatter, tossing their seeds to the ground. These are dispersal mechanisms—ways to distribute seeds for the next generation (Figure 4.1). Nothing happens when you walk through a field of

Figure 4.1. Some plant dispersal mechanisms.

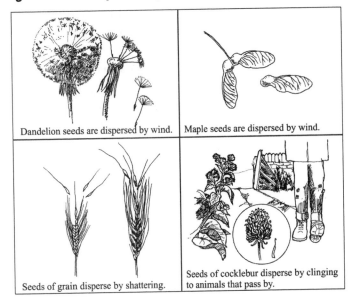

Dandelion seeds are dispersed by wind.

Maple seeds are dispersed by wind.

Seeds of grain disperse by shattering.

Seeds of cocklebur disperse by clinging to animals that pass by.

Topic: Natural Selection
Go to: *www.sciLINKS.org*
Code: GG15

Evolution is driven by **natural selection**—a process that results in the most fit individuals having the most offspring.

Domestication is driven by **artificial selection**—human decisions toward human goals.

wheat or corn (both domesticated grasses). No grain sticks to your pant legs; no seeds are thrown to the ground. How then could a wheat or corn plant disperse the seeds that will become the next generation? Wheat and corn are dependent on humans to collect the seeds and plant them—a dispersal mechanism of a different kind.

Domestication is really a form of **evolution**. Instead of changes being driven by **natural selection**, the changes of domestication are driven by **artificial selection**—meaning selection done by humans, toward human goals. Domestication almost always involves reproductive changes. Strategies that work well in nature are often inconvenient for farmers and other human caretakers. In nature, if a head of grain does not shatter, the seeds remain on the head. They don't reach the ground. They don't germinate. They don't become part of the next plant generation. In fact, natural selection would eliminate non-shattering heads of grain.

However, when humans found a plant with a mutation that meant the heads of grain didn't shatter, more of that plant's seed ended up in the harvest. More of it was planted for the next generation because the farmer was able to collect the non-shattering seeds more easily. Each generation, more and more of the non-shattering grain ended up in the harvest. Eventually, all the plants in a field were non-shattering, and the shattering types of plants disappeared from farmers' fields. Thus artificial selection often drives plants in different directions than natural selection.

Artificial selection and human preference change plants in consistent ways. Fruits become larger. Flavors become sweeter. Grains and fruits remain on the plant longer. Plants flower and mature at the same time, making harvests easier and more productive. Natural selection, on the other hand, is not directional and does not lead to a progression toward an ideal or goal. (An example of artificial selection is diagramed in Figure 4.3.)

Targets of domestication

Considering the hundreds of thousands of plants that exist in nature, it is remarkable that we are dependent on just a handful of domesticated plants for most of our food. Figure 4.2 shows the 32 crops for which more than 25 million metric tons were harvested around the world in 2004. Four crops—wheat, rice, corn, and potatoes—represent the majority of the harvest. Why are we dependent on so few crops, when there were so many to start with? The answer begins with which plants can be easily domesticated, as well as with taste, yield, and ease of growing.

68

Figure 4.2. World production (millions of metric tons) for 2004 (from FAOSTAT database).

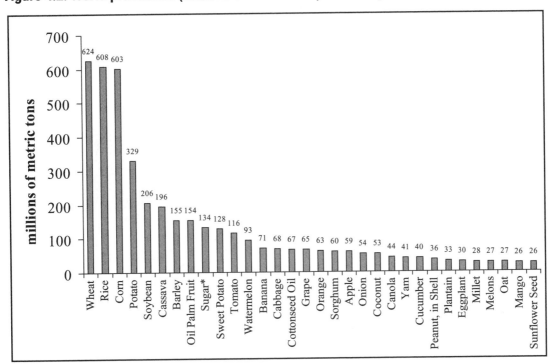

*2002 refined sugar equivalent

Not all plants are easily domesticated. For example, wild almonds and acorns suffer from the same major problem (from the human perspective). Their fruits are full of bitter, toxic compounds, which the plants use for defense and which interfere with human digestion. So why has the almond been domesticated while the oak has not? Both were eaten extensively by prehistoric people. Non-bitter forms of both trees exist in nature. But in almonds, bitterness is largely under the control of one gene. So the offspring of a non-bitter almond tree are likely to be non-bitter. Thus non-bitter almonds are relatively easy to select. On the other hand, many genes play a role in controlling the bitterness of acorns. When the acorns from non-bitter oaks are planted, the new generation still has bitter acorns. The critical trait that influences oak domestication is too genetically complex for non-bitter oaks to be easily domesticated.

THE POWER OF ARTIFICIAL SELECTION

Artificial selection is a powerful tool. The pressure of human selection has produced many different vegetables from the same plant, *Brassica oleracea.*

The original *Brassica* plant probably looked like a wild mustard plant. Broccoli, cauliflower, kohlrabi, brussels sprouts, cabbage, and kale are all modifications of the leaf, shoot, flower, or root system.

Figure 4.3. Artificial selection has produced many vegetables from the same wild mustard ancestor.

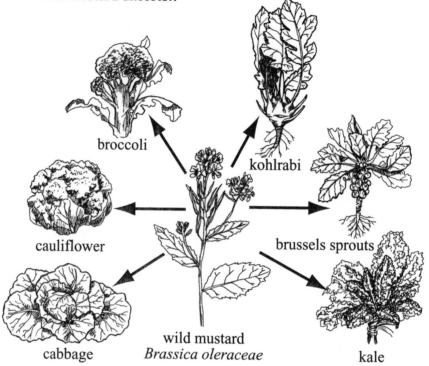

broccoli

kohlrabi

cauliflower

brussels sprouts

cabbage

wild mustard
Brassica oleraceae

kale

Timescale of change

Gradualism is the accumulation of small changes over time. It leads to slow, gradual evolution.

Evolution by **punctuated equilibrium** has bursts of change followed by periods of stability. It leads to much faster evolution.

How fast does domestication occur? Beginning with Darwin, people proposed that domestication, like all evolution, was the accumulation of small changes over time. This theory is often called **gradualism**. Many small, advantageous mutations would be selected for, and species would change slowly. More recently, people have proposed that evolution and domestication might occur with short bursts of radical change followed by periods of relative stability. This theory is called **punctuated equilibrium**. Domestication could also involve both kinds of change—rapid changes followed by slow changes or vice versa.

The process of domestication was different for each species. No one knows exactly how fast domestication of a species occurred because it happened a long time ago. However, the archeological and genetic records provide important clues. Prehistoric ears of corn and corncobs are visual evidence of how corn was domesticated. But how does genetic information help us understand domestication?

Corn: A genetic case study

The changes of domestication are genetic changes. For over a century, people studied, debated, and speculated about origins of corn. There was no obvious wild relative—nothing looked like the corn plants people knew. Eventually, scientists began to suspect that grassy weeds called teosinte, growing in cornfields, might be related to corn. Initially teosinte was considered a separate species. Further studies identified this grass, shown in Figure 4.4, as corn's nearest wild relative. Even though they look different, they have the same number of chromosomes and can cross in the field. They are now considered to be part of the same species. Genetic studies have shown that corn was domesticated from teosinte about 9,000 years ago.

Figure 4.4. Teosinte and corn.

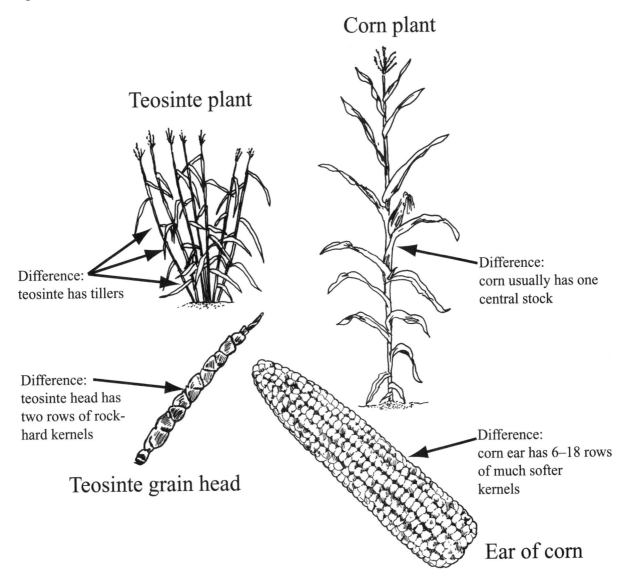

Corn plant

Teosinte plant

Difference: teosinte has tillers

Difference: corn usually has one central stock

Difference: teosinte head has two rows of rock-hard kernels

Teosinte grain head

Difference: corn ear has 6–18 rows of much softer kernels

Ear of corn

How, genetically, was the wild grass teosinte transformed into corn? Teosinte heads have two rows of rock-hard triangular seeds. Corn seeds or grains are softer and occur on cobs, sometimes with more than 20 rows. Teosinte has many tillers, or stems, growing from the same root base. Corn rarely has more than one main stalk.

Corn and teosinte seed heads or cobs are so physically different from one another that most people thought that many gradual changes over a long time must have been required for the domestication of corn (gradualism). They simply couldn't think of a few changes (really a few genes) that could result in such a different plant. To study the genetic basis for the differences, a group of scientists headed by John Doebley made crosses between teosinte and corn. Then they used a set of genetic tools called a QTL (quantitative trait locus) analysis to understand which genes were involved in domestication. (More on quantitative traits and QTL studies in Chapter 9.)

To everyone's surprise, Doebley's group found that the differences between corn and teosinte are controlled by a handful of genes (only five to ten). One of these genes accounted for a whopping 40% of the variation between corn and teosinte. Instead of finding support for slow change over a long time (gradualism), they found genetic evidence for a few genes with dramatic effects. The changes to so few genes could have happened very quickly (punctuated equilibrium)—possibly within a few generations.

How could rapid changes in the teosinte plant be caused by differences in a few genes? Most changes to genes (usually mutations) inactivate or disable a protein that the plant makes. (See Chapter 2 for details.) The plant needs most of the proteins it makes. Therefore, losing the ability to make a protein (like chlorophyll) is often fatal. In other words, most mutations are bad for the plant. Only occasionally do positive mutations occur. Therefore people thought that it would take a long time to build up the many small, positive mutations of gradualism. The Doebley teosinte study was exciting because the changes in phenotype resulted from as few as five positive mutations—this number of mutations is small and so the changes could have occurred in a short period of time. Thus, the teosinte study provided genetic evidence for the theory of punctuated equilibrium. With so few mutations being responsible for so large a change, people could envision the genetic basis for punctuated equilibrium's burst of rapid evolution.

Questions for further thought

<u>Evolution</u>: What is the definition of species? How could teosinte originally be considered a different species from corn if it is now considered the same species? What sort of information would be required to change a species classification?

> *Species classifications are categories we impose on organisms. Usually, species are considered separate if they cannot mate and produce viable offspring. A donkey and a horse can mate, but their offspring, a mule, is sterile. Thus donkeys and horses are considered separate species. When teosinte was discovered, it was believed to be a relative of corn, but not one close enough to mate with corn. Once scientists found evidence that the two are cross-fertile, they could not be considered separate species any more.*

<u>Genetics</u>: The radical difference between the grass-like teosinte and corn is thought to be controlled by as few as five or ten genes. Is each of these genes likely to have single effects (one for shattering, another for tillering, and still another for multi-rowed ears)? Or are they likely to be genes that have multiple effects (one gene affects both tillering and multi-rowed ears)?

> *The genes involved in the transition from teosinte to corn were likely genes with multiple effects.*

How could a gene have multiple effects?

> *For example, tb1, the gene which accounts for 40% of the difference between the teosinte and corn, suppresses tiller formation, causes ear formation, and suppresses tassel development. It is a regulatory gene. This means that it controls which other genes get turned on and off, and in which places. Therefore, it can have many different effects in many different places.*

Chapter 4 Teacher Notes

Overview and Concepts

Overview

The chapter explores the concept of domestication and the changes that occur in plants as they transition from wild to cultivated. Domestication is a form of evolution driven by artificial selection rather than natural selection. A box shows the power of artificial selection by looking at the members of the *Brassica* family. The chapter discusses two theories of evolution, gradualism and punctuated equilibrium, in terms of timescales of change. The chapter concludes by discussing genetic evidence about rates of evolutionary change from corn. Questions focus on evolution and genetics.

Activity 4 uses archeological and genetic evidence from corn to explore the timescale of evolution. Results show that corn has had periods of rapid change consistent with the theory of punctuated equilibrium, as well as the slow cumulative changes associated with gradualism.

Concepts covered

Evolution, domestication, gradualism, punctuated equilibrium, artificial selection, natural selection, genetic basis of domestication, archeology

Prior knowledge required

The text and activities of *Garden Genetics* are intended to apply and supplement textbook concepts. Students should have familiarity with the following:

- **Evolution:** The process by which modern organisms have descended from ancient organisms. Fundamentally about changes in relative frequencies of alleles in populations.
- **Evolutionary success:** Passing genes onto the next generation.
- **Natural selection:** The most "fit" organisms produce the most offspring.
- Evolution acts on **individuals** (will have many or few offspring) but is seen in shifts of allele frequencies in **populations**.
- **Gene:** A segment of DNA that codes for a particular protein. In an evolutionary context, that protein may confer an evolutionary advantage or disadvantage.
- **Simple genetic control:** A trait that is controlled by a single gene, like the pea characteristics studied by Mendel, or bitterness in almonds, as discussed in the text.
- **Complex genetic control:** A trait, like yield in wheat or bitterness in acorns, controlled by many genes.

Activity notes

Preparation prior to activity

- Students should be familiar with basic evolutionary concepts including natural selection and changes in populations over time.

Time frame

- One or two class periods

Materials

- Rulers
- Calculator (optional)

Teaching tips

- Students should answer all questions in the worksheet.
- Take some time to have students process the complex notion that corn shows good evidence for both quick and slow evolution within the same species.
- The end of the activity provides an opportunity to emphasize that science is about interpretation of data, and interpretation is limited to the best data available at the time. Scientists have been debating the origins of corn for a century!

Further reading

Domestication

Diamond, J. 2002. Evolution, consequences and future of plant and animal domestication. *Nature* 418: 700–707.

Harlan, J. 1976. The plants and animals that nourish man. *Scientific American* 235: 89–97.

Teosinte and maize

Doebley, J., and R. L. Wang. 1997. Genetics and the evolution of plant form: An example from maize. *Cold Spring Harbor Symposia on Quantitative Biology*, vol. LXII.

Archeological evidence from Tehuacan

Mangelsdorf, P., R. MacNeish, and W. Galinat. 1964. Domestication of corn. *Science* 143: 538–545.

Activity 4.
Corn and the Archeological Record
In the student edition, this activity begins on page 60.

Topic: Food Crops
Go to: *www.sciLINKS.org*
Code: GG16

Objective
Use predictions, genetic evidence, and the archeological record to determine a history of domestication for corn.

Background
Domestication (like evolution) can occur rapidly or slowly or with some alternation of the two rates. Genetic evidence tells us corn was domesticated about 9,000 years ago. Figure 4.5 shows actual sized illustrations of corn and teosinte, its wild relative.

Figure 4.5. Actual size drawings of teosinte and corn.

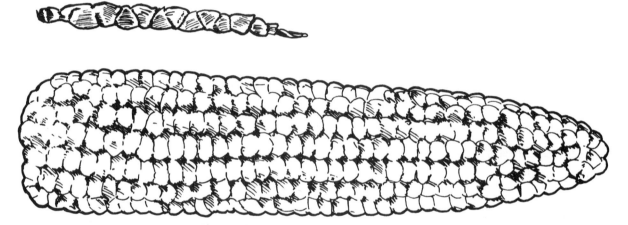

Activity

Part I. Predictions

Draw teosinte grain heads and corn ears on the timeline below to predict how corn might change if domestication occurred in the following ways.

1. Slow evolution, with small changes.
   Gradual progression of small changes over a long time.

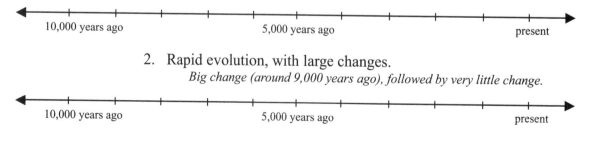

2. Rapid evolution, with large changes.
   Big change (around 9,000 years ago), followed by very little change.

3. Slow evolution followed by rapid evolution.
   Gradual progression followed by a big jump in size.

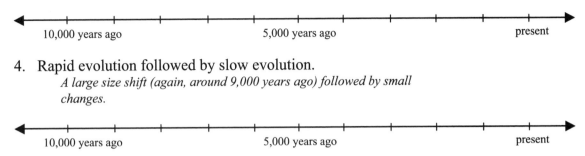

10,000 years ago   5,000 years ago   present

4. Rapid evolution followed by slow evolution.
   A large size shift (again, around 9,000 years ago) followed by small changes.

10,000 years ago   5,000 years ago   present

Part II. Evidence of domestication—genetic

There are two important lines of evidence to help us understand the domestication of corn: the archeological record and the genetic record. The chapter text reviews some of the recent genetic evidence.

5. Did scientists expect to find the effects of many genes (each providing small changes) or few genes (each providing large changes)? What about corn and teosinte led them to that expectation?
   Scientists expected to find many, many genes involved because corn and teosinte were so different.

6. What did John Doebley's genetic experiments show?
   Doebley's experiments showed a few (five to ten) genes responsible for the differences between teosinte and corn.

7. How is this genetic evidence interpreted in regard to rate of domestication?
   The genetic evidence is interpreted to mean the domestication event (the major, structural changes from teosinte to corn) took place rapidly, probably within a generation or two.

8. How long ago did the domestication events occur? Draw them on a timeline.
   The domestication events occurred about 9,000 years ago. There should be a major change from grass-like plants with 2-rowed triangular kernels to corn-like plants, with multi-rowed ears, full of rounded kernels, on the timeline.

10,000 years ago   5,000 years ago   present

Part III. Evidence of domestication— archeological

The archeological record provides physical evidence of the past. However, the archeological record has some limitations. Without an appropriate site and prehistoric corn or cobs, there is nothing to examine. If you have ever thrown an ear of corn onto a compost pile, it will be obvious that unusual circumstances are required to preserve corn kernels for thousands of years. Most importantly, the ear must be kept dry. Some of the most important archeological sites are caves, because the contents have been well protected from weather.

Furthermore, the archeologist is limited to studying the parts of the plant that remain behind. In the case of corn, the cob is the most durable part. Though whole ears with kernels thousands of years old have been found, most archeological corn samples are cobs or pieces of cob. Additionally, the story told by archeological evidence from one site is unique. A different site might yield different evidence.

In 1960, with the help of some local students, archeologist Richard MacNeish found several caves in the valley of Tehuacan, in the state of Mexico. MacNeish began digging (very carefully!) and within a week, found corn. From 1960 to 1963, archeologists and scientists came to Tehuacan to study the domestication and evolution not just of corn, but also of beans, squash, cotton, hunted animals, and the humans who lived there for thousands of years.

In the five caves of the Tehuacan valley, archeologists found 24,186 corn specimens. More than half (12,860) were whole or almost whole cobs. The corn specimens were deposited in layers, as various groups of people used the caves as shelter, over thousands of years. Each generation piled their garbage on top of that from the generation before, leaving a time sequence of the evolution of corn in the Tehuacan valley.

Each picture on pages 79 and 80 is a subset of the cobs found at a different level in the San Marcos cave in Tehuacan. The dates are provided for you from the original study. **The photos are actual size. Please determine the average size of the ears in each photo.**

Figure 4.6. Actual size photos of archeological corn from Tehuacan cave layers A and B.

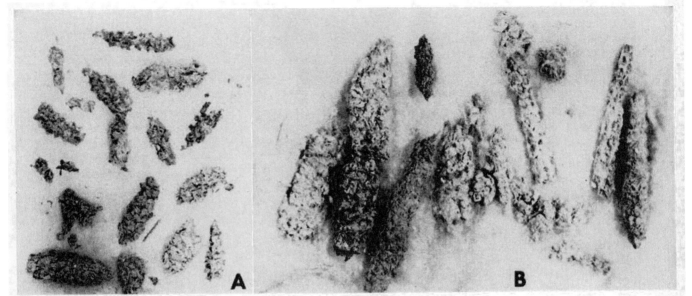

Reprinted with permission from Mangelsdorf, MacNeish, and Galinat. 1964. Domestication of corn. *Science* 143: 538–545. Copyright AAAS.

9. A   age: 7,200 to 5,400 years old   average size: *about 1.4 cm*

10. B   age: 5,400 to 4,300 years old   average size: *about 2.9 cm*

Figure 4.7. Actual size photos of archeological corn from Tehuacan cave layer C.

Reprinted with permission from Mangelsdorf, MacNeish, and Galinat. 1964. Domestication of corn. *Science* 143: 538–545. Copyright AAAS.

11. C   age: 3,500 to 2,900 years old   average size: *about 6.1 cm*

Figure 4.8. Actual size photos of archeological corn from Tehuacan cave layer D.

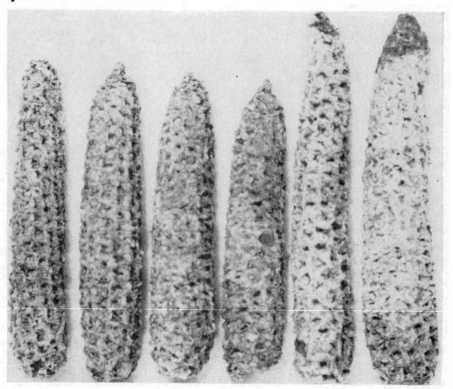

Reprinted with permission from Mangelsdorf, MacNeish, and Galinat. 1964. Domestication of corn. *Science* 143: 538–545. Copyright AAAS.

12. D   age: 2,700 to 2,200 years old   average size: *about 8.15 cm*

13. On your timeline, first show the changes suggested by the genetic evidence. (This is what you did in question 8.) Next, show on your timeline how the archeological evidence would influence the changes from teosinte to corn.

    Should show a gradual progression in size from 7,000 years ago to 2,000 years ago.

10,000 years ago   5,000 years ago   present

Part IV. Putting the evidence together

14. Given the genetic and archeological evidence, how would you describe the domestication of corn? Was it fast? Was it slow? Was it a combination of the two?

    Domestication of corn was a combination of the two. Around 9,000 years ago, there was a dramatic, rapid event in which the teosinte-form (tillering plant with many heads of grain) changed to the corn-form (a plant with one central stalk and few [usually one] very large, multi-rowed ears). Since then, there has been slow change as humans have gradually selected for larger and larger ears.

15. Does your timeline based on evidence agree with any of your predicted timelines? Why or why not?

> *The evidence agrees with the "fast, followed by slow" evolution scenario.*

A final note: You have just told a credible story of corn domestication (and evolution) based on two different kinds of evidence. In the last century, hundreds of studies were conducted to learn about the evolution of corn, but they did not all agree with one another. Like any scientist, you've drawn the best conclusions you can, given the evidence you have. This evidence reflects our current best knowledge about corn domestication. However, if you were given more evidence, like any scientist, you might have to adjust your conclusions.

16. How would you adjust your conclusions if a new archeological study found corn that looks like corn we eat today in a South American cave from 15,000 years ago?

> *If a new study showed much older archeological evidence from South America, you might conclude that domestication occurred separately and earlier in South America than it did in Mexico. The point of this question is that this is an exercise in interpretation. New evidence could change your perspective. (There are other reasonable answers too; e.g., the corn we grow today came from South America and the small Mexican ears were lost to extinction.)*

> *The evidence above is purely fictional. However, South American corn is highly diverse and different from Central American corn. Some scientists believe that corn came from South America or that it was domesticated in both places. Most modern evidence seems to refute these ideas and indicates that corn was domesticated in Central America and then moved to South America where it flourished and evolved.*

17. How would you adjust your conclusions if a recent genetic study showed large blocks of DNA in modern day corn that were similar to an entirely different species called *Tripsacum dactyloides*?

> *You could reasonably conclude that teosinte was not the only ancestor of corn. With this evidence, it would be reasonable to conclude that* Tripsacum *was an ancestor as well.*

> *Although the genetic evidence above is fictional, there is a controversy about whether teosinte was the sole ancestor of corn or whether both teosinte and* Tripsacum *were involved. The evidence for this controversy is based on the physical resemblance of a teosinte-*Tripsacum *cross to some of the earliest prehistoric ears of corn.*

The evidence in questions 1–15 represents the current majority opinion about the origins of corn, but some scientists disagree. All conclusions are interpretations of the data. No one really knows exactly how corn was domesticated. Questions 16 and 17 are included to illustrate that there has been a hundred years of debate on the origins of corn. New evidence requires new interpretation. Though the "evidence" presented is fictional, the questions represent real debates that have occurred.

THE RISKS OF IMPROVEMENT
Genetic Uniformity and an Epidemic

In the Mexican state of Jalisco, Don Paulo grows different kinds of corn (Figure 5.1). Mexico is the homeland for corn—the "Center of Diversity"—a place rich in corn genes and genetic diversity. Don Paulo's cornfields have short plants and tall plants, plants that mature quickly and plants that mature slowly, plants with large starchy kernels and others with small hard kernels. Yields are low, and the corn ripens at different times. Don Paulo harvests the corn by hand, so it doesn't matter if it matures at different times. His fields are on steep hillsides; he couldn't use a tractor even if he had one. The genetic diversity in his field is a good insurance policy—if a corn disease outbreak occurs, or a big storm blows through, some plants in his field are likely to survive. Don Paulo's yields are likely to be low even in a good year. But there will almost always be something to harvest, even in a bad year.

Topic: Plant Propagation
Go to: *www.sciLINKS.org*
Code: GG17

Crop improvement is driven by **artificial selection** in which humans make decisions about what kinds of plants they want.

The power of selection

Every year, Don Paulo saves the best seed from his harvest to plant again. This is a form of selection. He chooses seeds from plants that have characteristics he favors, such as large white grains, straight rows, and large ears.

Like Don Paulo, plant breeders select desirable traits in the plant populations they work with. Plant breeders select the best of a population of plants and use it as the parents of the next generation (Figure 5.2). By continuing to select the best, a plant breeder increases the frequency of those desirable genotypes. This is **artificial selection**.

Figure 5.1. Don Paulo in a Mexican cornfield.

Artificial selection differs from natural selection because humans do the selecting, instead of "nature" selecting the "fittest."

Selection improves whatever characteristic the breeder is working on, for example, ear size, yield, or resistance to a disease. Figure 5.2 shows that selection also results in genetic narrowing. Selection improves crops by eliminating the "undesirable" genotypes—the smaller ears, the lower yielding, or less disease resistant. This means that genetic diversity is lost with each round of improvement.

Figure 5.2. Effects of selection.

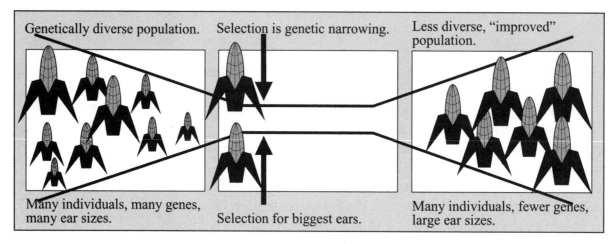

The downside of diversity

Topic: Genetic Variation
Go to: *www.sciLINKS.org*
Code: GG18

Is genetic diversity always a good thing? To Don Paulo, it is. But to farmers with rich, flat land, like in the midwestern United States, diversity has some drawbacks. Having different varieties in the same field may mean lower yields, plants that ripen at different times, and difficulty using tractors because the plants are too variable.

Farmers care about yield. Yield means money in their pockets. Without high yield, many farmers can't afford to stay in business. Therefore, when a new variety arrives that is better than the old varieties, farmers want to plant it. Figure 5.3 shows how much area in the United States was planted with the six most popular varieties of corn, cotton, soy, and wheat. In 1970, more than 70% of the corn-growing area in the United States was planted with only six corn varieties. What does this mean, when huge areas of land are planted to exactly the same variety? (Notice that by 1980, the area planted with the six most popular varieties had decreased to 43%—meaning that farmers were planting more different varieties. Something happened between 1970 and 1980 that made farmers realize the value of more diversity in the varieties they plant. More about this in Activity 5.)

Figure 5.3. Percent area planted with 6 most popular varieties of important crops, 1970 and 1980.

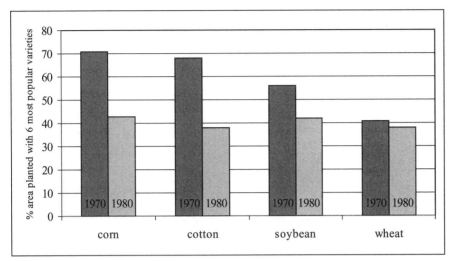

Pressure

Imagine a new variety of corn is created that is resistant to rust, a disease caused by a fungus. Farmers want to plant the variety because rust causes major losses in their crops. Suddenly, huge areas are planted with this variety.

Next try to predict what happens to the rust fungus. At the beginning, most of the rust-causing fungi die because they have no host plant and therefore no food source. However, there are a few fungi with a mutation or an adaptation that allows them to survive. Those few become the parents of the next generation of rust-causing fungi, many of which can survive on the new corn variety. Within a few generations there is a population of rust-causing fungi that can attack the corn that was bred to resist them. Thus, lack of diversity, or planting large areas of the same variety, has some major drawbacks when it comes to disease. It can create powerful natural selection pressure on insects, diseases, and other pests to change to forms that can survive on the new variety.

Corn hybrids

Hybrids take advantage of one of corn's unique traits: Corn can be pollinated by its own pollen (**selfed**) or by pollen from another plant (**crossed**). Making a hybrid requires both types of pollination. First a line of corn is selfed for many generations until it is homozygous, meaning it has two identical copies of the same allele at all of its loci. Then, two homozygous lines, called inbred lines, are crossed with each other. The resulting hybrid generation of plants will be heterozygous (one allele from each line). No one fully understands why, but that hybrid generation has about a 30% boost in yield. The yield gain disappears again in

A **hybrid** is a cross between two different things. A hybrid car is half gas, half electric. A hybrid plant results from a cross between two different parents. It has two different alleles at its loci, one from each parent.

Selfing is when a plant is pollinated by itself. In corn, pollen from the tassel of one plant is used to pollinate the ear of the same plant.

Crossing uses pollen from one plant to pollinate a different plant.

Figure 5.4. Impact of hybrid varieties on historical U.S. corn yield.

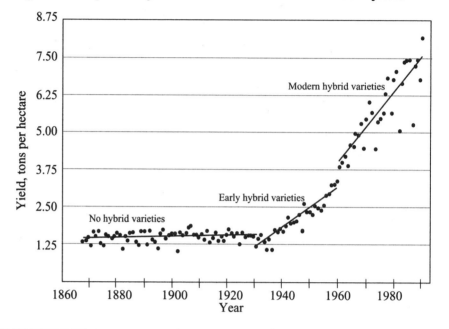

GREEN REVOLUTION

New crop varieties, fertilizers, pesticides, irrigation, and mechanization all contributed to increasing corn yield in the United States during the 21st century. The Green Revolution attempted to eliminate hunger worldwide by using similar methods to increase crop yields of other crops, like rice and wheat.

Green Revolution rice and wheat varieties have shorter stalks that can support large heads of grain without falling over. This new plant architecture is caused by one or a few mutations called dwarfing genes. When grown with fertilizers, these "dwarf" plants produce much higher yields.

The Green Revolution brought tremendous benefits in feeding a hungry world. In addition, with higher yields from existing farmland, less new land needed to be cultivated. This meant saving rain forests and other important ecosystems. However, the Green Revolution was not without problems. Crops were more uniform genetically and thus more subject to disease. Farmers became dependent on fertilizers and pesticides to produce high yields. And unfortunately, the benefits were not equally distributed across nations or socioeconomic groups; often only wealthier farmers were able to access the Green Revolution crops, fertilizers, and other technologies.

the next generation of plants, so farmers have a big incentive to keep buying new hybrid seed. (See figure 5.4)

So it seems easy. You take pollen from inbred plant B and use it to pollinate inbred plant A (Figure 5.5). But how do you keep the pollen from plant A from landing on the flowers of plant A and "contaminating" it?

Figure 5.5. Hybrid production.

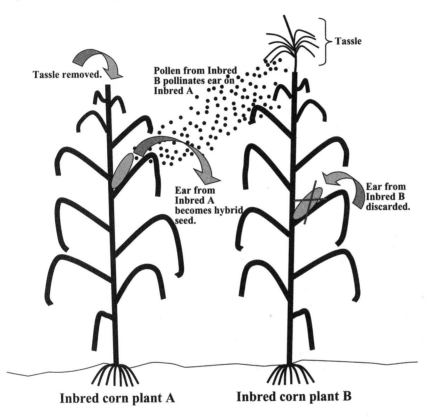

Inbred corn plant A   Inbred corn plant B

To prevent this, plant breeders **detassel**. As the word suggests, they remove the tassel from plant A, so its pollen can't contaminate the ear. This means that seed companies employed many young people, usually students, during the summer to detassel corn. It's hot, sticky work in the cornfields, and it was a major expense for seed companies.

You can imagine how excited seed companies would be to find a way to eliminate detasseling. In the 1950s, a mutant type of corn was found in Texas. It produced sterile pollen.

Think about that for a second. A plant that produces sterile pollen doesn't have to be detasseled! Male sterility is a very rare mutation in "nature." A plant that cannot produce pollen cannot be a male parent and is quickly eliminated from the gene pool. But corn breeders discovered the sterile pollen mutation and quickly bred it into their inbred lines. The mutation saved the seed companies lots of money and made hybrid production more reliable. By 1970, 85% of the corn planted in the United States had this single male-sterility gene, called T-cytoplasm.

What do you think happened? There have been plenty of other cases where large geographic areas have been planted with similar gene-types, and nothing happened. But in this case…(Activity 5 will explore what happened to T-cytoplasm corn in the United States).

Questions for further thought

Variation: Figure 5.2 shows changes that can occur with selection. Why is there still variability in yield after selection? If only a few individuals are selected, shouldn't the population that results from those individuals have very little yield variability?

> *The yield variability is caused by environmental effects. The genetic component of yield variation has been narrowed, but the environmental component has not. There will always be yield variability, even in a field of genetically identical hybrids, caused by variation in soil moisture, nutrient availability, heavy metals, sunlight, and other environmental factors.*

Genetics: Why does selfing make populations homozygous? (Hint: Use Punnett's squares to cross individuals with themselves and see what happens.)

> *If an individual starts out homozygous for an allele (TT or tt) when it crosses with itself, there are no other allele combinations. For example, if a tt individual is selfed (tt x tt) the only allelic combination for the offspring is tt—the t allele is "fixed." If an individual is heterozygous and is selfed, the next generation could be TT, tt, or Tt. Of the offspring with TT and tt, 50% will be fixed in a homozygous state. The Tt offspring will self again in the next generation. With each generation, half of the heterozygotes are changed to homozygotes. After a few generations, the plants will be fixed for alleles at all loci.*
>
> *Note: Mendel's "true-breeding" plants were homozygous.*

Chapter 5 Teacher Notes

Overview and Concepts

Overview

This chapter explores the role of genetic diversity in crops. Using hybrid corn as an example, it discusses selection—the genetic narrowing that accompanies gains in traits like yield and disease resistance—and the ecological and evolutionary consequences of genetic uniformity in crops.

Activity: Students re-enact a class action lawsuit from the 1970s in which farmers sued corn seed companies because of an epidemic caused by lack of genetic diversity in crop. Through acting as the trial's witnesses, students explore social, political, and economic consequences, as well as the ecological and evolutionary pressures, caused by lack of genetic diversity. They also learn about the interaction of nuclear and cytoplasmic (mitochondrial) DNA.

Concepts covered

Genetic diversity, genetic narrowing, natural and artificial selection, coevolution of plant and pathogen populations, hybrid corn, cross and self-pollination, plant structures, agriculture, Green Revolution, cytoplasmic (mitochondrial) DNA.

Prior knowledge required

The text and activities of *Garden Genetics* are intended to apply and supplement textbook concepts. Students should have familiarity with the following:

- **Mendelian crosses:** When Mendel crossed **true-breeding** (homozygous) tall and short plants, the resulting generation had one allele from each parent.
- **F1 or hybrid generation:** The result of Mendelian crosses, where each plant has one allele from each parent, is called the F1 or hybrid generation. See Chapter 1 for more information and examples.
- **Genetic diversity:** The range of alleles in a population, species, or group of species.
- **Genotype:** A representation of the genetic make-up of an individual.
- **Phenotype:** A phenotype is the physical expression of a genetic trait. A phenotype can be structural, physiological, behavioral, or biochemical—it is not just an organism's physical appearance. (Though that is certainly the easiest type of phenotype to identify!)

- **Resistance:** The ability of an organism to defend itself against drugs, pathogens, or parasites—for example, antibiotic resistance in bacteria. The term is also often used to describe plants that can survive environmental conditions like drought, frost, and water-logged or salty soil.
- **Mutation:** A change in the hereditary material of an organism (usually DNA).
- **Fungus:** An organism made of eukaryotic cells with cell walls, which gets its food by absorbing organic substances from detritus or other organisms.

Activity notes

Preparation prior to activity

- You may want to review the witness materials in Part III of the activity.
    - If you want further information about the epidemic, please see the references on page 93.
- Think about what you want the students to assess in their papers. The paper described in the activity is intended to prompt students to synthesize the arguments presented by the defense and the prosecution and to explain how they would vote as a "member of the jury." Be sure they address the big-picture issue about genetic diversity and the dangers of genetic uniformity.
    - Students have also successfully written papers evaluating the content and presentation of the trial.
    - Students could also conduct peer evaluation. They could evaluate each other's presentations or papers (for clarity, content, and delivery) and hand in the evaluations with their final paper.

Time frame

- The hearing should take 2–3 days to hold in class. You may want to play the role of the judge and keep everyone to their time limits. Typically a witness is given 2–5 minutes with an optional 1–2 minutes for cross-examination (if you decide to allow cross-examination!).

Materials

- A gavel can be an entertaining and useful prop.
- Set up your classroom as a courtroom, with a witness "box" and tables for the prosecution and defense.
- Internet access. Many of the witnesses have "search terms" at

the beginning of their material. It is important to review with students that not all information on the internet is credible. Generally, information from educational (.edu) and government (.gov) websites is accurate. All of the internet search terms have been tested using the Google search engine. Using quotation marks in searches enables the search engine to search for specific phrases. Therefore, students should use quotation marks where they are included with the search terms. You may also want to point out to students that using the Google Images search is a good way to find pictures to support their testimony.

Potential problems and teaching tips

There are 16 roles described in the activity.

If your class is larger, you can:

1. Assign more than one person to each role. (The lawyer role is easily shared between 2–3 students, especially if you allow cross-examination.)
    - The role of the geneticist expert witness who discusses T-cytoplasm and mitochondrial DNA could easily be split into two roles. These are complicated concepts.
2. Add some roles. There are important issues not covered here, such as:
    - History of "single gene catastrophes." *Newsweek*'s June 9, 2003 article "Crisis in the Cupboard" is an excellent overview of events like an epidemic in Brazilian citrus and the Irish Potato Famine.
    - Where does the U.S. corn crop go? How much is used by industry, for food, for animal feed? Check out: *www.ohiocorn.org* and *www.ksgrains.com/corn/ CornClass04.pdf*.

If your class is smaller, you can:

1. Assign more than one role to each person.
2. Eliminate some witnesses:
    - Some, like the seed store manager or the corn futures trader, are less important than others.
    - The geneticist expert witness who discusses T-cytoplasm and mitochondrial DNA handles some very complicated concepts. You may want to eliminate the mitochondrial DNA and T-cytoplasm details.
    - The trial will take significantly longer, but be more realistic, if you allow cross-examination. In pilot classes, cross-examination was an opportunity for dramatic, quick-thinking students to take the stage; they were not

always students who usually excelled in science class. This was also a place for laughter, and a source of some nervousness that forced students to be prepared!

- Students can either choose their own roles, or you can assign roles.
- Students should not be allowed to read the information from Part III verbatim as testimony during the trial. They should assimilate it and present it in their own words. Using drawings, figures, tables, and charts will help them present their information quickly and clearly. They may add supplemental information. There are internet search terms listed for most witnesses.
- Students should look up the underlined terms in the text describing their roles.
- Most of the information about the United States corn crop is given in bushels per acre. It might be useful to have students convert measurements to T/ha (the metric equivalent). This is a more complicated exercise than it might appear because bushels/acre is a measure of <u>volume</u>/area, and T/ha is <u>weight</u>/area. Conversion is a three step process (Figure 5.6):
  1. First the bushels must be converted to weight (lb). Conversion: 56 lb corn/bushel.
  2. Then the pounds must be converted to metric tons. Conversion: 1 lb = 0.45 kg = 0.00045 T.
  3. Finally, convert the area units from acres to hectares. Conversion: 1 acre = 0.40 hectares.
     Therefore, for corn, one bushel/acre = 0.063 T/ha.

Figure 5.6. Calculations for conversion from bushels per acre to tons per hectare.

$$\frac{1 \text{ bushel}}{\text{acre}} = \frac{56 \text{ lb}}{\text{bushel}} \times \frac{0.00045 \text{ T}}{\text{lb}} \times \frac{1 \text{ acre}}{0.40 \text{ ha}} = \frac{0.063 \text{ T}}{\text{ha}}$$

Further reading

Hybrid corn

Duvick, D. 2001. Biotechnology in the 1930s: The development of hybrid maize. *Nature Reviews Genetics* 2: 69–74.

Problems of genetic uniformity

Margolis, M., I. Mackinnon, S. Schafer, J. Cochrane, and M. Hastings. 2003. Crisis in the cupboard. *Newsweek* June 9, 2003, p. 48.

Southern corn leaf blight epidemic (SCLB)

Doyle, J. 1985. *Altered harvest.* New York: Viking Press.

Tatum, L. A. 1971. The southern corn leaf blight epidemic. *Science* 171: 1113–1116.

Ullstrup, A. J. 1972. Impacts of the southern corn leaf blight epidemics of 1970 and 1971. *Annual Review of Phytopathology* 10: 37–50.

Activity 5.

Trial

In the student edition, this activity begins on page 75.

Objective

Recreate the courtroom trial in which U.S. farmers sued seed companies for crop losses in 1970 caused by the southern corn leaf blight (SCLB) epidemic.

Background

In 1970, an epidemic swept through the corn crop in the United States. After an unusually warm, wet spring, a previously rare disease, southern corn leaf blight (SCLB), began to cause problems in farmers' cornfields in the southern part of the United States. In Florida, Georgia, Alabama, and Mississippi, many farmers lost most of their corn crop. As the warm weather moved north toward the major corn producing states, the disease moved with it.

The plants vulnerable to SCLB had the male sterile gene known as T-cytoplasm. More than 80% of the U.S. corn crop in 1970 had this gene. Ultimately, the epidemic caused the loss of 15% of the U.S. corn crop—a loss worth more than one billion dollars.

Within a few short years, lawsuits were filed in the states of Indiana and Iowa against seed companies. They were class action lawsuits on the behalf of many individual farmers who were harmed by the crop losses of 1970. The farmers alleged that the seed companies had behaved irresponsibly in releasing corn varieties that all had the same gene for T-cytoplasm, and therefore should be financially responsible for the farmers' loss.

Activity

Part I. Trial format

You will reconstruct the class action trial against the seed companies. Everyone will have a role to play. Using the materials provided on pages 96–107, and any others you care to supplement from your own research, each "witness" will present part of the story. The class will act as the jury. At the end of the trial, you, as a juror, will present your opinion in the case as a 2–3 page paper. Be sure you address the importance of genetic diversity and the consequences of genetic uniformity in the paper.

In a trial, both sides have time to present their cases. The trial begins with opening statements from the lawyers. Then the prosecution, arguing on behalf of the farmers, will call all their witnesses, in an order to be determined by the lawyers. After the prosecution is done, the defense will call all their witnesses. Then the trial ends with the closing arguments from the lawyers.

Witnesses should speak briefly, answering the questions they are asked in their own words. If they don't know the answer to a question, they should say so. Whenever possible, they should use visual aids (pictures, tables, graphs, charts) in presenting their information.

Part II. Roles and overview

Table 5.1 shows an overview of the roles in the trial. Following the table you will find the specific information for each individual witness's testimony. Witnesses are responsible for learning the material for their own testimony. Lawyers will also read the information and will ask questions of the witnesses to elicit the information. Witnesses should present this information in their own words and can supplement it with their own research or with visual aids like drawings, charts, and graphs.

Please look up underlined terms if you do not already know what they mean and answer the underlined questions in your testimony.

Table 5.1. Overview of roles and responsibilities for trial.

Prosecution (arguing on behalf of the farmers)		
Student	**Role**	**Responsibility**
	Prosecution lawyer(s)	Responsible for opening statement, closing statement, organization of the prosecution witnesses, cross-examination of defense witnesses (if applicable).
	Farmer 1	Describe crop losses—personal and national.
	Expert witness: pathologist 1	Describe how southern corn leaf blight (SCLB) occurs in the field.
	Expert witness: pathologist 2	What causes SCLB? Describe the different races of blight before and after 1970.
	Expert witness: nursery manager from Florida	Noticed that T-cytoplasm hybrids had problems with SCLB but the few varieties without T-cytoplasm did not.
	Expert witness: Philippine scientist	Published two papers in late 1960s detailing a possible connection between T-cytoplasm and vulnerability to a new strain of SCLB.
	Expert witness: geneticist	What is T-cytoplasm? What is mitochondrial DNA? How does it work?
	Expert witness: corn breeder	What is a hybrid? How do corn breeders make them? Why is T-cytoplasm used? Are there alternatives to T-cytoplasm?
	Expert witness: seed store manager	Describe varieties available. How many of them had T-cytoplasm in 1970? What percentage of the corn area in the United States was planted with T-cytoplasm?
	Expert witness: trader in corn futures	Describe how corn is traded and what corn futures are. Describe the effect of SCLB epidemic on corn futures.
Defense (arguing on behalf of the seed companies)		
Student	**Role**	**Responsibility**
	Defense lawyer(s)	Responsible for opening statement, closing statement, organization of defense witnesses, cross-examination of prosecution witnesses (if applicable).
	Seed company president	What is the goal of a seed company? (Produce high-quality seed at a reasonable price.) How do you do it?
	Seed company corn breeder 1	No known problems with T-cytoplasm. No known vulnerabilities.
	Seed company corn breeder 2	Few, if any, people in the United States knew about the Philippine papers. Those who knew discounted them.
	Expert witness: pathologist	Race T of SCLB was virtually unknown before 1970.
	Seed company executive	Reaction to the problem. Eliminate T-cytoplasm from seed stocks at tremendous cost to the companies.

Part III. Roles and material

Farmer 1: Overview of crop losses—personal and national

Internet search terms: Southern corn leaf blight 1970 epidemic "crop loss"

In the spring and summer of 1970, SCLB began to show up in farmers' fields in Florida, Georgia, Alabama, and Mississippi. By June, we knew it was an epidemic that was spreading to Louisiana and Texas. Losses in the Gulf region of the South were commonly 50% or more in fields with T-cytoplasm. People became very worried when they realized that more than 80% of the U.S. corn crop was susceptible (because it had T-cytoplasm).

Weather patterns favored the spread of the disease. The weather was warm and wet, with northerly winds blowing spores up into Kentucky, Ohio, Indiana, and Illinois (where 85% of U.S. corn is grown) by late June and July. In August, there were reports of SCLB in Wisconsin, Minnesota, and Canada.

People worried. How much of the crop would be lost? Would there be enough to meet U.S. food needs? Would there be enough to feed all the animals in the United States that eat corn? Would there be enough for the industries that use corn? Would there be a similar or worse epidemic next year? Could anything be done to stop the disease? If resistance to the disease could be found, how many years would it take before that resistance made it into new seed? Rumors began that the corn grain and plants were toxic to humans and animals. The rumors were false, but frightening. The states with early disease problems immediately began experiments feeding SCLB-infected grain to animals that showed the infected grain was undesirable, but safe to eat.

The United States keeps stocks of grain in silos around the country to buffer just such a crisis. In 1970, the reserves were adequate to make up for the shortfall. But would they be adequate if such a problem occurred in 1971 and 1972 as well? There probably would have been enough to survive two years of bad blight.

Prices of corn and corn products rose. Prices of meat and other grains rose as well.

Epidemic Facts
July 1970 estimate of U.S. corn crop: 4.82 billion bushels.
December 1970 estimate of U.S. corn crop: 4.11 billion bushels.
Market price = $1.50/ bushel.
Loss (710 million bushels × $1.50) = about 1 billion dollars in crop losses because of disease.

Average U.S. yield in 1969: 83.9 bushels/acre.
Average U.S. yield in 1970: 71.7 bushels/acre.
Some southern states lost more than 50% of their corn crop (though those states do not count for much of the national production).

Expert witness—Pathologist 1: How SCLB occurs in the field.

Internet search terms: Southern corn leaf blight "in the field," southern corn leaf blight symptoms, southern corn leaf blight description

Moisture is critical for development of an outbreak of SCLB. For the disease to enter the plant, only a thin film of moisture on the leaves, stalks, or husks is necessary. The fungus enters through the stomata and produces a toxin that attacks the mitochondria. This destroys the cell's ability to utilize energy from glucose. (Why?) Within 24 hours, tan, cigar-shaped spots called lesions begin to appear on leaves. By passing spores from one plant to another, the disease can wipe out a field in 10 days.

Under optimal conditions (20–30 degrees C and damp weather), the fungus can begin reproducing itself within 60 hours of landing on a plant and thus can complete a generation in 3 days. The spores can survive temperatures of 28 degrees C below zero, meaning they can survive winter in the field. In some cases, the disease can also penetrate seed, causing the seed to produce diseased seedlings or to not germinate at all.

Weather plays a critical role in the spread of SCLB. Cool, dry weather stops the spread of the disease.

> *Stomata:* Pores in the leaf's surface that allow air necessary for photosynthesis into the leaf.
> *Mitochondria:* The "powerhouse" of the cell—where energy (glucose) is broken into ATP to fuel cellular processes.
> *Why does attacking the mitochondria destroy the cell's ability to utilize energy from glucose?*
> Because the mitochondria, which are the site of efficient, oxidative ATP production, are destroyed.

Expert witness—Pathologist 2: What causes SCLB? Describe the different races of blight before and after 1970.

Internet search terms: Southern corn leaf blight "race T," southern corn leaf blight "race O," *Bipolaris maydis* "race T," *Bipolaris maydis* "race O"

SCLB is caused by a fungus with the Latin name *Bipolaris maydis*. Historically, the disease was of only minor significance, causing average crop yield losses of about 1 to 2.3% in the United States. Hybrids were relatively resistant to the common strain of SCLB. Different strains of SCLB are referred to as "races." In 1970, race T of SCLB caused a 15% loss of the national corn crop.

Infection of corn depends on the amount of the different types of the fungus, the genetic background of the plant, and the reproductive rates of both the fungus and the plant. When a new plant variety is introduced, the balance shifts. Diseases to which the new variety is resistant are suppressed. Diseases to which the new variety is susceptible will thrive and multiply. Often, it is impossible to know exactly how the balance will shift until after the variety has been released and is planted on thousands and thousands of hectares.

What happened to corn is similar to what happened to wheat in the 1950s. In 1953, a wheat stem rust race called 15B destroyed 65% of the U.S. durum wheat crop and 25% of the bread wheat crop. In 1954, the same race of rust destroyed 75% of the durum wheat crop and 25% of the bread wheat crop. Race 15B was found in surveys of wheat rusts in very low frequencies from 1942 to 1953. During these years, it adapted, changed, and accumulated the genetic traits it needed to become an epidemic.

Before 1970, SCLB caused only minor losses in corn. Prior to 1970, SCLB was caused by "race O" of the fungus, and it left relatively small brown areas on plant leaves. The epidemic in 1970 was caused by "race T," which was previously unknown. Race T produced a stronger infection with longer, browner spots on leaves. It could also infect stems and ears.

> *Durum wheat*: Durum wheat is hard wheat used to make noodles.
> *Bread wheat*: Bread wheat has a much softer grain and is used to make bread.

Expert witness—Nursery manager from Florida: Noticed that T-cytoplasm hybrids had problems with SCLB but the few varieties without T-cytoplasm did not.

In 1968, about 100,000 kg of seed were infected with SCLB on seed farms in Iowa and Illinois. Seed farms produce the seed corn that farmers will plant the next year. (This is where hybrids are made.) At the time, seed farmers called SCLB "ear rot" because SCLB was not known to infect ears of corn before this. Instead, they thought the "ear rot" might be a combination of two other familiar diseases. In fact, this was probably the first strike of the new strain of the disease. The losses were small, however, and people discounted them as part of normal fluctuations in diseases.

In 1969, farm managers on the same midwestern seed farms noticed much more severe problems. Ears rotted inside their husks, leaves had ugly brown lesions spreading on them, and stalks fell over. Nursery managers in Florida (where winter crops of seed corn are planted to help produce seed corn faster) noticed more SCLB in the corn plants. They knew the disease was caused by a fungus, but that was all they knew. It didn't behave like other familiar diseases (even the types of SCLB with which that they were familiar).

By 1970, the problem was obvious in cornfields. The Florida fields have narrow plots of different varieties planted right next to each other. You could look down the row and see which plants had T-cytoplasm by looking for the blight. Those that had T-cytoplasm were infected. Those that didn't have T-cytoplasm were healthy.

Further tests in the greenhouse that took the fungus from infected fields and exposed plants in otherwise disease-free environments showed that SCLB was the culprit! And it was causing heavy losses in plants with T-cytoplasm.

Expert witness—Philippine scientist: Published two papers in the 1960s detailing a possible connection between T-cytoplasm and vulnerability to a new strain of SCLB.

Internet search terms: southern corn leaf blight epidemic "Philippine plant breeders"

As early as 1961, two Philippine scientists reported that corn with T-cytoplasm was more likely to become infected with SCLB. In 1965, Philippine scientists showed stronger proof of the vulnerability. Both articles were published in the journal *Philippine Agronomy*, which was not read by many scientists in the United States. However, some people argue that the seed companies should have read these studies and seen the dangers that might lie ahead.

A 1972 study by the National Academy of Sciences in the United States dismissed these reports noting that the scientists from the Philippines did not warn of an epidemic. The report also pointed out that scientists are trained NOT to extrapolate from local data to worldwide epidemics. The fact that the problems were noticed in a tropical environment made it easy for scientists to dismiss the results as a local, tropical problem, unlikely to occur in the United States.

Expert witness—Geneticist: What is T-cytoplasm? What is mitochondrial DNA? How does it work?

Internet search terms: cytoplasmic inheritance T-cytoplasm, maternal inheritance T-cytoplasm, mitochondrial DNA

T-cytoplasm was first described in 1952. It was found in Texas (accounting for the "T" in T-cytoplasm) in a line of corn called Golden June.

Geneticists and breeders were immediately intrigued by the sterile male flowers it produced. Male sterility can be caused by genes in the <u>nucleus</u> or by genes found in the <u>cytoplasm</u> (more specifically in the <u>mitochondria</u> or the <u>chloroplasts</u>, which are found in the cytoplasm). Nuclear genes are the ones we usually study. An individual has two copies of each nuclear gene—one from the mother and one from the father. Mitochondrial genes, like T-cytoplasmic male sterility, are inherited only from the mother. Maternal inheritance means the genes are passed from mother to offspring in the cytoplasm of the egg cell, without contribution from the father.

The people making hybrids have a fundamental problem. To make hybrid crosses, they want plants without pollen (so the hybrid crosses aren't self-contaminated—see Chapter 5 text). But to make hybrid seed, plants must make pollen. A corn variety that doesn't make pollen can't pollinate the ears around it, and those ears then won't make seed. If there is no seed in a field, a farmer has nothing to harvest. Obviously, that would make for a very bad variety!

As the name suggests, cytoplasmic male sterility is caused by a gene (called tcms) found in the cytoplasm (really in the mitochondrial DNA). The intriguing thing about the tcms gene is that the expression of its phenotype (sterile or not sterile) is controlled by genes in the nucleus, even though the gene is found in the mitochondria. This gives plant breeders a "switch" that can be turned on and off. This way, corn breeders can make hybrids with the pollen "switched off." Then, in the next generation, they can "switch" the pollen back on. These nuclear genes, the "switches," are called fertility restorers. The fertility restorer genes suppress the male sterile genes, allowing the plant to make functional pollen again. Therefore the fertility-restored hybrid will have no problems making pollen or grain.

<u>Expert witness—Corn breeder: What is a hybrid? How do corn breeders make them? Why was T-cytoplasm used?</u>

Internet search terms: USDA timeline corn hybrid, detasseling hybrid production, hybrid corn production

Advantages of T-cytoplasm:
- Avoids the substantial cost of detasseling, whether manual or mechanical.
  - Manual, summer detasseling crew costs: finding, training, paying, and supervising detasselers. (At the peak, more than 125,000 people/day detasseled corn in hybrid production fields in the United States!)
  - Mechanical costs: machinery, maintenance, and operational costs.

- Greater precision because human error can lead to missed tassels and contamination.
- Works even during poor weather conditions when detasseling is not effective.

These cost savings could be passed along to the farmer, through the cost of seed.

In 1970, at least 80% of the United States corn crop contained T-cytoplasm.

Expert witness—Seed store manager: Describe varieties available. How many of them had T-cytoplasm in 1970? What percentage of the corn area in the United States was planted with T-cytoplasm?

In 1970, more than 80% of the United States corn crop had T-cytoplasm. Nearly all commercial varieties had T-cytoplasm. In fact, the problem even extended beyond the United States.

No one knew it before 1970, but SCLB could enter the corn seed, not just the corn plant. This raised worries that the blight was being exported to other countries in seed exports. In 1971, SCLB was reported in Latin America, Africa, Japan, and the Philippines. At the time the United States was exporting 46.8 million pounds of seed, worth about $5 million a year. But no one could prove whether or not the blight was being exported, since no one was checking the seed. By the time people knew to check seed, the problem (presence of the tcms gene in seeds) had largely been eliminated.

Prices for corn seed jumped because of the blight. Seed without the tcms gene was scarce and therefore more expensive. In 1969, the U.S. price for hybrid corn seed was $13.70/bushel. By 1974, the price was $25.00/bushel. (Part of the increase was caused by high inflation rates in the United States.)

Expert witness—Trader in corn futures: Describe how corn is traded and what corn futures are. Describe the effect of SCLB epidemic on corn futures.

Blight developed in the high corn production areas of the Midwest in July and August 1970. People began to fear that the harvest plus our national reserves would not be adequate to meet demand. (Did you know that we keep national reserves of important commodities like corn and oil that we might need in an emergency?)

Stocks from previous years: 999 million bushels. The 1970 crop fell 700–800 million bushels short of expectation, and therefore, prices rose. High corn prices spilled over into other grains, like sorghum, barley, oats, and wheat, which could be used instead of corn as animal feed.

News stories about the spread of the disease began to scare investors. The price of "corn futures" on the Chicago Board of Trade began to rise steeply. Corn futures are the price for a contract for a bushel of corn at the *future* harvest. People began to trade corn futures madly. Volumes of trade increased and so did prices. When the blight was confirmed to be in midwestern states, panic struck. At the peak, 193 million bushels of corn were traded in one day, topping a record that had stood for 122 years. The Dow Jones index for commodity futures had its highest one-day advance in 19 years. Prices of other grains and livestock soared as well. The blight boosted the price of corn 20% (increased $0.30 on a price of $1.50/ bushel).

Seed company president: What is the goal of a seed company? How is it accomplished?

Goal: to produce and sell high-quality seed at a reasonable price.

To do so, seed companies employ corn breeders, entomologists, agronomists, geneticists, pathologists, field workers, salespeople, and many others!

- Corn breeders: make crosses, design varieties, and invest years in developing varieties with new and/or improved traits.
- Entomologists: study insect interactions with the crops.
- Agronomists: study how to best manage the crop for high yield, high quality, and resistance to diseases.
- Geneticists: use the latest techniques to understand corn genetics. Which genes are involved in important traits like yield and disease resistance?
- Pathologists: study corn diseases and help look for new resistant genes.
- Field workers: plant, weed, water, harvest, and otherwise take care of the thousands of hectares of fields required to produce our hybrid seeds.

Producing a hybrid variety takes an average of eight years, large areas of land, and millions of dollars of investment. For example, seed companies start with 50,000 to 60,000 new experimental hybrids every year. They select the best 10% of the hybrids to continue working with each year. Of the 50,000 hybrids they start with, fewer than 10 will be released as commercial varieties. That's roughly 1 of every 5,000 hybrid varieties the companies try. All of that means seed companies make large investments in people, land, and time for every hybrid released.

Seed company corn breeder 1: No known problems with T-cytoplasm. No known vulnerabilities.

In 1965, to everyone's best knowledge, there were no disease-related differences between T-cytoplasm and regular cytoplasm corn varieties in the United States. Seed companies even tested T-cytoplasm varieties against known variants of SCLB, but they didn't test with Race T of the SCLB, because they didn't know about Race T.

By early 1970, someone had isolated, identified, and reported Race T. Reports in 1970, using data from the new strain of SCLB, warned of epidemic possibilities, but by then the epidemic was already underway. Simply put, seed companies were unaware of the problem in time to warn their customers. The seed sold in 1970 was produced in 1969 and parent stocks were produced in 1968.

Genetic sameness may mean vulnerability to disease. However, for years, breeding programs have been managing this vulnerability without major problems. To do this, they keep a steady stream of new varieties coming out, so no one genotype dominates the entire production area. There is always a new variety ready should an old one become susceptible to disease. Corn breeders all over the world are in contact with one another as they keep tabs on the disease problems and pressures in their area.

Historically, corn has been less susceptible to disease than other crops like wheat and oats. This is probably because it is out-crossing (meaning that a corn crosses with another corn plant, as opposed to crops like wheat and rice where a plant must pollinate itself) and it has a wealth of genetic diversity. However, hybrid varieties are not as diverse as "wild" corn and have some of the same problems as crops that do not out-cross.

Seed company corn breeder 2: Few if any people in the United States knew about the Philippine papers; those who knew discounted them.

Seed company scientists believed that the susceptibility to SCLB in the Philippine studies was caused by the tropical environment. The studies were small-scale and in a very different environment than the United States. Tropical areas have more problems with disease than the United States because warm temperatures incubate disease-causing agents, especially fungal ones like SCLB. Simply put, scientists didn't think problems in the Philippines would apply to the United States.

Tropical environments have no winter. Winter plays an important role in killing off pathogens. In non-tropical areas like the United States, to survive winter, pathogens end up synchronizing their life cycles. Therefore, pests in a place with winter, like the United States, are much easier to control, because they are all vulnerable at once. This is another reason scientists expected SCLB in the United States to be different from SCLB in the Philippines.

Expert witness—Pathologist: Race T of SCLB was virtually unknown before 1970.

The pathogen responsible for the epidemic of SCLB we call Race T, because it only caused disease on plants with T-cytoplasm. Race T was virtually unknown before the epidemic. Scientists were surprised and shaken at the strength of the outbreak. Presumably Race T existed, but at levels that were difficult to detect. Furthermore, there was no way to detect it without the plants on which its unique symptoms appear (T-cytoplasm plants). It's a circular problem—scientists couldn't see Race T until they had plants that were susceptible to it. But until they had plants that were susceptible, they didn't even know Race T existed.

Before this case, there was no evidence of susceptibility to disease being caused by cytoplasmic genes. Understanding of the genetic basis for resistance and susceptibility to disease was based on genes in the nucleus. Immediately after 1970, a great deal of research was launched to better understand cytoplasmic genetics and inheritance.

Rapid reproduction rates of pathogens mean their population can grow fast when conditions (environment and genetics of the host plant, like corn) are favorable. This can happen with little or no warning signs beforehand.

Seed company executive: Reaction to the problem. Eliminate T-cytoplasm from seed stocks at tremendous cost to the companies.

By 1970, when the epidemic began, seed companies understood that the problem was caused by T-cytoplasm. At the time, most seed was grown during the summer in the Midwest. In 1970, seed production had already begun to shift away from heavy reliance on T-cytoplasm and back to manual detasseling. Seed produced in the traditional way, by detasseling, is resistant to the T race of SCLB. In the winter of 1970/1971 (after the epidemic), seed companies had plantings everywhere they possibly could, including Florida, Hawaii, Argentina, and Mexico. Their goal was to increase non-T-cytoplasm seed stocks so there would be enough non-T-cytoplasm seed for the 1971 planting. (These plantings were very expensive, especially because of the short notice.) In some cases, 1971 seed was 20–30% lower yielding than 1970 seed. However, the lower yield was preferable to the risk from seed that resulted in a 50% loss from some fields.

In 1971, there was only enough non-T-cytoplasm seed to plant 23% of the nation's corn crop. Most of that seed went to the South, where disease pressures were most intense and damage had been most severe. The idea was to create a buffer zone to block progression of the disease north.

Seed companies also sold mixtures of 50% susceptible and 50% resistant seed. Some farmers complained damage was still high in their fields.

In 1971, much of the United States was planted to susceptible varieties of corn, and the infestation of SCLB was light. The weather helped the situation—1971, unlike 1970, had a cool, dry spring and somewhat drier summer conditions. There were some local outbreaks, but overall, the national crop had only minimal losses in 1971. By 1972, susceptible seed had been eliminated from the system and detasseling was back in style!

Certainly farmers, scientists, and seed companies learned their lesson. Look back at Figure 5.3. In 1970, more than 70% of the corn-growing area in the United States was planted with only six corn varieties. By 1980, the area planted with the top six varieties had decreased to 43%—meaning that farmers were planting far more varieties. And those six varieties didn't share a gene for cytoplasmic male sterility!

Part IV. Optional extra role and material

Optional extra expert witness for the prosecution—Geneticist: Details of how T-cytoplasm works.

How does this work? The cytoplasmic gene has two alleles: male sterile (MS) or normal (N) (Figure 5.7). All plants with N cytoplasm will always be "male fertile," meaning they make viable (normal) pollen. If a plant has N cytoplasm, it doesn't matter what fertility restoring genes it has in the nucleus (Rf genes), it will always make normal pollen.

Plants with MS cytoplasm can either have normal (male fertile) or sterile pollen. Male sterile plants, those where fertility is "switched off," must also have two recessive alleles of the nuclear gene rf. If a plant with male sterile cytoplasm has even one of the dominant fertility restoring nuclear alleles, Rf, then it too will be able to produce pollen.

Figure 5.7. Interactions of genes in cytoplasm and nucleus to produce male sterility.

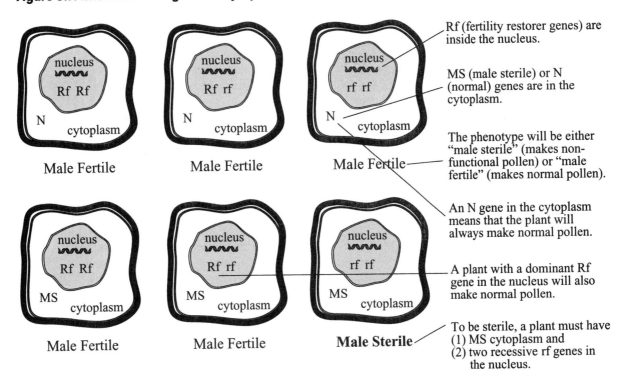

Rf (fertility restorer genes) are inside the nucleus.

MS (male sterile) or N (normal) genes are in the cytoplasm.

The phenotype will be either "male sterile" (makes non-functional pollen) or "male fertile" (makes normal pollen).

An N gene in the cytoplasm means that the plant will always make normal pollen.

A plant with a dominant Rf gene in the nucleus will also make normal pollen.

To be sterile, a plant must have
(1) MS cytoplasm and
(2) two recessive rf genes in the nucleus.

GENETIC ENGINEERING

Do you eat genetically engineered foods? Though you might not know it, the answer is probably yes. Recent studies estimated that about 60% of food products in grocery stores in the United States contain ingredients from genetically engineered plants. How is that possible? Are all the plants we eat genetically engineered?

Interestingly enough, genetically engineered varieties of only 12 crops have been approved for commercial production. The three most important of those plants—corn, soybean, and canola—account for almost all of the genetically engineered food we eat. Genetically engineered foods aren't labeled in the United States, so how do you know whether or not you're eating them?

As a rule of thumb, anytime you're eating something that contains corn, soy, or canola, you can assume that some of it is genetically engineered. The systems for moving crops from farmers to processing plants do not keep genetically engineered crops separate from non-genetically engineered crops—so anything containing corn can be assumed to have some genetically engineered corn in it. However, very little sweet corn (only 3–5%) is genetically engineered, and there are no genetically engineered popcorns on the market. The box on page 110 shows a partial list of products that are made from corn and soy.

Focus on genetically engineered corn

Since genetically engineered corn was introduced in 1996, farmers have been planting more and more of it. Figure 6.2 shows that in 2003, 40% of the corn area in the United States had genetically engineered varieties.

Why do farmers plant genetically engineered varieties? They have to pay quite a lot for the seed, so there must be a reason they want it. Most of the genetically engineered corn in the United States and other countries has one of two characteristics to address one of two problems: The varieties are either **herbicide resistant** to combat weeds or they contain **Bt genes** to combat some insect predators.

Herbicide resistance involves inserting a gene that makes plants immune to herbicide.

Bt genes make bacterial proteins that are toxic to many insect predators.

SciLINKS.
THE WORLD'S A CLICK AWAY

Topic: Genetic Engineering
Go to: www.sciLINKS.org
Code: GG19

PRODUCTS MADE FROM CORN AND SOY

Where do you find corn and soy products? Nearly everywhere! And in many places you might not suspect. The following list contains some (not all) of the products made from corn, soy, or both. Corn and soy are the source of many of the unpronounceable ingredients in your food!

ascorbate (vitamin C)	aspartame	beta-carotene (vitamin A)	caramel
carotenoids	cellulose	cobalamin (vitamin B12)	corn flour
corn masa	corn meal	corn oil	corn starch
corn syrup	cystein	dextrin	dextrose
fructose	glucose	glutamate	gluten
hemicellulose	high fructose corn syrup	inositol	invert sugars
lactoflavin	lactose	lecithin	leucine
lysine	maltose	methionine	modified starch
mono- and diglycerides	monosodium glutamate (MSG)	niacin	phenylalanine
riboflavin (vitamin B2)	sorbitol	soy flour	soy isoflavones
soy isolate	soy lecithin	soy oil	soy protein (vitamin E)
textured vegetable protein (TVP)	threonine	tocopherol	tryptophan
vanilla extract (contains corn syrup)	vegetable oil	xanthan gum	zein

FIGURE 6.1. LABEL WITH CORN AND SOY PRODUCTS.

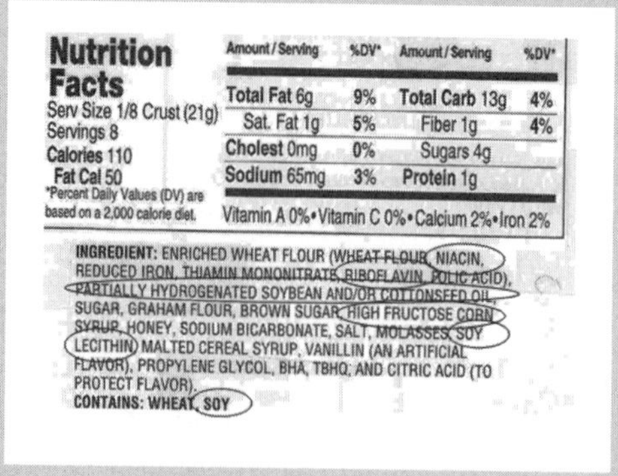

Figure 6.2. Percent of U.S. corn area planted with genetically engineered corn varieties. (The dip in 2000 was due to the rejection of genetically engineered foods by the European countries. Farmers feared they would not be able to sell their genetically engineered crops.)

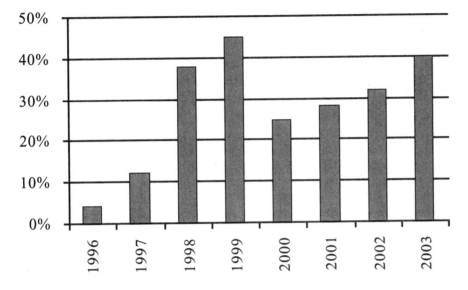

In herbicide-resistant corn, a gene is inserted that makes corn immune to the effects of herbicides like Roundup. A farmer can spray an herbicide-resistant field and know she'll kill all the weeds in her fields, but she won't kill her crop. This means less work for the farmer.

Insect protection: A plant that makes its own pesticide?

Bt genes come from a common type of soil bacteria called *Bacillus thuringiensis*. The bacteria produce a protein toxic to insects. The protein ingested by insects is actually harmless, but it is quickly cut by an enzyme in their guts to a smaller, deadly form. The small pieces bind to receptors in the insect digestive system. These bound proteins disrupt the insect's digestive system, ultimately killing it. There are many different Bt toxins that exist in nature, and each affects a different group of insects. The Bt genes commonly used in genetically engineered crops today affect moths, butterflies, beetles, and their larvae. For many years, organic farmers have used bacteria that produce the Bt protein as an organic insecticide to protect their crops.

A plant engineered to express Bt genes often produces the toxin, in essence a pesticide, in all its tissues—leaves, stems, roots, grain, and pollen. That means that the chances are high that humans are eating the pesticide. However, the toxin is not considered to be harmful to humans because our digestive systems lack the toxin receptors that insects have. Furthermore, the Bt protein is quickly broken down to harmless components in *our* digestive systems.

SCI/LINKS.
THE WORLD'S A CLICK AWAY

Topic: Biological Pests
Go to: *www.sciLINKS.org*
Code: GG20

Topic: Biological
Pest Control
Code: GG21

Bacteria genes in a corn plant?

The **DNA** of all organisms is made up of the same bases (A, C, G, and T), whether it comes from bacteria, fish, or corn plants. Therefore, a segment of DNA from bacteria, if inserted properly into a corn plant, will lead to production of the same proteins it encoded in bacteria.

By carefully choosing and carefully inserting the gene from the bacteria that encoded the Bt toxin, scientists were able to "engineer" a plant that produced a bacterial toxin. Genetic engineering is time-consuming and expensive but many seed companies and farmers think it is worth the costs. Many plant breeders see genetic engineering as simply another tool for creating new and improved crop varieties.

Unintended consequences?

What happens when the pollen from the genetically engineered corn plant blows in the wind? The pollen has the Bt toxin (though recent varieties have much less of the toxin than early Bt corn varieties had). At pollination time, corn pollen is everywhere—the puddles around cornfields have a yellow pollen layer on top of them, and so does everything else. What happens to something like the larvae of the monarch butterfly? In some places, monarch larvae are looking for milkweed to eat at the time that corn plants are producing all that pollen. The pollen is deposited on milkweed too. The larvae only feed on milkweed, but if there's corn pollen on it, they'll eat the pollen as well (Figure 6.3).

Studies in 1999 showed that Bt pollen can be toxic to monarch butterfly larvae. This came as a terrible surprise to some people who argued that Bt genes would not have impacts beyond the cornfield.

Further studies published in 2001 concluded that most tested Bt corn varieties didn't cause problems for monarch butterfly larvae. Rain quickly washes pollen off milkweed leaves. In many places the time when the monarch larvae are eating milkweed does not overlap with the time when corn pollen is being dispersed. Bt genes from genetically engineered corn seem to have far smaller impacts on monarch larvae than a single application of pesticide to the same field. On the other hand, field corn is not often sprayed for the pests that Bt corn varieties control, because the pests eat their way into the center of the corn stalk where pesticides do not penetrate well.

Regardless of the conclusions about Bt effects on monarch larvae, the studies raise the important issue of unintended consequences of genetically engineered plants. No new technology is without risks. And people are concerned that the risks of genetically engineered plants could be high.

DNA (deoxyribonucleic acid) is the double-stranded series of bases (A, C, G, and T) that compose genes and encode proteins.

Figure 6.3. Monarch butterfly larvae eating corn pollen on a milkweed plant.

Who is in charge?

In the United States, a number of government agencies regulate food, plants, pesticides, and agriculture. The Food and Drug Administration (FDA) regulates food. The Environmental Protection Agency (EPA) regulates pesticides. The U.S. Department of Agriculture (USDA) regulates agriculture. Who regulates a plant that makes its own pesticide? Is it a plant? Is it a pesticide? Who decides if the food from it is safe? You will find your own answers to these questions in the activity that follows.

Genetically engineered crops cross boundaries that traditional crops do not. Thus, these crops pose new and challenging regulatory issues.

Question for further thought

Ecology: For years, organic farmers have used organic pesticides containing Bt bacteria. "Organic" in this case means pesticides that occur in nature and are not created from chemicals. How might the widespread use of genetically engineered Bt crops impact the effectiveness of these organic Bt bacteria pesticides? Think about ecology and resistance.

> *Many farmers using Bt crops over wide areas could lead to insects developing resistance to Bt. If this happens, then the organic Bt pesticides will no longer be effective.*
>
> *As a precaution, farmers using Bt crops are required to plant "refuges" of plants without the Bt gene. In this way, insects will not be subject to such strong selection pressures for developing resistance to Bt. Furthermore, there are many Bt genes, each of which affects a different insect. So the Bt in genetically engineered organisms used over a wide area may have some genetic variability and may or may not be the specific Bt protein that the organic farmers are using.*

Chapter 6 Teacher Notes

Overview and Concepts

Overview

This chapter focuses on genetically engineered foods. Bt corn has bacterial genes that encode a protein toxic to many insects. Therefore the corn plant makes its own pesticide. The chapter explores the DNA basis for this genetically engineered plant, as well as discusses unintended consequences and regulatory issues concerned with Bt corn.

In Activity 6, students will hold a congressional hearing and write an opinion paper on the basis of the testimony they have heard. The students will also testify as the "experts" in the hearing, using internet-based resources about genetic engineering background, regulatory and distribution issues, potential risks, and potential benefits.

Concepts covered

Genetic engineering, herbicide resistance, Bt genes, pesticides, DNA, ecological consequences of Bt crops to insect populations, coevolution of plant and insect populations, U.S. regulatory agencies (EPA, USDA, FDA), Congressional hearing, food distribution system

Prior knowledge required

The text and activities of *Garden Genetics* are intended to apply and supplement textbook concepts. Students should have familiarity with the following:

- **Congressional structure and function:** Congress is the legislative body that makes laws, both at the state and national levels. There are two legislative bodies: the House of Representatives and the Senate.
- **Congressional hearings:** The testimony of witnesses before a Senate, House, or joint committee of the U.S. Congress. Hearings provide legislators with information required to explore topics of current interest, or investigate areas of public concern.
- **DNA (deoxyribonucleic acid):** A double strand of base pairs (A, C, G, and T) that stores and transmits genetic information from one generation to the next.
- **Genes:** The unit of inheritance; a segment of DNA that encodes a protein.
- **Protein:** One or more amino acids encoded by DNA. The chain of amino acids then folds into a 3-D structure. Many of the important components of an organism are made up of proteins (structures like muscles, as well as enzymes and defense compounds).

Activity notes

Preparation prior to activity
- You may want to look over the websites listed.
- If students have limited internet access, you may want to print some of the websites (each about a page) for them to have printed resources.
- Think about what you want the students' paper to assess. The paper described in the activity is intended to prompt students to synthesize the arguments for and against genetic engineering and to explain how they would vote as a "member of Congress."
  - Students have successfully written papers evaluating the content and presentation of the hearing as well.
  - Students could also incorporate an element of peer evaluation. They could evaluate each other's presentations (for clarity, content, and delivery) and hand in the evaluations with their final paper.

Time frame
- The hearing should take 2–3 days to hold in class. You will probably need to play the role of the Congressional leader and keep everyone to their time limits and call the next "expert."

Materials
- Internet access
- A gavel is an entertaining and useful prop.

Potential problems and teaching tips
- You may want to have students hand in their notes with their papers, as a way of evaluating how well they took notes.

There are 22 roles described in the activity.
If your class is larger, you can:
1. Assign more than one person to each role.
2. Subdivide roles. Some, like the "corn and soy" or the "horizontal gene transfer/weediness" role, are easily divided.
3. Assign someone to organize and sum up each section of the hearing.
4. Add some roles. There are additional materials on the geo-pie website about the following:
   - GE canola
     http://geo-pie.cornell.edu/crops/canola.html
   - GE cotton
     http://geo-pie.cornell.edu/crops/cotton.html

- Other crops: potato, squash, papaya, tomato, sugarbeet, rice, flax
  http://geo-pie.cornell.edu/crops/eating.html
- Delayed fruit ripening
  http://geo-pie.cornell.edu/traits/fruitrip.html
- Pollen control systems
  http://geo-pie.cornell.edu/traits/polcont.html
- Crops producing pharmaceuticals
  http://geo-pie.cornell.edu/issues/prodigene.html
- "Terminator Technology"
  http://geo-pie.cornell.edu/issues/terminator.html
- Urban legends about GE
  http://geo-pie.cornell.edu/media/media.html
- Important issues not covered here that could be assigned as roles include corporate patents on genes, nutritionally engineered crops like "golden rice," global inequity in access to technology, varieties, and hunger.

If your class is smaller, you can:
1. Assign more than one role to each person.
2. Eliminate some topics that may be less important (e.g., antibiotic resistance, nicotine-free tobacco) or for which there is less information (plant-based vaccines, drought tolerance, viral resistance).

Activity 6.

*Congressional Hearing on Genetic Engineering**

In the student edition, this activity begins on page 95.

Objective

Hold a Congressional hearing to determine whether or not genetic engineering of food plants should be banned.

Activity

Part I. Congressional hearing

A Congressional hearing is one of the ways lawmakers seek information to help inform the laws they make. A series of experts are called to give their opinions about a list of subjects the Congressional committee wants to learn about.

In this case, you will be the experts called before Congress. Each of you will be responsible for learning about a certain aspect of genetic engineering and then presenting your findings. As an expert, you're not necessarily arguing for or against genetic engineering. Your job is to present balanced information as accurately as you can.

When you are called to speak in front of "Congress" you will have four minutes. Be sure your information is organized and concise. Please use visual aids (pictures, graphs, tables) whenever possible.

The class (with you as a part of it) will also serve as Congress. At the end of the hearing, you will be asked to submit your informed opinion in the form of a paper.

Topic: Food Safety
Go to: *www.sciLINKS.org*
Code: GG22

Part II. Roles

Person	Topic	Resources
Organizational Unit: Background		
	What are the GE foods on the market?	*http://geo-pie.cornell.edu/crops/eating.html*
	In what food products do corn and soy appear? What percentage of corn and soy products is genetically engineered?	*http://geo-pie.cornell.edu/crops/ingredients.html* *http://geo-pie.cornell.edu/crops/soybeans.html* *http://geo-pie.cornell.edu/crops/corn.html*
	What are the GE crops NOT in the marketplace?	*http://geo-pie.cornell.edu/crops/eating.html#eating* *http://geo-pie.cornell.edu/traits/traits.html*
	Please explain why many people see GE as an extension of plant breeding. What is the major difference between traditional plant breeding and GE?	*http://beyonddiscovery.org/content/view.page.asp?I=171* *http://beyonddiscovery.org/content/view.page.asp?I=187*

* This activity was created in collaboration with Nicole Bernati at Ithaca High School.

	How are genetically engineered foods labeled? How are GE foods labeled in other countries?	*http://geo-pie.cornell.edu/issues/labeling.html* *http://geo-pie.cornell.edu/regulation/FDA.html#labeling* *http://geo-pie.cornell.edu/issues/intllabeling.html* *http://geo-pie.cornell.edu/issues/ANZlabels.html*
Organizational Unit: Regulation and Distribution		
	Does our food distribution system have a way to keep GE separate from non-GE foods? (Starlink case study.)	*http://geo-pie.cornell.edu/issues/starlink.html*
	What is the FDA? What is the role of the FDA in regulating GE foods and crops? Are there differences in GE requirements for human food versus animal feed?	*http://geo-pie.cornell.edu/regulation/reg.html* *http://geo-pie.cornell.edu/regulation/FDA.html* *http://vm.cfsan.fda.gov/%7Elrd/biocon.html*
	What is the EPA? What is the role of the EPA in regulating GE foods and crops? Who regulates a plant that produces its own pesticide? Is it a plant or a pesticide? Which agencies are responsible for regulating each?	*http://geo-pie.cornell.edu/regulation/reg.html* *http://geo-pie.cornell.edu/regulation/EPA.html*
	What is the USDA? What is the role of the USDA in regulating GE foods and crops?	*http://geo-pie.cornell.edu/regulation/reg.html* *http://geo-pie.cornell.edu/regulation/APHIS.html*
Organizational Unit: Potential Risks		
	What is "horizontal gene transfer"? What are the risks it poses? How can it be controlled? Does GE increase the chances that a crop may "escape" the field and become a weed? How likely is it? What are the risks associated with "weedy" crops?	*http://geo-pie.cornell.edu/issues/hgt.html* *http://geo-pie.cornell.edu/issues/pollenbio.html* *http://geo-pie.cornell.edu/issues/gmofree.html* *http://geo-pie.cornell.edu/issues/triple.html* *http://geo-pie.cornell.edu/issues/weeds.html*
	What are the risks of GE foods to people with food allergies? Who regulates and tests for allergic food qualities? Are these tests stringent and effective?	*http://geo-pie.cornell.edu/issues/allergy.html* *http://geo-pie.cornell.edu/issues/brazilnut.html* *http://geo-pie.cornell.edu/issues/convallergy.html*
	What are the risks of GE plants producing toxic substances? Do conventional crops have toxins in them? Please describe.	*http://geo-pie.cornell.edu/issues/toxins.html* *http://geo-pie.cornell.edu/issues/convtoxins.html* *http://geo-pie.cornell.edu/issues/pusztai.html*
	What are some of the potential risks from antibiotic resistance? What methods are available to deal with these risks?	*http://geo-pie.cornell.edu/issues/antibiotic.html*
	What are the potential effects of GE on non-target insects? Have any cases been documented?	*http://geo-pie.cornell.edu/issues/monarchs.html*
	Has enough research about GE foods been done? Has the research asked the right questions?	*http://geo-pie.cornell.edu/issues/science121500.html*

Organizational Unit: Current and Potential Benefits		
	What are the current benefits of GE use of Bt genes? What are the potential problems in terms of evolution of insect resistance to over-used pesticides like Bt? How does the use of GE Bt impact organic farmers who have used Bt on their crops for many years?	*http://geo-pie.cornell.edu/traits/traits.html* *http://geo-pie.cornell.edu/traits/bt.html*
	What is herbicide resistance? What are the current benefits from GE use of herbicide resistance?	*http://geo-pie.cornell.edu/traits/traits.html* *http://geo-pie.cornell.edu/traits/herbres.html*
	What are the current and potential benefits of GE in reducing pesticide use? Please give an example where GE has reduced pesticide use, and another example where GE is associated with increased pesticide use.	*http://geo-pie.cornell.edu/issues/pesticide.html* *http://geo-pie.cornell.edu/issues/pestnum.html* *http://geo-pie.cornell.edu/issues/glyphosate.html*
	What are the potential benefits of GE in terms of resistance to viral diseases that have no other cure? Please give an example.	*http://geo-pie.cornell.edu/traits/virusres.html*
	How can GE alter plant nutritional qualities? What is altered oil content? What are the current benefits from GE use of altered oil content?	*http://geo-pie.cornell.edu/crops/rice.html* *http://geo-pie.cornell.edu/crops/canola.html* *http://geo-pie.cornell.edu/traits/altoil.html*
	How can GE eliminate chemicals known to be harmful? Describe the case of nicotine-free cigarettes.	*http://geo-pie.cornell.edu/crops/tobacco.html*
	What are the potential benefits in solving problems like plant growth in drought or salt conditions? Please give an example.	*http://advance.uconn.edu/2001/011119/01111912.htm*
	What are the potential benefits of GE in terms of plant-based vaccines? Please describe an example.	*www.nature.com/nsu/020715/020715-16.html*

Part III. Notes

Use this form to take notes on the arguments presented about various topics. You will use this information to write your paper, so your notes are important!

Person	Topic	Arguments
Organizational Unit: Background		

Organizational Unit: Regulation and Distribution		

Organizational Unit: Potential Risks		

Organizational Unit: Current and Potential Benefits

Part IV. Opinion paper

At the end of the hearing, you will be asked to submit your informed opinion as a member of Congress about genetic engineering, in the form of a paper.

The paper will be 2–3 pages long, double spaced, and will present what you think are the two strongest arguments for genetic engineering and the two strongest arguments against genetic engineering. The paper will conclude with your opinion about whether or not genetic engineering of food plants should be banned. Make sure your opinion is well supported by arguments. Be sure you take notes during the hearing so you will remember the information you have heard.

SWEET GENES IN CORN

One of the joys of summer is sweet, fresh, crisp corn on the cob. Little did you know, this corn contains a puzzle. Most corn is starchy—just think of tortilla chips, which are made of corn. Usually, corn doesn't taste sweet. In fact, more than 75% of the weight of a kernel of popcorn is starch. Why isn't corn on the cob starchy? What makes sweet corn sweet?

Leaves: A sugar factory

In all plants, sugar comes from **photosynthesis**. The leaves of a plant are like a factory for capturing the energy of the Sun and converting it into sugar. Plants make the sugar **glucose** ($C_6H_{12}O_6$) using carbon dioxide (CO_2) from the air, water (H_2O) from the soil, and energy from the Sun. The Sun's energy is captured by light-absorbing chloroplasts inside the plant's cells. Through a variety of chemical reactions, the captured energy ends up stored in the bonds between the atoms of the sugar glucose.

Inside a cell, sugar can be changed into a variety of forms. All sugars have a similar chemical structure. They are made up of rings of carbon atoms. Changes between different types of sugars are simply a matter of joining and separating carbon rings. For example, corn makes the sugar glucose. A corn plant also contains **fructose**, a different type of simple sugar often found in fruits and juices. The corn plant transports sugar in the form of **sucrose** from the leaves where it is produced to the other plant parts. Sucrose, also known as table sugar, is made up of one glucose molecule plus one fructose molecule. **Enzymes** are the agents within the cell that convert one carbohydrate form into another by connecting or disconnecting the sugar groups.

Starches are long chains of sugars. The sugar chains can be straight or branched (see Figure 7.1). Starches are assembled from sugars by enzymes that join sugar groups together. Starches can easily be broken back into sugars by a different set of enzymes. Together, the sugars and

Photosynthesis is the process of taking the Sun's energy, in combination with water and carbon dioxide from the air, to make sugars, oxygen, and water.

Topic: Photosynthesis
Go to: www.sciLINKS.org
Code: GG23

Carbohydrates are sugars and starches made up of carbon, hydrogen, and oxygen. Carbohydrates are converted from one form to another by **enzymes**. **Glucose**, **fructose**, and **sucrose** are all sugars.

starches are called **carbohydrates**. (The name comes from the fact that they are a combination of carbon, hydrogen, and oxygen.) The starch in a corn kernel is roughly 75% amylopectin and about 25% amylose.

Figure 7.1. Common carbohydrate forms within plant cells.

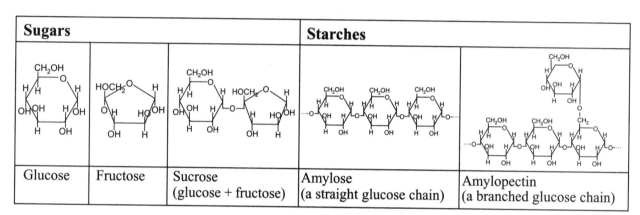

Sugars			Starches	
Glucose	Fructose	Sucrose (glucose + fructose)	Amylose (a straight glucose chain)	Amylopectin (a branched glucose chain)

The sugar shuffle

Why does the plant need all these different forms of carbohydrates? It seems more complicated than necessary. The plant's basic job is to reproduce itself. The seed is its way of doing so. In essence, the seed is the plant's "lifeboat." The plant puts all the resources necessary for survival into this lifeboat and then casts it loose. The most essential thing the plant puts into the lifeboat is enough food to nourish the seedling until it can produce its own food. That food is carbohydrate. So for many plants, the point of photosynthesis is to load carbohydrate into the seed.

Why not just send sugar to the seed? Sugar is water soluble. When you put a spoonful of sugar (sucrose) into water, it dissolves. So moving sugar around the plant is not much more difficult than moving water. In fact, sugar (sucrose) is the form of carbohydrate that is most easily transported in the plant. Sugar moves out of the leaf, where it is highly concentrated, by **diffusion**. The sugar moves down a **concentration gradient** from an area of high sugar concentration to an area of lower sugar concentration.

After diffusion, the sugar concentration would be the same inside and outside the seed, and the sugar solution would stop moving. Therefore, no more sugar would enter the seed. How then do seeds manage to capture sugars at concentrations greater than in other parts of the plant? (Remember, loading that seed "lifeboat" up with carbohydrate is critically important to the survival of the next generation!)

The corn plant has two solutions to the problem of building up sugar in its seeds. First, the corn plant can *actively* pump sugar out of the leaf and into the seed using **ATP energy**. Second, the seed is full of

The movement of molecules of a substance down a **concentration gradient** (from an area of high concentration to an area of lower concentration) is called **diffusion**.

SCiLINKS
THE WORLD'S A CLICK AWAY

Topic: Diffusion
Go to: *www.sciLINKS.org*
Code: GG24

an enzyme, called starch synthase, which turns sugar into starch. Thus, the plant can pack the seed full of sugar, which in turn is transformed into starch. In starchy corn, starch synthase converts sugars into starch, and the plant can keep packing carbohydrate into the "lifeboat."

A sweet treat

All of that explains why a corn kernel is starchy. Why then is sweet corn sweet? Sweet corn is not the same *genetically* as starchy field corn. Sweet corn contains a gene, called su1 (for "sugary"), that blocks the conversion of sugar to starch in the kernel. The su1 gene encodes a defective copy of the enzyme needed to convert sugar into starch. Therefore at the immature, corn-on-the-cob stage, sweet corn's kernels are full of sugar and water—creating the sweet taste of summer corn. However, if that same sweet kernel is left to reach full maturity, it dries and shrivels up. Sweet corn seeds become shriveled because they have very low starch reserves to fill the endosperm in the center of the seed (see Figure 7.2). Without the water that fills the kernel at the corn-on-the-cob stage, the sugars have very little bulk to fill the seed.

ATP is the **energy** that organisms use to fuel life processes. An **active** process requires energy. A **passive** process (like diffusion) does not require energy.

Figure 7.2. Kernel profiles of starchy and sweet corn.

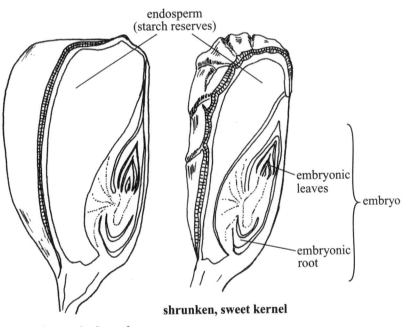

The sweet mutation was first described in 1901, and was one of the first mutations in corn to be officially described. Since then, plant breeders and farmers have been breeding it into their sweet corn varieties, which are eaten fresh, canned, or frozen. For years, sweet corn was a local crop—people ate it in areas very close to where it was grown. It had to be eaten quickly before the ears lost their sweetness. The ears lose their sweetness because sugars in the kernel are slowly converted into starch after the ears are picked. In the 1950s, sweet corn breeders began looking for a different genetic system that would hold its sweetness longer. They turned their attention to a different gene, called sh2 ("shrunken" because of its shriveled appearance).

Corn breeders had known about sh2 for a long time. They knew it produced even sweeter corn than the su1 gene. However, they considered it impractical for making sweet corn varieties because sh2 seed had terrible problems. It was so shrunken and shriveled that the plants could barely get started. Remember that the amount of carbohydrate in the seed lifeboat plays an important biological role. Plants grown from the sh2 gene grew slowly and had problems with mold and disease. Basically, the sh2 gene left its seed with so few reserves that it couldn't produce plants with good ears of corn.

The sweet corn breeders, however, were persistent. For years, they worked with the natural variation in other genes and eventually selected plants with the sh2 gene that could also compete and produce good ears. These varieties are now sold under the names " super-sweet" and "x-tra sweet." Because these varieties are sweeter, and the sugars last longer, farmers in Florida and California can now produce sweet corn that can be transported long distances. So if you see sweet corn in the grocery story in New York in February, you can bet that it has the sh2 gene and that it has had a long journey!

SC*LINKS*
THE WORLD'S A CLICK AWAY

Topic: Biochemical Processes
Go to: www.sciLINKS.org
Code: GG25

XENIA—POLLEN PAINTING

When you read the planting instructions for sweet corn, they recommend you plant it more than 150 m from other corn. Why?

Corn has an interesting phenomenon called **xenia** (pronounced "zeen-eeya"). The pollen "paints" the seed with the pollen plant's characteristics. Seed from white corn pollinated by blue corn will be blue. Seed from sweet corn pollinated by starchy corn will be starchy.

How does it work? Before fertilization, the endosperm of what will become the seed has two sets of chromosomes from the female parent (2n). Once the kernel is fertilized, it gains a third set of chromosomes from the male parent (n): $2n + n = 3n$. This means the endosperm has three sets of chromosomes. Therefore kernels reflect the male parent's genes too! And if the male parent is starchy, the sweet corn won't be as sweet.

The two sweet mutations occur at different genes. A sweet su1 variety has starchy alleles at the sh2 locus, and vice versa. Since they are both recessive genes, neighboring corn, even if it is sweet, might not have the same sweet recessive mutation. Therefore even sweet corn can make other sweet corn starchy.

How do su1 and sh2 work?

Both the sugary (su1) gene and the super-sweet gene (sh2) block steps in the same **biochemical pathway**. Biologists often talk about biochemical pathways as the "route" that one substance, like sugar, takes in order to become another substance, like starch. Each of the "steps" in the pathway, shown as an arrow in Figure 7.3, is really a chemical reaction controlled by a particular **enzyme**. A gene that blocks a step in the pathway is really a mutant, defective gene that leads to a dysfunctional version of the enzyme (see Chapter 2 for details). If a plant lacks the enzyme that executes a step in the pathway, the whole pathway is blocked.

Each step in the pathway converts one type of carbohydrate into another (shown in bold print). Each conversion is done by a different enzyme (shown as an arrow). The su1 and sh2 genes encode defective copies of enzymes needed to perform a conversion. Therefore, the plant accumulates glucose, instead of starch.

The plant transports sugar as sucrose. In the cells of the seed, the sucrose is first broken down to one form of glucose. A second enzyme that is defective in sh2 plants then converts the first form of glucose into a second form of glucose (Figure 7.3). The two glucoses have slightly different chemical structures. The second form of glucose is then chained together to make the starches amylose and amylopectin. (See Figure 7.1 to remind yourself how the glucose and starches look.) The su1 gene makes a defective copy of an enzyme that converts glucose into amylopectin. If a plant has the su1 gene, it will have glucose, and the starch amylose, but no amylopectin. Remember that in a normal kernel of corn, about 75% of the starch is amylopectin. This is why old-fashioned su1 sweet corn tastes sweet. But it is also why su1 sweet corn loses its sweetness over time. The sugars in su1 sweet corn are slowly converted into amylose. Sh2 sweet corn stays sweet longer because it can't make either amylose or amylopectin.

Amylose is a straight chain starch that plays a role in the firmness of cooked foods (Figure 7.1). Amylopectin is a branched glucose chain that has an important role in thickening starchy foods. Amylopectin is also important because it affects the ability of starchy foods to hold fat and protein molecules that lead to better texture and flavor. Tortillas made with higher levels of amylopectin are softer. Therefore neither sh2 nor su1 sweet corn would make very soft tortillas!

A **biochemical pathway** is a way to describe the series of chemical reactions required to convert one compound (like sucrose) into another compound (like starch). Each of the "steps," shown by arrows in Figure 7.3, is performed by a different **enzyme**.

Figure 7.3. Biochemical pathway for creation of starch from sugar (sucrose).

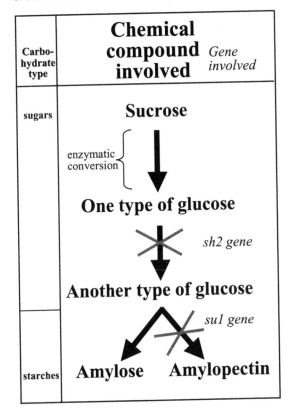

Questions for further thought

Experimental Design: Scientists have used the xenia effect to study how pollen moves in cornfields. Can you describe how they might do so? (Hint: They use blue corn and white corn. Blue is dominant over white.)

> They plant white corn next to blue corn and then count blue kernels on the ears harvested from the white corn plants. Blue kernels in the white corn show how far the pollen traveled.

Evolution: What would happen to the su1 or sh2 gene in nature?

> Both genes would be very disadvantageous in nature. They produce weak seedlings, which would grow slowly and would be over-shadowed by seedlings from normal, starchy corn. The su1 and sh2 genes would be selected against and would eventually disappear. However, even starchy corn would have trouble surviving "in nature," because of changes that occurred during domestication. (For example, the seeds stay on the ear, rather than shattering and falling to the ground. See Chapter 4 for more details.) We humans select for things that nature would never favor. However, because humans also care for and plant the seed, the system works.

Genetic Diversity: Why do farmers keep growing sweet corn with the su1 gene, if the sh2 gene is sweeter?

> Some people prefer traditional sweet corn from the su1 gene, complaining that the sh2 gene is too sweet and doesn't have enough "corn" flavor. Su1 corn is thought to have better creaminess, to be less watery, and to have a better "feel" in the mouth. Furthermore, the two types grow well in different environments. The sh2 varieties are vulnerable to many diseases and need to be planted in warm soil. Therefore, they are rarely planted in the northern parts of the United States.

Taking it further: Why don't varieties have BOTH the sh2 and the su1 genes? Wouldn't they be sweetest of all?

> They might be sweetest, but the two genes together would leave the seed with so few reserves that it would be nearly impossible to germinate and produce a healthy enough plant to have ears. There is a third sweet gene called "sugary enhancer" (se) with more complicated genetics. The se gene is sometimes combined with the sh2 gene to get varieties with better corn flavor (coming from the se gene), in addition to the sweetness and storage advantages of the sh2 gene.

Biochemical pathways: Why does su1 sweet corn lose its sweetness if it sits for days without being eaten?

> The su1 gene results in a blockage in the pathway from sucrose to starch (by encoding a defective copy of an enzyme), but it only blocks the creation of one type of starch (Figure 7.3). The type of starch blocked is the dominant type of starch formed (amylopectin). However, the enzyme that creates amylose, the other type of starch, will slowly convert the available sugars into starch. That's why old sweet corn loses its sweetness and becomes chewy. Super-sweet varieties that capitalize on the sh2 gene block the conversion of sugar to starch completely (Figure 7.3). That's why these varieties stay sweet much longer.

Chapter 7 Teacher Notes

Overview and Concepts

Overview

The chapter begins with consideration of sugars made by the plant during photosynthesis and the movement of those sugars within the plant by diffusion along concentration gradients and by other processes. By exploring the genetic basis of sweet corn, students learn about the biochemical pathway that leads to conversion of sugars into starches. Sweet corn genes encode defective copies of enzymes that convert sugar into starch. A box (p. 128) discusses pollen painting (xenia) in corn.

In the activity, students design and implement their own experiment to test the effect of seed reserves on germination and seedling growth using starchy, sweet, and super-sweet corn seeds.

Concepts covered

Diffusion, photosynthesis, genes leading to production of proteins, mutation, defective genes leading to blockage of biochemical pathways, germination and seed reserves, experimental design

Prior knowledge required

The text and activities of *Garden Genetics* are intended to apply and supplement textbook concepts. Students should have familiarity with the following:

- **Photosynthesis** is the process of taking the Sun's energy, in combination with water and carbon dioxide from the air, to make sugars, oxygen, and water.
- **Diffusion** is the movement of molecules of a substance down a concentration gradient (from an area of high concentration to an area of lower concentration).
- A **mutation** is a genetic change in the DNA code.
- **Genes** are made up of DNA and encode proteins.

Activity notes

Time frame

- Activity: Two class periods, plus a week for observation. One class period will be used for starting the activity (might not take the entire period) and another to finish the activity. Students will need to take data over the course of a week. Depending on temperature (and rate of germination) students may need to observe their seeds for two weeks.

- Preparation: Order the seeds several weeks before the activity. You will need one type of seed from each category. Seed sources are listed below. Extra seed can be kept fresh for up to a year in a refrigerator. If you are reusing old seed, test it ahead of time to be sure it germinates.

Materials
- Disposable gloves
- Paper towels
- Soil and containers
- Water source
- Dark location
- Ruler
- Scale (optional)
- Three types of corn seeds: sh2, su1, and starchy

Seed Sources

Company	su1 variety	sh2 variety	starchy (field corn) variety
Willhite (yellow varieties) www.willhiteseed.com P.O. Box 23 Poolville, TX 76487 1-800-828-1840 - Toll Free 817-599-5843 - FAX	Seneca Horizon Bonanza Golden Cross Bantam Jubilee Merit	Marvel	Reid's Yellow Dent
Willhite (white varieties)	Silver Queen	How Sweet It Is	Hickory King Trucker's Favorite
Johnny's (yellow) www.johnnyseeds.com 955 Benton Ave Winslow, ME 04901 1-800-879-2258 - Toll Free	Tablemaster Sugar Buns Kandy Kwik	Northern X-Tra Sweet	Northstar

Additional su1 varieties: Bellringer, Biqueen, Bold, Bonus, Butter & Sugar, Chalice, Dynamo, Early Cogent, Elite, Excalibur, Honey and Cream, Legacy, Lumina, Quick Silver, Seneca Chief, Silver Ice, Spirit, Sprint, Stylepak, and Sundance.

Additional sh2 varieties: Bandit, Cabaret, Candy Store, Challenger, Crisp N' Sweet, Dazzle, Even Sweeter, Fantasia, Frontier, Ice Queen, Krispy King, Landmark, Max, Pinnacle, Punchline, Rustler, Showcase, super-sweet, super-sweet Jubilee, super-sweet Jubilee Plus, Suregold, Sweetie 82, Top Notch, Twice as Nice, and Zenith.

Safety Notes

- Many corn seeds are sold already treated with a fungicide to improve germination in cold soils. The fungicide is toxic and students should not ingest treated seeds or handle treated seeds with bare hands. Fungicides are usually improbable colors like pink or blue so it is obvious that the seeds have been treated. When ordering seed from some sources, you can request untreated seed.
- Students should wear gloves when handling seed.
- Students should wash their hands immediately after handling the seed.
- Under no circumstances should a student taste or touch a seed.
- All students should wash their hands after the activity.

Lab notes

- Because of the fungicide issues, if you want students to make observations about seeds, put them in petri dishes and seal the dishes shut with tape or parafilm. This enables students to handle and observe the seeds without touching them.
- Disposal:
    - The plants grown in the dark will be long, spindly, and possibly smelly. They can simply be thrown away when you are finished with them. If plants have been grown in the light as well, students may enjoy observing these as they continue to grow. Unless you have access to a tall greenhouse, however, it is unlikely that your corn plants will ever set seed.
    - If containers and soil were used, they can be reused. Containers should be washed out with soap and water. Ideally, to prevent acquiring soil-borne diseases, soil should be autoclaved or baked in an oven between 180 and 200 degrees. The soil (not the oven) should be above 180 degrees for at least 30 minutes. (Higher temperatures can produce toxins.) Alternately, the soil can be sterilized in the microwave—90 seconds per kilogram (2.2 pounds) on full power.

Taking it further

Sweet seeds on the cob and Mendelian genetics.

Carolina Biological sells ears of corn that are segregated for color genes (purple and white) and sweet (sweet and starchy) genes. These ears give classic di-hybrid crosses (2 dominant genes and 2 loci) and give either a 9:3:3:1 ratio or a 1:1:1:1 ratio (from a backcross). You could also use these ears for an activity like Activity 1 in Chapter 1, where students use the ratios to deduce the behavior of genes and parentage. (White color and the su1 genes are recessive.)

Sugar and water content.

Sweet corn seeds are shriveled because sugary contents are much less bulky when they dry than the contents of starchy field corn (usually grown for animals or industrial uses in the United States). Students could track changes in sweet corn, especially in the winter, and see what happens as they dry down. As a class, you could track weight loss to see how much of the weight of corn on the cob is water. If you have the ability to find fresh (starchy) field corn, it would be interesting to compare sweet to starchy corn.

Carbohydrate solubility.

A good demonstration of the different solubility of sugar and starch is to stir a spoonful of sugar and a spoonful of cornstarch (or flour) into two cups of water. The sugar dissolves. The starch mixes, creating a cloudy solution, and will eventually settle out. The results with flour are similar to cornstarch. This makes a very concrete demonstration of why the plant transports carbohydrates as sugars, not starches.

Carbohydrate conversion.

Using the classic iodine (10% KI) stain for amylose (does not stain amylopectin) students should be able to deduce whether sweet corn from the store is sweet (su1 gene) or super-sweet (sh2 gene). Sugars in the sweet (su) corn will be slowly converted to amylose. Sugars in the sh2 kernels should not be converted to amylose or amylopectin. Students could stain several kernels from the same ear for several consecutive days to see the sugar conversion over time. (Students must cut the kernels off the ear for the dye to penetrate the waxy seed coat.)

Further reading

Sugary genes and starch production pathways

Whitt, S., L. Wilson, M. Tenaillon, B. Gaut, and E. Buckler. 2002. Genetic diversity and selection in the maize starch pathway. *Proceedings of the National Academy of the Sciences* 99: 12959–12962.

Activity 7.

Sweet Seeds

In the student edition, this activity begins on page 109.

Objective

Design an experiment to test the effects of the su1 and sh2 genes on seed germination.

Background

Seeds contain all the material necessary to start the next generation off properly. The genetic material contains all the instructions the plant will need for growth. The endosperm has the nutrients the seed will need until it can begin producing its own food through photosynthesis. The seed coat protects the seed from bacteria, fungi, mold, and other threats.

Figure 7.4. Corn seeds germinating.

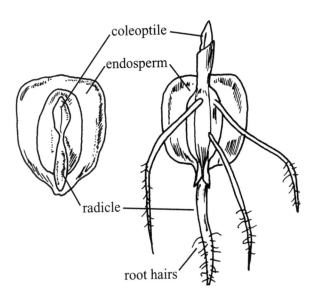

What does a seed need to germinate or sprout? Primarily it needs water, air, and suitable temperatures. If the environment is too cold or too hot, the seed will not germinate. Temperature and water requirements help the seed to germinate under circumstances that give it a good chance of surviving. Germinating in the middle of winter, or under the Sun in the desert, would not give most seedlings a good chance to survive.

Does a seed require light? Most seeds germinate under the soil, in the dark, so light is not essential. Shortly after germinating, the part of the embryo that will become the root, called the radicle, grows down. The coleoptile, the part of the embryo that will become the leaves, grows up. Until the plant reaches the light and unrolls its first leaf, all the energy for the growing plant comes from the starch reserves in the endosperm (see Figure 7.4).

Normally, corn is planted a few centimeters deep. For the seed to grow, the soil must be moist. Some varieties of corn planted by Native Americans in the southwestern United States grow more than 40 cm before they reach the light. The seeds are planted deep where the soil is moist. Just think of the amount of energy reserved in the endosperm that is required for the seedling to grow up to the soil surface!

What happens to sweet corn seeds with their shrunken, shriveled endosperms that lack sufficient reserves to get the seed started? You will design your own experiment to test the effects of the sweet genes on germination.

Materials
- Gloves
- 3 types of corn seeds: sh2, su, and starchy
- Paper towels
- Soil and containers
- Water source
- Dark location
- Ruler
- Scale (optional)

Safety Notes
- Many corn seeds are sold already treated with a fungicide to improve germination in cold soils. The fungicide is toxic. If your seed is pink, green, or blue, it has definitely been treated with fungicide. If your seed is not colored, assume that it has been treated unless you are specifically told otherwise.
- You MUST wear gloves when handling seeds.
- When you have the gloves on, do not touch your face, your skin, or someone else's skin.
- You MUST wash your hands immediately after taking off the gloves.
- Under no circumstances should you taste a seed, or touch a seed without gloves.
- You should wash your hands AGAIN after the activity.

Activity

Part I. Design your experiment

Sweet corn seeds have smaller amounts of starchy reserves to start seedlings. You will design your own experiment to see how much the different seeds will grow with the starch reserves they have.

1. Formulate a hypothesis about how corn seedlings from kernels with starch, sweet, and super-sweet genes will grow. A hypothesis is a possible explanation or an educated guess about what you will find. It is a starting point for your experiment.

   Most students will hypothesize that seedlings from starchy kernels will grow the longest (because they have the most carbohydrate reserves), seedlings from sweet kernels will grow the second longest, and seedlings from super-sweet kernels will grow the shortest distance.

   This is a good time to discuss that in science, finding evidence that does not support your hypothesis is just as powerful as finding evidence that does support it. Some of the most interesting discoveries in science have been made this way! The key is to set up an experiment so that results will give you a clear answer and to be open-minded if things do not go as expected.

2. How will you plan your experiment to investigate your hypothesis?

   The seedlings will grow for a surprisingly long time in the dark, using their reserves (up to 24 inches, for longer than two weeks).

   2a. What do you plan to do?

   Students will have different plans for how to investigate their hypotheses. The basic plan should involve germinating seeds of all three types (or at least two) in the dark for at least 10 days. If students germinate their seeds on paper towels (rather than soil) results will be much easier to measure.

   2b. What supplies will you need? How will you get any that are not already available in the classroom?

   Obviously, you can constrain students' projects by constraining their materials. In general, students usually stick to the materials you provide with this experiment: seeds, dark place, paper towels, soil and containers (optional), rulers, and sometimes a scale. In the past, some students have tried germinating their seeds underwater (not successfully) and on sponges (successfully).

   2c. How do you plan to schedule the project?

   Students will plant the first day and then measure growth at intervals thereafter. Make sure students think about who will measure and how long it will take. Make sure their plans are consistent with the amount of time you wish to devote to the project over the next two weeks.

2d. How will you measure your results?

Typically, students measure the length of the radicle and the coleoptile. Some students weigh the seedlings, but this must be done very carefully to not damage the seedlings. (Change in weight reflects water taken up by the growing plants. Most of a plant cell is a central, water-filled vacuole that is important for rigidity. The plant is not photosynthesizing, so net levels of carbohydrate do not change.)

This is a good opportunity to be sure that students have thought about what and how they will measure. Though it seems obvious, some students have planted haphazardly in soil and later realized they couldn't measure radicle length, nor could they effectively measure coleoptile length since they didn't know how deep they had planted their seeds. If students plant in soil, they must plant at a consistent depth or they will be unable to measure radicle length.

This is also a good opportunity to discuss what students will do with their data. What will they do when they have measurements for more than one plant in a category? Should they take averages? How will they keep a list of measurements that correspond to the LABELED plants? (Of course, this means they must label their seeds!) Make sure they think about what to do with the numbers once they have them! (Are they going to graph? Average? Present a table?)

You may want to insert a lesson about repeatability and "operator error." If two different people take the same measurement, will the measurement be the same? Probably not, since students rarely are explicit about what they will measure. (For example, if they plan to measure radicle length, where exactly does the radicle start? Where does it end? Will they measure branching roots? What if the branching roots are longer than the radicle?) Students have no trouble deciding how to handle these small problems, but they are rarely explicit about it!

3. Evaluate your experiment.

This would be a prime opportunity for students to peer review each other's questions or discuss them in small groups. You could have student groups pair off and present their projects to each other. Then they can reconvene with their own group to improve their projects. Depending on how much time you want to devote to this, you could have groups present a "research proposal" to the class and have the class critique each other. Students will be more helpful to one another in their critiques if they focus on the questions below.

3a. Does your experiment test the effect of seed reserves on the seedling growth?

For example, an experiment that planted seeds at a standard depth in soil in the light and then measured coleoptile length of the emerging seedling is confounded by light. Once the emerging coleoptile reaches the light (even if it is not under a grow light or in a sunny window), the coleoptile turns green and begins to photosynthesize. Therefore,

138

the experiment is not testing the effect of seed reserves on growth at all. To test seed reserves, the plants must be grown in the dark.

3b. Does your experiment frame a clear question?
In the example above, the question is confounded by the ambient light. Make sure that the students are actually testing what they are supposed to be testing (effect of seed reserves on seedling growth).

3c. Does your hypothesis answer the clear question?
Students should double-check that their hypothesis answers the question. It seems obvious, but some students struggle with this concept.

3d. Is the proposed experiment feasible given the time and materials at hand?
This is an opportunity to make sure that students have a time frame in mind that is compatible with the time and materials you have available. If they're planning to be measuring the plants outside of class time, make sure they think about who will do so and when. If they're planning on taking three days to run their experiment while you're expecting it to take three weeks, they should adjust their plans.

Common problems: Students don't think about how to measure results. Students also often have trouble with the idea of replication and with using more than one plant of each type. Make sure students have thought about how to deal with weekends and holidays.

3e. What are your controls?
Controls in this experiment are a bit tricky. The simplest approach is to have students consider the "starchy" seed a control. (It controls for the effect of the reduced sweet seed reserves.)

3f. Be sure you have considered the following review questions. Do you need to re-evaluate your experiment after answering these?
The purpose of these questions is to ensure that the students don't confound their experiments with light, as in the example in 3a.

- Where does the energy for plant growth come from once the plant's leaves reach light?
  The Sun, via photosynthesis.

- Where does the energy for plant growth come from BEFORE the plant reaches the light?
  Seed reserves.

- Therefore, if you want to test the effects of the energy contained within seeds on seedling growth, what variable must you eliminate from your experiment?

Students must eliminate light. If there is light, then the plant begins to photosynthesize, and you can no longer say that the only source of energy for the seedlings is seed reserves.

Part II. Data and results

4. You need to document initial differences between the seed types. Do they have the same mass? Do they look the same?

    Students should document initial differences between the seeds. Mass is important, because this gives a strong indication of initial carbohydrate reserves. The amount of water in each seed should be comparable between seeds and should not confound measurements. Other measures like length, diameter, number of wrinkles, photographs, or drawings can be left to your (or the students') discretion.

Characteristic	Starchy corn	su1 gene corn	sh2 gene corn
1. for example: seed weight (10 kernel average)			
2. number of wrinkles (average)			
3. drawing or photograph			

5. Use this space to record your data.

    Students may want to create a data sheet that has a space for each labeled seed/seedling and the measurements they plan to take. For example, if students were measuring coleoptile and radicle length every three days, their first two data sheets might look like this:

    Note: Measurement should correspond to the same plant. Many students will write down a list of numbers without any idea which number pertains to which plant.

plant	Day 3						Day 6					
	Starchy		Sweet		Super-sweet		Starchy		Sweet		Super-sweet	
	coleoptile (cm)	radicle (cm)	coleoptile (cm)	radicle (cm)	coleoptile (cm)	radicle (cm)	coleoptile (cm)	radicle (cm)	coleoptile (cm)	radicle (cm)	coleoptile (cm)	radicle (cm)
1												
2												
3												
4												
5												
6												
7												
8												
9												
10												
average												

6. Make a table here to summarize your data. Include calculations such as averages for length measurements.

    If students have made a data sheet, this step is simply a matter of tallying the columns. Some students will want to do this on a computer; others will be happy doing it by hand. To ensure that students take individual measurements, ask them to show their averaging calculations.

    For example, if students were measuring coleoptile length and radicle length, their data for the first measurement might look like this.

	Day 3						Day 6					
	Starchy		Sweet		Super-sweet		Starchy		Sweet		Super-sweet	
plant	coleoptile (cm)	radicle (cm)	coleoptile (cm)	radicle (cm)	coleoptile (cm)	radicle (cm)	coleoptile (cm)	radicle (cm)	coleoptile (cm)	radicle (cm)	coleoptile (cm)	radicle (cm)
1	2.4	2.7	2.6	2.2	2.1	2.4	6.4	8.2	5.4	5.7	4.2	5.3
2	3.0	3.1	1.0	1.8	1.2	1.8	5.2	7	4.7	4.6	3	4.2
3	0.0	0.0	2.0	2.3	0.8	0.9	7.4	9.2	6.4	6.2	5.2	6.2
4	1.7	1.6	0.0	0.2	1.4	1.3	6.8	8.6	5.8	5.9	4.6	5.7
5	2.7	2.7	2.3	2.6	2.4	2.0	6	7.8	4.8	4.8	3.8	4.8
6	1.9	2.2	1.7	1.4	1.6	1.9	6.2	8	5	5.2	5	5.7
7	1.8	1.9	0.0	0.0	0.9	1.1	5	6.8	0	0	3.4	4.5
8	2.2	2.1	2.5	2.1	0.0	0.2	6.2	8	6.6	6.3	5.4	6.5
9	2.0	2.4	2.1	2.6	1.8	1.9	7.2	9	6.5	6.4	5.2	6.3
10	2.3	2.5	1.3	1.8	0.0	0.0	5.6	7.4	4.4	4.4	0	0
average	2.0	2.12	1.55	1.7	1.22	1.35	6.2	8.0	5.0	5.0	4.0	5.0

7. Graph your data.

    For example, if students were measuring coleoptile and radicle length, their graphs might look like this:

Figure 7.5. Sample student data.

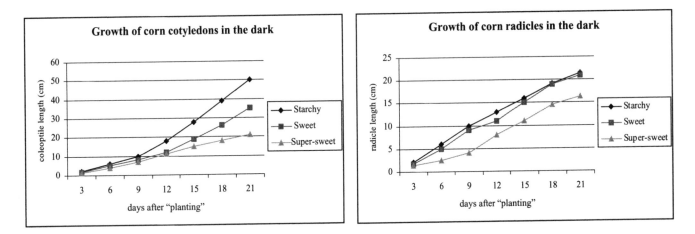

Part III. Conclusions

8. What conclusions can you reach? (What did you learn from your experiment? Was your hypothesis correct? Can you think of any other possible explanations for your results?)

   This is a good place to emphasize that it is easy to draw conclusions... but in science those conclusions must be based on data.

9. Did you have any unexpected results? What were they and why do you think they happened?

   Hypothetical set of expected results:

   - *Coleoptile length: Starchy kernels will grow the longest, su1 kernels will grow measurably less, sh2 kernels will grow the least of all.*
   - *Radicle length: All kernels will reach similar lengths because the purpose of the radicle is to grow until it reaches water. Once it reaches water, the plant is better served by increasing the number of roots, rather than increasing the length of only one.*
   - *Coleoptile growth rate: Starchy kernels will grow the fastest and most vigorously. Sh2 kernels will grow the slowest and least vigorously.*
   - *Radicle growth rate: Though the ultimate length of the radicle may not show variation for the different kernel types, the rates of growth should. Starchy kernels will grow the fastest. Sh2 kernels will grow the slowest.*
   - *Germination rates: The sh2 kernels will have the lowest germination rates. They are most susceptible to mold, disease, and age of seeds. Note that germination rates depend strongly on seed age and health, not just genetics.*

   It's also important to encourage students to come up with thought-out explanations for why results were not as expected (e.g., Might results be due to the biology of the organisms, due to some fault with the procedures, or due to multiple factors?). If students attribute unexpected results to "experimental error" make sure they are specific about what they think went wrong and why.

10. How could you improve your experimental design? (Are there ways your experiment could be improved to better answer the initial question? Did you come up with questions you can't answer using your data?)

    Encourage students to think creatively and critically here! Was it a good experiment? Would more seeds, more time, or a different experimental setup have improved their experiment? Was it truly dark in the location they used? Could their controls have been better? Were the measurements students took helpful? What else could they have measured?

    This is also a good time to point out that scientists often run an experiment more than once, especially when they are fine-tuning their investigative technique. (Were they measuring the right thing? Is there a better

*measurement technique? Should the plants be a different age? Would a
different environment give the same result?)*

*This is also a good time to process and get feedback about the challenges
of dealing with data. Did students collect the data they needed? How did
they decide what to do with it? Did the conclusions from the data show the
same conclusions they could see for themselves? (If not, were they taking
the right data?) What would happen if they had ten times as much data?
(The results might be clearer, because any one anomalous plant would
have less impact on the mean. However, more data can make things more
complicated to manage. With more data it is essential to have a good plan
for what to do with it!)*

11. Based on what you know about seed reserves and sweet genes in
    corn, are there other questions you would like to investigate with
    the techniques you developed in this experiment?

    *For example, does temperature affect germination and seedling
    development? Seedlings could be grown on paper towels, in the dark in a
    drawer, and in a refrigerator. Sample prediction: Super-sweet seedlings
    will be most sensitive to cold and will stop developing in the cold before
    any of the other seedlings.*

    *Another example: Is growth rate (not just growth) affected by seed
    reserves? Seedlings could be grown on paper towels, in the dark, just as in
    this experiment, but instead of measuring length, students would measure
    the rate of change (cm grown/day). Prediction: Seeds with fewer reserves
    (super-sweet) will grow more slowly than seeds with substantial reserves.*

    *The hypothesis about seed reserves and growth rates could be extended
    to assess individual variation between seeds of the same type (i.e., will
    starchy seeds with larger reserves grow further and more quickly than
    starchy seeds with smaller reserves?)*

Part IV. Applying what you've learned

12. What does your experiment tell you about the effect of sweet
    genes (compared with starchy genes) on germination?

    *Sweet genes lead to smaller seed reserves and thus fewer resources for the
    germinating seed. For this reason, germination under cold, wet, disease-
    laden field conditions is more challenging for sweet corn compared to
    starchy corn, which has more reserves.*

13. Are there differences in germination ability between the su1 gene
    and the sh2 gene? If so, describe. If not, why do you think they
    don't differ?

    *Student answers will vary according to their results. The sh2 gene is
    likely to have lower germination ability or growth capacity—in fact,
    plant breeders have known about the sh2 gene for many years, but it is
    only recently that germination rates in the field, through selection and
    improvement, have become high enough to be commercially viable.*

14. What do you think would happen if sweet corn breeders tried to make a variety with both the su1 gene and the sh2 gene in it?

> *Plant breeders have attempted this, but the plant has so few reserves that germination is very, very poor—especially in cold soil, where the plants grow slowly and pathogens have a long time to attack the seeds.*

SECTION 3
Tomatoes

CENTERS OF DIVERSITY

What country do you think of when you think about a tomato? For most people, Italy immediately springs to mind. Red pasta sauce, red pizza sauce— it's hard to imagine Italian food without the tomato. How long do you think the tomato has been in Italy, given how widespread it is in Italian cooking?

Interestingly, the tomato is a relative newcomer to Italy. Originally, the tomato came from the Americas. It didn't arrive in Europe until the 1500s. The Spanish explorers found it in Central America and brought seeds back to Spain. The tomato is first mentioned in print in Europe in 1544, roughly 50 years after Columbus set sail for the New World.

Even after the tomato arrived in Europe, it was regarded mostly as a curiosity. People grew the plants because they were novel and interesting to look at. It never occurred to people to *eat* the red fruits! (Botanically, the tomato is a fruit because it is the structure that contains the plant's seeds.) In fact, it seemed wise *not* to eat the tomato, since it is a member of the nightshade plant family, which includes many poisonous plants. It wasn't until 1692, 200 years after Columbus headed for the New World, that the tomato first appeared in a European cookbook. Even then, recipes called for sparing use, only for flavoring.

In the 1600s and 1700s, the Pilgrims bound for North America carried the tomato back to the New World. However, suspicions about it persisted. In 1820, Colonel Robert Gibbon Johnson decided to put an end to all the suspicion. He declared that he would eat an entire bushel of these "nonpoisonous" fruits. People came from far away to watch his death by poisoning. You can imagine how surprised they were when he lived! Within a few short years, the tomato became increasingly popular, appearing in gardens, seed catalogues, and foods throughout the New World.

It is surprising that we think of Italy when we think of tomatoes, given that Italians have only eaten tomatoes for about 300 years, while South Americans have grown and eaten tomatoes for thousands of years!

Figure 8.1. What country do you think is the origin of the tomato?

Geographic patterns

It's difficult to imagine how different the world must have been, even just 100 years ago. Transportation was time-consuming and difficult. People rarely traveled far from home. People's diet was limited to foods that grew locally and that were in season. An orange in the middle of winter was a rare luxury rather than a common occurrence.

Explorers have always recorded the plants they saw in journals and brought seeds home. But it wasn't until the early 1900s that botanists began systematically traveling around the world to collect edible plants. A Russian named Nikolai Vavilov was one of these collectors.

From 1916 to 1940, Vavilov made many trips around the world, collecting thousands of plants. He and his colleagues carefully catalogued and transported the plants to storage facilities in Russia.

Vavilov was interested in collecting plants from places with the most genetic diversity. He realized that crop plants exhibited amazing diversity in some regions, while other regions had very little diversity. From these observations, he came up with the theory of the **center of origin**. A center of origin is the place where a food plant was **domesticated** from its wild relatives. He concluded that a place like Peru, which has the highest diversity of tomatoes, was likely the site of domestication of the tomato. In other words, Vavilov proposed the idea that the center of origin for tomato is the same as its **center of diversity**.

Vavilov noticed that the same places had high diversity not just in one food plant, but in many different crops. For example, where he found many tomato varieties, he also found many potato varieties. Thus he concluded that there were a few of these centers of origin for all of agriculture—each of them giving rise to many food plants. He described seven centers: Central Asia (including China), South Asia (including India), the Middle East, the Mediterranean, Africa, Central America, and Andean South America. These were the places, he argued, where agriculture arose (Figure 8.2).

Changes to Vavilov's centers of origin ideas

Vavilov's ideas about agricultural centers of origin are still important today, and the basic concept is still accepted. However, detailed genetic and geographic studies have given us some important modifications of his theory.

Many crops, like wheat and barley, have a clear center of origin. However, others, like yam and cotton, do not. Yam appears to have been domesticated separately in Africa, Asia, and South America. Cotton seems to have been domesticated separately in Mexico, South America, Africa, and India.

Vavilov first suggested that the geographic center of diversity of a plant is also likely its center of origin.

Domestication is the change from a wild to a cultivated plant. A domesticated plant is dependent on humans for its survival.

Figure 8.2. Vavilov's proposed centers of origin.

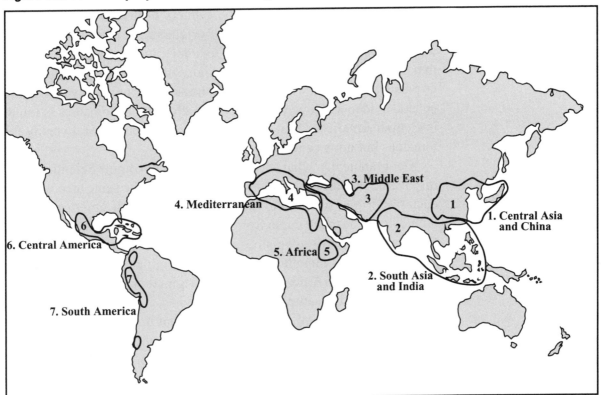

INTERSECTION OF SCIENCE AND POLITICS: NIKOLAI VAVILOV'S LIFE

In 1916, Vavilov began his worldwide plant collection trips. What happened in Russia in 1917? The Communist Revolution overthrew the tsar. This was the beginning of the Soviet Union.

Scientists faced a new, difficult political reality. Scientists were educated, elite people under the old regime. Under the communist government, educated, elite people often were put in work camps in Siberia to be "re-educated." Very few returned alive. However, scientists like Vavilov were in an unusual position. The Soviet Union needed their skills to increase crop yields in order to feed its people. Therefore, Vavilov was able to continue working on genetic diversity and crop breeding through the 1920s and 1930s.

However, by the late 1930s the political climate had changed. Science, like all other aspects of life in the Soviet Union, had become politicized. Genetics and heredity were rejected as "elitist." Vavilov became the object of a slander campaign by one of his former students, Trofim Lysenko.

In 1940, Vavilov was arrested, interrogated for 11 months, and eventually sentenced to death for political crimes. In 1943, he died in a Stalinist prison cell. Ironically, after devoting a life to plant breeding and fighting hunger, he died of malnutrition-related disease while in prison.

Other crops, like corn and tomato, have clear centers of origin and two (or more) centers of diversity. Centers of diversity can arise independently in the original center of origin and in a secondary site to which a crop was transported. For example, most people believe that tomatoes were domesticated in the Andes of South America, probably in present-day Peru. The Peru hypothesis is supported by fossil and genetic evidence. However, a very rich diversity of tomatoes is found in Central America. Thus, Central America is a center of diversity for tomatoes but not a center of origin.

Geographically, what constitutes a center of origin? Scientists have discovered that crops do not always come from the same area within a center of origin, such as the Andean region of South America. For example, tomatoes may come from the coastal areas near the base of the Peruvian Andes, while potatoes appear to come from higher altitudes within the Andes mountains. In this case, both potatoes and tomatoes are from the South American center of origin, though their source areas are not exactly the same.

The central idea of Vavilov's theory, that the center of origin of a crop is likely to be found at its center of diversity, remains the starting point for research on crop origins. In many cases, his theory holds true. In other cases, the center of origin is not in the same place as the center of diversity. Regardless, Vavilov's ideas give us an important starting point for understanding the geographic distribution of diversity.

Chapter 8 Teacher Notes

Overview and Concepts

Overview

The chapter discusses genetic diversity of food plants in the context of the geographic regions from which they originate. The center of origin is the site where the plant was domesticated. The center of diversity is the site where maximum genetic diversity is found.

In Activity 8, students create graphs from data in tables and use the graphs to understand which biomes have been the most important sources for annual and perennial plants and why. They also use tables and maps to locate the geographic origins of food plants.

Concepts covered

Genetic diversity, geography, domestication, biomes, drought, annual and perennial plant growth strategies

Prior knowledge required

The text and activities of *Garden Genetics* are intended to apply and supplement textbook concepts. Students should have familiarity with the following:

- **Evolution:** Students will better understand the activity if they are familiar with the notion that evolution is driven by natural selection—a process that results in the most fit individuals having the most offspring.
- **Artificial selection:** In contrast to natural selection, artificial selection is selection done toward human goals (like larger fruits). See Chapter 4.
- **Domestication:** A domesticated plant or animal is dependent on humans for its survival. Humans have become part of its ecosystem. See Chapter 4.

Activity notes

Time frame

- One class period

Materials

- Calculator
- Graph paper
- A large wall map of the world would be helpful.

Further reading

Geographic origins

Harlan, J. R. 1992. "Views on agricultural origins" (chapter 2) and "Space, time, and variation" (chapter 7). In *Crops and man.* Madison, WI: American Society of Agronomy.

Activity 8.
Where Does It Come From?
In the student edition, this activity begins on page 125.

Objective
Use tables and graphs to understand the relationship between food plants and the biomes they originated in. Use tables and maps to understand the geographic origins of food plants.

Background
Plant centers of origin are related to the ecology of geographic regions. Which **biomes**, or environments with characteristic climates and communities of plants and animals, are most important for agriculture?

Some biomes are inhospitable for agriculture even today. The Arctic tundra is too cold and dry for farming. Reindeer were domesticated there by native people, and there is some forestry, but no farming. It would be an unlikely origin for agricultural plants.

A **biome** is an environment with a characteristic climate and biotic community of plants and animals.

Activity

Part I. Biomes and food plants

1. Table 8.1 shows which biomes contributed which of the most important foods consumed worldwide. Graph the food contributions that originated in each biome (see Figure 8.3 for sample graph).

Topic: Biomes
Go to: *www.sciLINKS.org*
Code: GG26

Table 8.1. Source biomes for common food plants (from FAOSTAT database and Harlan 1992).
(MT = millions of metric tons, or megatons.)

Source Biome	Crop	2004 world production (MT)	Plant part consumed	Annual or perennial?
Costal areas				
	Tomato	108.5	fruit	annual
	Cabbage	62.5	leaves	annual
	Coconut	49.6	seed	perennial
	Sugar Beet	24.6	tuber	annual
Dry shrubland				
	Wheat	572.9	seed	annual
	Barley	132.2	seed	annual
	Canola	33.2	seed	annual
	Oat	25.5	seed	annual
	Rye	21.2	seed	annual
	Onion	51.9	bulb	annual
				(continued on p. 154)

(continued from p. 153)

Source Biome	Crop	2004 world production (MT)	Plant part consumed	Annual or perennial?
Prairie				
	Sunflower	23.9	seed	annual
Savanna				
	Maize	602.6	seed	annual
	Rice	576.3	seed	annual
	Cassava	184.9	tuber	perennial
	Sweet Potato	136.1	tuber	annual
	Watermelon	81.8	fruit	annual
	Sorghum	54.5	seed	annual
	Cottonseed Oil	53.7	seed	annual
	Yam	39.6	tuber	annual
	Peanut	34.1	seed	annual
	Millet	23.3	seed	annual
	Beans	18.3	seed	annual
	Triticale	11.0	seed	annual
Temperate forest				
	Soybean	179.9	seed	annual
	Grape	61.0	fruit	perennial
	Apple	57.1	fruit	perennial
Tropical mountains				
	Potato	307.4	tuber	annual
Tropical rain forest				
	Sugar Cane	142.9	stem	perennial
	Banana	69.8	fruit	perennial
	Orange	64.1	fruit	perennial
	Plantain	32.2	fruit	perennial
	Mango	25.8	fruit	perennial
	Coffee	7.4	seed	perennial
Total		3,898.9		

Figure 8.3. Sample student graph of biome contributions to world food production.

Category sums: coastal areas 245.3MT, dry shrubland 836.9MT, prairie 23.9MT, savanna 1845.2MT, temperate forest 298.0MT, tropical mountains 314.8MT, tropical rain forest 334.8MT.

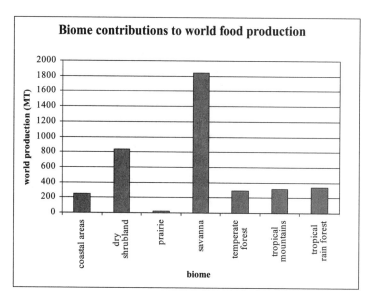

154

2. Which two biomes are the origin for the largest quantity of food?

   The savanna and dry shrublands have the food plants that are the largest quantity of what the world eats today.

3. What do the climates of these two biomes have in common? (Use Table 8.2.)

   The savanna and dry shrublands both have a hot, dry season.

Table 8.2. Climate descriptions of agricultural biomes.

Biome	Water availability	Temperature
Coastal areas	wet	varies
Dry shrubland	dry summer, wet winter	hot summer, cool winter
Prairie	dry summer, wet winter	hot summer, cold (below-freezing) winter
Savanna	wet season, dry season	always hot
Temperate forest	wet	cool season and warm season
Tropical mountains	wet	cold season and warm season
Tropical rain forest	very wet	always warm

4. Do any other biomes share these same features? If so, which?

   The prairie also has a hot, dry season. However, instead of a cool, wet productive winter, prairies have frozen, biologically unproductive winters.

5. How much of world food production comes from crops that originated in the biome(s) of question 4?

   The prairie contributed plants that make up less than 0.6% of today's world food production. Prairies were not an important source of food plant biodiversity, at least in part because of the cold winters mentioned in question 4.

   Currently, the prairies are very important sites of U.S. agriculture. However, prairie agriculture is a recent development. Historically these grasslands burned periodically and the prairie grasses survived by having a strong, shallow mat of roots under the soil, from which they could quickly regenerate after a fire. Despite the ecological importance of this root mat, it was nearly impossible to penetrate and therefore grasslands were sites of grazing and hunting, but not sites of agriculture. The prairies were not farmed until the invention of the steel plow, a tool strong enough to cut through the root mat.

6. In what part of the year does plant growth occur in the biomes of questions 2 and 4? (Use Table 8.2 and think about both temperature and water. How well do plants grow when temperatures are below freezing? How well do plants grow when the climate is hot and dry?)

Most biological growth in the dry shrublands and savannas occurs during the wet season. Most plant growth in the prairie happens during the cooler, wet spring, and a little bit of growth occurs during the hot, dry summer.

7. What relationship do you see between growing season and the number of plants each biome has contributed?
   The prairie, with its frozen winters and hot, dry summers, does not have much opportunity for plants to grow. The dry shrublands and savannas, with their warm, wet growing seasons, are the most important contributors of food plants!

An **annual** plant completes its entire life cycle within one year. The life of a **perennial** plant lasts more than one year.

Water is critical for plant survival. In drought-prone biomes, many plants transfer energy into a seed, which can survive the drought inside its protective seed coat. The more energy the plant packages into the seed, the better the chance that the seed will germinate successfully the following season. Grains, such as wheat and corn, share this strategy. An **annual** plant is one that completes its entire life cycle—from seed to plant to seed again—within a year. Another successful drought strategy is to transfer all the plant's resources belowground to a tuber, root, or bulb. Potatoes, carrots, and onions share this "annual" strategy. Technically, potatoes and onions aren't annuals because the same plant can grow again from the tuber in the next wet season. However, from an agricultural perspective, they are annuals since they can be harvested and planted anew each year. Thus, the parts of these annual plants where sugars are stored so that plants survive from one year to the next—seeds, roots, and tubers—have high energy reserves and have become important sources of food for humans.

Perennial plants, like trees and shrubs, live much longer than one year. Some produce an annual crop of fruits or nuts that we harvest.

8. Table 8.1 shows whether agricultural plants are annual or perennial. Graph the amount of food produced by annual plants versus perennial plants. (See Figure 8.4 for sample graph.)
   Category sums: annual plants 3204.1MT, perennial plants 694.8MT.

9. Which plant strategy is more important for agricultural production?
   Annual plants are far more important for world agriculture. Humans are largely seed-eaters.

10. Which biomes have been the most important sources for annual plants? (Refer to Table 8.1.)
    Dry shrublands and savannas.

11. What important climate feature do these biomes share? (Refer to Table 8.2.)
    Drought.

156

Figure 8.4. Sample student graph of annual and perennial growth habit and world food production.

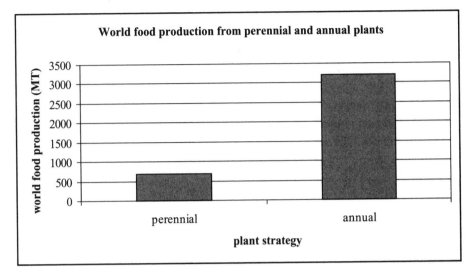

12. Why is climate important for producing annual plants? (Think about how plants survive until the next generation.)

    Plants transfer their energy resources to a seed or tuber to avoid the dry season. We harvest and store the seeds and tubers and consume the plant energy.

13. Which biomes have been the most important sources for perennial plants? (Refer to Table 8.1.)

    Tropical rain forests and temperate forests.

14. What important climate feature do these biomes share? (Refer to Table 8.2.)

    Ample water.

15. What part do we eat of the perennial plants from these biomes? (Refer to Table 8.1.)

    We eat the fruit. (The exception is coffee, where we consume an extract of the seeds. However, we don't consume coffee for calories, but instead for its stimulating properties.)

Perennial plants typically do not face the biological challenge of severe drought. Therefore they can make a long-term investment in woody growth and can drop leaves to survive cold winters. The perennial plants' "problem" is dispersal. How does an apple tree move its seeds far from itself so the new seedlings don't compete with the parent tree and with each other? Many of the food plants from this biome have solved their dispersal problems in the same way. They focus their energy on making their fruits attractive to animals that might help in dispersal. Humans and other animals eat the fruits and help transport the seeds to new locations.

16. In conclusion, which biomes have been the most important source of agricultural food plants and why?

The dry shrublands (like the Mediterranean) and savannas have been the most important source of annual plants. Agriculture depends on annual plants. The annual strategy is a good one for avoiding the droughts of these biomes.

Part II. Centers of origin and food plants

17. Use Table 8.3 to fill in the geographic region of origin for the following food plants:

Food plant	Plant part consumed	Annual or perennial?	Source biome	Geographic center of origin
apple	fruit	perennial	temperate forest	*Middle East*
avocado	fruit	perennial	tropical rain forest	*Central America/South America*
bean	seed	annual	savanna	*Central America/South America*
beet	root	annual	coastal	*Middle East*
cabbage	leaves	annual	coastal	*Europe*
carrot	root	annual	dry shrubland	*Europe*
chocolate (cacao)	seed	perennial	tropical rain forest	*Central America*
coffee	seed	perennial	tropical mountains	*Africa*
corn	seed	annual	savanna	*Central America*
cranberry	fruit	perennial	wetland	*North America*
okra	fruit	annual	savanna	*Africa*
orange	fruit	perennial	tropical rain forest	*India*
peach	fruit	perennial	woodland	*China*
potato	tuber	annual	tropical mountains	*Central America/South America*
raspberry	fruit	perennial	temperate forest	*North America*
rice	seed	annual	savanna	*China/India*
spinach	leaves	annual	unknown	*Middle East*
sugar cane	stem	perennial	tropical rain forest	*Pacific Islands (India/Indochina, Pacific Islands group)*
sunflower	seed	annual	grasslands	*North America*
tomato	fruit	annual	coastal	*Central America/South America*
vanilla	seed	perennial	tropical rain forest	*Central America*
walnut	seed	perennial	temperate forest	*Middle East*
watermelon	fruit	annual	savanna	*Africa*
wheat	seed	annual	dry shrubland	*Middle East*
yam	tuber	annual	savanna	*China, Africa, India*

18. Give two examples of food origins that surprised you. Explain why.
    Many acceptable answers… the point is to get students to process the above information, rather than just looking it up.

19. Several of the food plants listed in Table 8.3 have more than one center of origin. Find five plants with multiple centers of origin.

Food plant	First area of geographic origin	Second area of geographic origin
tomato, bean, cotton, squash, avocado, guava, papaya, cassava, jicama	Central America	South America
rice, yam	India	China (yam also has third center in Africa)
turnip, canola	China	Africa
jack bean	South America	India

20. What do you notice about the two centers of origin, geographically? (Are they isolated from one another? Close to one another?)
    Multiple centers of origin are often linked to one another by land. For example, many crops have centers of origin in South and Central America (bean, cotton, cassava, jicama, papaya, avocado, pepper, and squash). Jack bean is the exception—its two centers of origin (South America and India) are separated by water.

21. How can a plant have two centers of origin? Explain.
    The plant could have originated separately (in two different places). More likely, however, the plant arose in one region (one center of origin) and then was carried to the other, where it continued to evolve (two centers of diversity).

Table 8.3. Geographic centers of origin for various food plants (from Harlan 1992).

Geographic center of origin	Crop						
	Cereals	Legumes	Roots and tubers	Oil crops	Fruits and nuts	Vegetables and spices	Stimulants
Central America	corn	bean	sweet potato, cassava, jicama	cotton	papaya, guava, avocado, pineapple, prickly pear	pepper, squash, tomato, vanilla	cacao
North America			Jerusalem artichoke	sunflower	strawberry, raspberry, grape, cranberry, pecan		tobacco

(continued on p. 160)

(continued from p. 159)

Geographic center of origin	Crop						
	Cereals	Legumes	Roots and tubers	Oil crops	Fruits and nuts	Vegetables and spices	Stimulants
South America		peanut, bean, lupine, inga, jack bean	arracacha, achira, yam, cassava, jicama, potato, oca, anu, ullucu	peanut, cotton	cashew, pineapple, guanábana, chirimoya, Brazil nut, papaya, guava avocado	pepper, squash, tomato	coca, mate
India, Indochina, Pacific Islands	Asian rice	pigeon pea, jack bean, winged bean, moth bean, rice bean	yam, arrowroot, taro	coconut	bread fruit, orange, lime, tangerine, grapefruit, mango, banana	cucumber, nutmeg, eggplant, plantain	
China	Asian rice, proso, foxtail millet	soybean, adzuki bean	turnip, yam	canola	chestnut, quince, persimmon, lychee, apricot, peach	Chinese cabbage, ginger	tea, ginseng, camphor
Africa	African rice, pearl millet, sorghum, teff, fonio	cowpea, hyacinth bean, groundnuts (Bambara, Kersting's)	yam	oil palm, castor bean	watermelon, melon, baobab	okra	coffee
Middle East	wheat, barley, rye, oat	pea, chickpea (garbanzo), lentil, lupine	turnip, carrot, radish, beet	canola, safflower, flax, olive	fig, hazelnut, walnut, pistachio, date palm, almond, grape, apple, pear, plum, melon	onion, leek, garlic, lettuce, saffron, parsley	poppy, digitalis, belladonna, licorice

22. Map the crops of Table 8.3 onto Figure 8.5. Connect the crop pictures to their regions of origin and add the names of food plants from the table if they are not already pictured on the map.

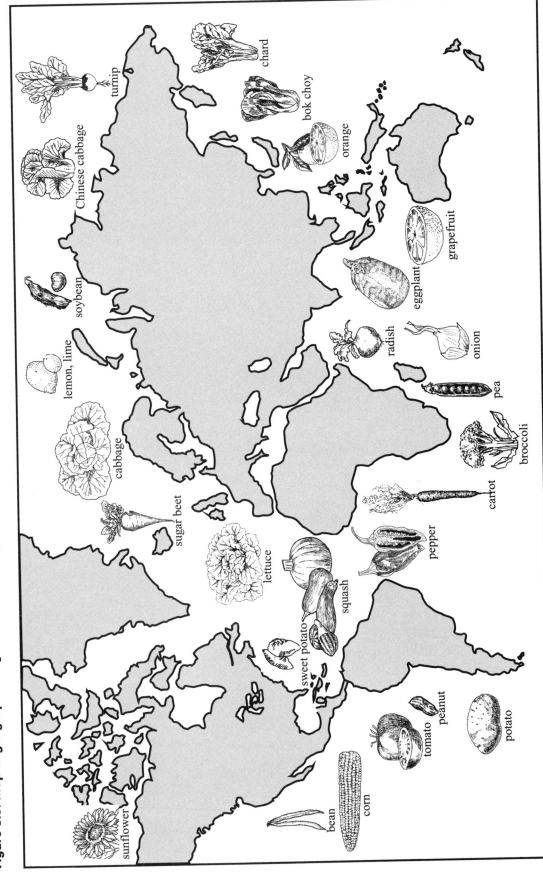

Figure 8.5. Map of geographic origins of some food plants.

QUANTITATIVE TRAITS

Our world holds an astonishing array of diversity. Everyone knows about red tomatoes. Many people are also familiar with the orange and yellow tomato varieties. But few of us have seen the little known varieties that are green, purple-black, blue, and even white when they are ripe. Some tomatoes look like peaches, complete with fuzzy skin and peachy color. The sausage tomato is a long, red cylinder. The yellow pear variety is bite-sized and shaped like a pear. There are tomatoes named for peaches, pears, cherries, plums, and currants. Some have ridges like pumpkins. Others are perfectly smooth. Many of these varieties have been around for more than a century. Their seeds are sold as "heirloom" tomatoes. Gardeners all over the world grow them for their intriguing looks and novel flavors. Look at the different types of tomatoes to the right in Figure 9.1.

With all this variety in color, shape, and size, it's no wonder that these traits are controlled by more than one gene. Most of the traits that people care about in plants (like yield, color, and flavor) are complex. They are not controlled by a single gene, like Mendel's wrinkled peas or the bitterness gene in cucumbers. Instead, these complex traits are controlled by many genes, each having a small effect. Nowhere can you find a color gene that has red, orange, green, yellow, and purple alleles. Instead color is influenced by dozens of different genes, making dozens of proteins. Each of those proteins has a small effect on color.

Gene hunting

It's easy to understand why plant breeders would want to discover the genes involved in yield, fruit size, or flavor. People have been improving crops for these complex traits for centuries. Until recently, though, we did not have the right tools to isolate the effect of specific genes on a complex trait like yield.

Traditionally, to understand the behavior of traits and genes, plant breeders made crosses between mutant and normal **phenotypes** and

Figure 9.1. Diversity in tomato shape.

SciLINKS
THE WORLD'S A CLICK AWAY

Topic: Observing Traits Molecularly
Go to: *www.sciLINKS.org*
Code: GG27

A **phenotype** is the physical expression (often visible) of an individual's genes.

Figure 9.2. Crosses and behavior of single-gene and multiple-gene traits.

If you make a cross between...	And the offspring are...	What type of gene do you have?
A smooth (SS) tomato and a fuzzy (ss) tomato	Offspring are all the texture of one parent [smooth (SS)].	A dominant Mendelian gene.
A round (Rr) tomato and a flat (rr) tomato	Offspring are the shape of both parents [round (Rr) and flat(rr)].	A dominant Mendelian gene.
A yellow-flowered (YY) tomato and a white-flowered (yy) tomato	Offspring are between the parents [cream-colored flowers(Yy)].	An incompletely dominant Mendelian gene.
A small tomato (many genes) and a large tomato (many genes)	Offspring are a continuous range of sizes (many genes).	Many genes.

A Mendelian trait is controlled by a single gene. Mendelian traits can be **dominant**, **recessive**, or **incompletely dominant**.

Quantitative traits are controlled by many genes.

looked at the offspring. This approach worked well with single-gene, **Mendelian traits**. For example in Figure 9.2, when a mutant fuzzy-skinned tomato crossed with a normal smooth-skinned tomato, and all the offspring have the smooth-skinned phenotype of one parent, it is a clear case of **dominance**. If a mutant flattened tomato is crossed with a normal round tomato and the offspring have both the flat and round phenotypes of the parents, the situation is equally clear, and also indicates a dominant gene. A third single-gene scenario, **incomplete dominance**, allows for three phenotypes: the parental yellow-flowered and white-flowered as well as cream-flower offspring.

However, things are not always so simple! What happens when a cross of a small tomato and a large tomato gives offspring that range in size from small to large, with many sizes in between? The situation can no longer be explained by one gene. Suddenly, plant breeders are trying to understand the behavior of many genes, all acting together to create one phenotype. Until quite recently, plant breeders and scientists didn't have the tools to find the different genes involved and separate the effects of each.

New techniques

Why can't plant breeders simply look at a plant's DNA to find the multiple genes involved in quantitative traits? Unfortunately, DNA is not something we can see easily. With a microscope, you can sometimes see chromosomes, but not genes or DNA. Even if you could see DNA, what would a gene look like? DNA is just a sequence of base pairs. There is no visible information in those base pairs about which sections of DNA are coded into proteins and which are not. Only 28% of a tomato's total DNA, or **genome**, is actually in genes. The rest is **non-coding** DNA that we don't understand well. Some people call it "junk" DNA, though it likely serves an unknown purpose.

Furthermore, there is a lot of DNA! A tomato has 637 million base pairs. Compared to other organisms in Table 9.1, like corn or humans, that is a small genome. However, it would still take years to carefully examine every gene.

So scientists have come up with a short cut. They use **genetic markers** (also called molecular markers) to focus in on sections of DNA, instead of trying to look at every base pair. These markers are the equivalent of bookmarks placed throughout the plant's genome. They are short (50–500 base pairs) sequences of DNA, usually at known places on the plant's chromosomes. Markers allow scientists to narrow down the locations of genes.

Table 9.1. Genome size.

Organism	Genome size
bean	637 Mb
tomato	**953 Mb**
chicken	1,130 Mb
corn	**2,671 Mb**
peanut	2,800 Mb
mouse	3,010 Mb
human	**3,190 Mb**
pea	4,000 Mb
grasshopper	13,400 Mb
wheat	16,979 Mb
lily	124,852 Mb

Some DNA **codes** for genes that make proteins. Other DNA is **non-coding**.

A **genome** is an organism's complete DNA, including both genes and non-coding DNA.

Genetic markers are short sequences of DNA in an organism's genome.

Topic: Genes and Chromosomes
Go to: www.sciLINKS.org
Code: GG29

WHY ARE GENETIC MARKERS CALLED MARKERS?

Historically, plant breeders used visible phenotypes, like purple-colored leaves, to "mark" desirable invisible phenotypes, like resistance to a disease. These "markers" were rare—occurring, for example, only when the genes for purple-colored leaves and disease resistance were located close together on the chromosomes.

Genetic markers also mark phenotypes, but in this case, the marker does not cause a phenotype of its own. It is just a section of DNA, probably not in a gene, chosen because the sequence of its end points and its location are known (Figure 9.3). Instead of looking at all of the roughly 79 million base pairs of DNA on a chromosome, researchers can look at short sections of about 500 base pairs of DNA in 10 marker locations. Because the genetic markers are DNA, at the marker location, an individual will have an "allele." The individual could have one of up to four alleles—up to two from the mother and up to two from the father. The roughly 7 million unknown base pairs of DNA in between markers are called bins.

Figure 9.3. Tomato genetic markers.

Tomato DNA: 1 chromosome ~79 million base pairs

| ATCCCGCCCGCCC | CGACGACGACGA | TACTAGGGAGAT | GCCGCCGCCGCC | CATCATCAGCAT |

Tomato genetic markers: short section of DNA (~500 base pairs) in a known location on the chromosome

Tomatoes have 12 **chromosomes**, shown on the map in Figure 9.4. Chromosome 1 shows nine markers, labelled m1 through m9, and represented by a bar across the chromosome. Between the markers are unknown areas of DNA called **bins**. Markers can have several alleles, just like genes have alleles. The alleles are slightly different lengths of DNA found at the same location. It is these differences at the same location that allow researchers to do quantitative trait loci or QTL studies.

Figure 9.4. Tomato chromosome map with bins. Markers are only labeled on the first chromosome. Unlabeled markers are represented by bars on other chromosomes.

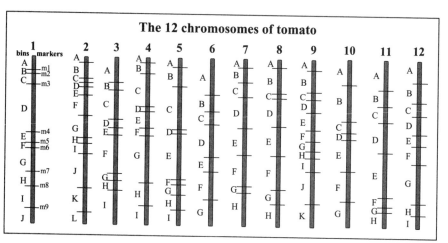

Quantitative trait loci (QTL) studies

So how do plant breeders find the genes involved in quantitative traits? They begin by making a cross between two very different types of plants. For example, researchers interested in genes involved in tomato fruit weight crossed a wild tomato (which has tiny, green tomatoes) with a cultivated tomato (which has large, red fruits) The next generation is the hybrid generation (also called F1 generation), where plants are genetically similar to each other (but not identical, because the parents weren't homozygous at all loci) and similar in appearance to the wild tomato. The hybrid generation is then crossed back to a cultivated tomato again to create the backcross 1 generation (BC1 generation).

The plants of the backcross 1 generation are genetically different from one another—each has a different combination of genes from the wild and cultivated tomato parents. The BC1 generation is again backcrossed to the cultivated tomato to create the BC2 generation. With each cross back to the cultivated tomato, the resulting generation has a larger number of genes from cultivated tomato and a small number of genes from the wild tomato. The plants of the BC2 generation are each genetically distinct and will show differences in fruit weight, as well as in many other characteristics. The BC2 generation will be more physically and genetically similar to the cultivated tomato than to the wild tomato (see Figure 9.5).

Figure 9.5. QTL study to find tomato fruit size genes.

Generation	Populations involved	Action taken
Parental (P) Generation	Wild tomato (small fruit) X Cultivated tomato (large fruit)	
Hybrid (F1) Generation	The F1 generation is genetically similar (but not identical).	X The F1 generation is crossed to the cultivated tomato again.
Backcross 1 (BC1) Generation	Each plant in the BC1 generation is genetically different.	X The BC1 generation is crossed to the cultivated tomato again.
Backcross 2 (BC2) Generation	Each plant in the BC2 generation is genetically different. (The BC2 plants are more similar to the cultivated tomato than the BC1 generation.)	(1) Measure fruit weight. (2) Analyze DNA sample with genetic markers.

From each plant in the BC2 generation, the researchers take both a measurement of fruit weight and a DNA sample (Figure 9.6). The genetic markers shown in Figure 9.4 are used on the DNA sample from each plant. By comparing each plant's markers and fruit weight, the researchers are able to pinpoint areas of the genome that are associated with fruit weight. In Figure 9.6, markers 1 and 2 always have allele A in heavy tomatoes and always have allele B in light tomatoes. Therefore there is a QTL for fruit weight in the bin between markers 1 and 2. Because there are 107 markers, finding these associations requires powerful computers and complicated statistics. (Another reason these studies couldn't be done until recently!)

Figure 9.6. Measurements and DNA analysis on BC2 generation.

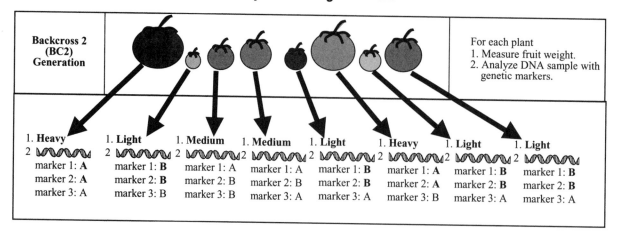

The relationship between marker and fruit weight is only an association—genetic variation near that marker coincides with variation in tomato weight. The markers don't *cause* the variation, but a gene near the marker might.

The results from these quantitative trait locus (QTL) studies are highly specific because they depend on the alleles present in the parents, the markers used to detect them, and the environment in which the plants were grown. In a different tomato population or environment, other genes might be involved. To control for the highly specific results, scientists compare plants grown in different environments or compare studies to look for bins that have been identified multiple times as having QTLs for a trait like fruit size. If the same QTL shows up in multiple studies, it is more likely to be important.

Scientists studying tomatoes have looked at QTLs for fruit weight, fruit shape, and fruit color, as well as flavor and sweetness (Table 9.2). In all cases, many genes are involved. For example, 28 different QTLs were associated with fruit weight in at least two studies.

Table 9.2. Examples of QTL studies in tomato.

Trait	QTLs appearing in more than two studies	Major QTLs (>20% in at least one study)
Fruit weight	28 QTLs	6 major QTLs
Fruit shape	11 QTLs	5 major QTLs
Fruit color (lycopene)	8 QTLs	1 major QTL

Figure 9.7. QTLs, variation, and QTLs of major effect.

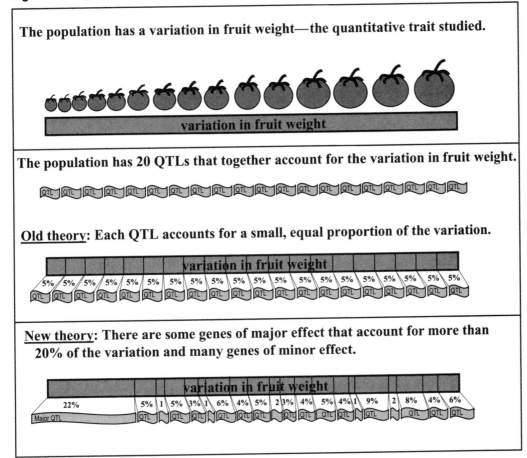

Genes of major effect

Historically, scientists believed that quantitative traits were controlled by many genes, all contributing equally to the phenotype (Figure 9.7). Data from QTL studies show that most QTLs do not account for more than 20% of the variation in a trait. However, it is common to discover one or two QTLs that account for larger amounts of the variation (up to 70%). These QTLs are called **major QTLs**. Six of the fruit weight QTLs in Table 9.2 are major in at least one study. That means that though there may be many genes involved in a trait like fruit weight, some genes have greater effects than others. How? Researchers are only beginning to understand the function of the proteins that these genes encode and how they interact with one another to produce quantitative traits.

In the case of tomato fruit weight, one major QTL, called fw2.2, accounts for about 30% of the variation. All large-fruited tomato varieties have one version, while all small-fruited varieties have a different version of the QTL. When crossed, the small-fruit allele was

A major QTL accounts for more than 20% of the variation in a trait.

Topic: Genome Mapping
Go to: www.sciLINKS.org
Code: GG30

somewhat dominant (remember there are lots of other genes involved also) to the large-fruit allele. When you consider that dozens of QTLs are involved, 30% is a very big proportion! If each of the 28 QTLs from Table 9.2 accounted for an equal proportion of the variation in fruit weight, each would contribute 3.6% of the variation. Therefore, a QTL that accounts for 30% of the variation indicates the presence of an important gene.

Naturally, people wanted to know how this important gene worked. But first they had to find it. The early QTL studies located fw2.2 in bin B on chromosome 2. But that bin contained millions of DNA base pairs. Further studies zoomed in closer and closer (Figure 9.8) until researchers could identify "Candidate gene A," a 1.8 kb (1,800 base pairs) section of DNA. But how could they be sure that this was the important fruit weight gene?

Figure 9.8. Fine mapping studies zoom in on the region with the major fw2.2 gene or genes for fruit weight.

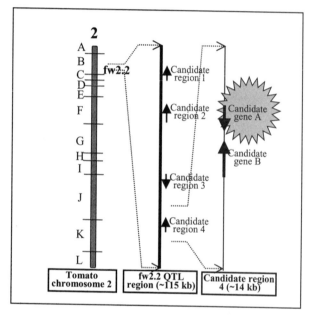

Genetic sequence is the reading of base pairs in a section of DNA (for example, ACGGG...).

To prove they had found the gene, scientists did something very clever. They copied the "small-fruit-causing" version of the gene and used genetic engineering to insert it into a "large-fruit-type" tomato plant. When the previously large-fruit-type plants grew only small fruit (under identical conditions) the researchers knew they had found the fruit weight gene they were looking for!

Fw2.2 does *what*?

At that point, researchers knew the DNA sequence of the gene. Using powerful databases, they were able to compare fw2.2 to other **genetic sequences** from plants and animals (see Activity 2 for more details). One sequence in the database matched fw2.2 closely. To everyone's surprise, the matching gene was a gene involved in human cancer. How could that be possible? It seemed ridiculous until people compared the effects of both genes.

The small-fruit allele appears to be a protein that regulates cell division. In small tomatoes, the gene switches cell division in the fruit on and off. Evolutionarily, this makes sense. The small fruits are large enough to contain hundreds of seeds, and small enough to be transported by birds or rodents. From the tomato's perspective, there is no reason to invest in making larger fruits. Especially if further investment makes the fruits too big to be transported by birds and rodents!

The large-fruit allele disables the protein that stops cell division. In other words, large tomatoes have many more cell divisions than small ones. Cancer is also often the result of unregulated cell division. It's remarkable that a similar process can have such different effects!

The fw2.2 gene has importance beyond just tomato weight. Remember that one of the important differences between wild tomatoes and the domesticated tomatoes that grow in our gardens is fruit size. When humans began to select wild tomatoes for characteristics that appeal to us, fruit size was at the top of the list! Remember that all large tomatoes have one version of fw2.2 while all small tomatoes have another. In other words, fw2.2 is an important gene in the evolution and domestication of cultivated tomatoes.

Review

The interesting and important gene fw2.2 was discovered through a QTL study. QTL studies are a way of investigating quantitative traits, where many genes have an effect on a trait. Until recently, it was difficult to pinpoint the genes involved in quantitative traits. With powerful computers and DNA markers, QTL studies are now possible. The fw2.2 gene accounts for 30% of the variation in fruit weight. That's a large amount considering the dozens of genes involved in controlling fruit weight. However, that still leaves 70% of the variation controlled by the many other genes.

Questions for further thought

<u>Mendelian genetics:</u> What would happen if a true-breeding fuzzy, flat tomato was crossed with a true-breeding smooth, round tomato (see Figure 9.2)?

Using the notation from Figure 9.2, the fuzzy, flat tomato (ssrr) is crossed with the smooth, round tomato (SSRR) and the offspring are all smooth, round di-hybrid tomatoes (SsRr).

If these di-hybrid tomatoes are selfed (or crossed to one another) the offspring will have 9 smooth, round tomatoes (SSRR, SsRR, SsRr), 3 smooth, flat tomatoes (Ssrr, SSrr), 3 fuzzy, round tomatoes (ssRr, ssRR), and 1 fuzzy, flat tomato (SSrr).

<u>Quantitative genetics:</u> When researchers were testing to be sure they had found fw2.2, why did they take the small-fruit-causing gene and put it into a large-fruit plant? (Remember that the small-fruit allele was somewhat dominant to the large-fruit allele.)

If they had inserted a large-fruited allele into a small-fruited plant, the tomato size would not have changed because of the other genes influencing fruit weight. The plant would still have had two copies of the small-fruited allele, and the large-fruited allele wouldn't have had much, if any, effect. Because the small-fruit allele is somewhat dominant, it would have over-ridden the new allele. By putting the "somewhat" dominant allele into a large-fruited plant (recessive background), one copy of the allele would have immediate, visible results.

Chapter 9 Teacher Notes

Overview and Concepts

Overview

The chapter begins with single-gene Mendelian traits and compares them to quantitative traits where many genes are involved in determining phenotype. Quantitative trait loci (QTL) studies use molecular markers to pinpoint which sections of DNA are associated with variation in a trait like tomato fruit size. Some genes that impact quantitative traits have more effect on the trait than other genes. Questions review and apply Mendelian and quantitative genetics.

Activity 9 explores the QTLs involved with color, a quantitative trait, in tomatoes. Students begin by mapping the QTLs found on tomato chromosomes. Then they map mutant genes known to affect tomato color by causing blockages of biochemical pathways and look for places where known color genes coincide with QTLs for tomato color.

Concepts covered

Quantitative and single-gene traits, dominance and incomplete dominance, genome, genetic markers, chromosome maps, crosses, back-crosses, quantitative trait loci (QTL) studies, genetic sequence, domestication, biochemical pathways

Prior knowledge required

The text and activities of *Garden Genetics* are intended to apply and supplement textbook concepts. Students should have familiarity with the following:

- Crosses and segregation ratios of single-gene **Mendelian genetics**.
- A **phenotype** is the physical expression of a genetic trait. A phenotype can be structural, physiological, behavioral, or biochemical—it is not just an organism's physical appearance. (Though that is certainly the easiest type of phenotype to identify!)
- **DNA** is made up of **base pairs**.
- DNA encodes proteins. **Proteins** are the actors within the cells.
- An **enzyme**, a type of protein, acts as a catalyst in biological reactions.
- The process of **photosynthesis** uses chlorophyll and other chemical compounds to capture light energy.

Activity notes

Preparation prior to activity

- This activity presents very recent research that may not be familiar to most teachers. If you are unfamiliar with molecular markers, quantitative traits, and QTL studies, take some time to familiarize yourself with the text, the activity, and perhaps the papers listed under the further reading section.

Time frame

- One class period. (You may wish to budget a second class period for discussion of the chapter text and/or the activity.)

Materials

- Colored pens or pencils

Teaching tip

- Working through the questions for the activity, as a class, through discussion, or in small groups may help students handle the complexity of the material.

Further reading

QTL studies in tomato

Grandillo, S., H. M. Ku, and S. Tanksley. 1999. Identifying the loci responsible for natural variation in fruit size and shape in tomato. *Theoretical and Applied Genetics* 99: 978–987.

The fw2.2 gene

Frary, A., T. C. Nesbitt, A. Frary, S. Grandillo, E. van der Knapp, B. Cong, J. Liu, J. Meller, R. Elber, K. Alpert, and S. Tanksley. 2000. fw2.2: A quantitative trait locus key to the evolution of tomato fruit size. *Science* 289: 85–88.

Tomato fruit color (for activity)

Liu, Y., A. Gur, G. Ronen, M. Causse, R. Damidaux, M. Buret, J. Hirschberg, and D. Zamir. 2003. There is more to tomato fruit colour than candidate carotenoid genes. *Plant Biotechnology Journal* 1: 195–207.

Activity 9.

Mapping Tomato Color

In the student edition, this activity begins on page 145.

Objective

To map the results from a QTL study of color in tomato in order to understand the genetics of tomato color.

Materials

- Colored pens or pencils

Background

The study of color in plants is more important than you might think! Plant pigments have impacts on human health, as well as on the plant's ability to capture sunlight and protect its tissues. In tomatoes, as in many other plants, color is determined by a group of pigments called carotenoids. Carotenoids are familiar to us as vitamins and nutritional supplements. Beta-carotene, a carotenoid, is a precursor to Vitamin A and is responsible for yellow color in carrots, squash, and sweet potatoes. Lycopene is the carotenoid pigment that makes tomatoes red. Lycopene has recently been in the news for its antioxidant properties, which may be important for healthy hearts.

Color pigments also play an important role in plants. Chlorophyll, which captures the Sun's energy to convert carbon dioxide (CO_2) into sugars, is one such pigment. Other pigments help protect the plant from damage caused by the Sun's light—sunlight can harm plant tissues just like it can harm human skin.

Because of the importance of carotenoids to humans and plants, scientists have studied the biochemical pathways involved in making them. Figure 9.9 shows the tomato carotenoid biochemical pathway. The arrows represent enzymes—the actors within the cell that convert one pigment into the next. An enzyme converts phytoene into gamma-carotene. Another enzyme is responsible for converting that into lycopene.

Many pigments and enzymes are involved in determining tomato color. And many genes are involved in making those pigments and enzymes. (Pigments and enzymes are just proteins, after all. And genes encode proteins.) Therefore, it is not surprising that color in tomatoes is a quantitative trait.

Figure 9.9. Biochemical pathway for color pigments phytoene, gamma-carotene, lycopene, delta-carotene, and beta-carotene.

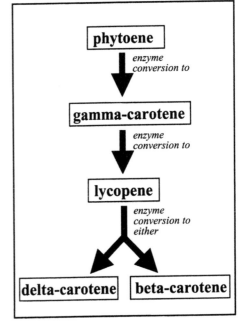

Activity

Part I. QTL study

Since color is an important trait, it's not surprising that plant breeders were interested in understanding where the many color genes could be found in the tomato genome. To find the color genes, plant breeders did a QTL study.

1. The first step was to make a cross. Since this study was about color, what important difference must have existed between the two parents they crossed?

    The two parents should have been different for the trait of interest—color.

Figure 9.10. QTL study to find tomato color genes.

Generation	Populations involved	Action taken
Parental (P) Generation	Green tomato X Red tomato	
Hybrid (F1) Generation	The F1 generation is genetically similar (but not identical.)	X The F1 generation is crossed to the red tomato again.
Backcross 1 (BC1) Generation	Each plant in the BC1 generation is genetically different.	X The BC1 generation is crossed to the red tomato again.
Backcross 2 (BC2) Generation	Each plant in the BC2 generation is genetically different. (The BC2 plants are more similar to the red tomato than the BC1 generation.)	(1) Measure fruit color. (2) Measure lycopene levels. (3) Measure carotene content. (4) Analyze DNA sample with genetic markers.

A **spectrophotometer** measures light intensity and color (or more specifically, the wavelength of light).

The researchers crossed a wild tomato relative with green fruits and a commercial tomato variety called M82 with red fruits (Figure 9.10). Interestingly, wild relatives have useful genes to improve characteristics like color, even though their own color is not desirable in commercial tomatoes. The researchers grew the F1 and BC1 generations, making the crosses shown in Figure 9.10 until they reached the BC2 generation.

Next, the researchers needed to measure the BC2 generation for color, lycopene content, and carotene content—the traits of interest in this study. Lycopene and carotene are measured by grinding up the tomato, separating the compounds chemically, and measuring lycopene and carotene content with a **spectrophotometer**. To measure color, they used a scale from 1 to 5 where 1 = yellow, 2 = orange, 3 = light red, 4 = red, and 5 = dark red.

- A + sign indicates the QTL is associated with redder color, more lycopene, or more carotene.

- A − sign indicates the QTL is associated with less color, less lycopene, or less carotene.

- Multiple + or − signs (+++, or −−) indicate a stronger association.

Chromosomal bin locations for:		
Color	**Lycopene**	**Carotene**
2C (−)	2K (+)	10E (++)
2K (+)	3C (−−)	12C (++++)
3C (−−)	5A (+)	
4F (−)	6A (+)	
4H (+)	11A (+)	
6A (+)	12B (+)	
6E (−)	12C (−−)	
7B (−)		
7F (+)		
8C (+)		
8E (−)		
8F (−)		
9G (+)		
10B (+)		
10E (−)		
11B (+)		
12C (−−)		
12H (−)		

The next step was to look for QTLs associated with tomato color, lycopene, and carotene levels. The list to the right shows the locations on the tomato chromosome map (QTLs) that are associated with color, lycopene, and carotene levels in the tomato crosses. The QTLs can be associated with positive values for the trait (redder color, more lycopene, or more carotene) or negative values for the trait (less red color, lower lycopene or carotene levels). Some associations are stronger than others. In the list, stronger association between QTL and trait are shown with more + or − signs.

2. Use the list and the map of tomato's 12 chromosomes in Figure 9.11 to map QTLs for color, lycopene, and carotene. Draw the color QTLs in red, lycopene QTLs in green, and carotene QTLs in blue on the map. Use multiple + or − signs to show strength of the association.

Figure 9.11. Chromosome map for exercise: Teacher Version.

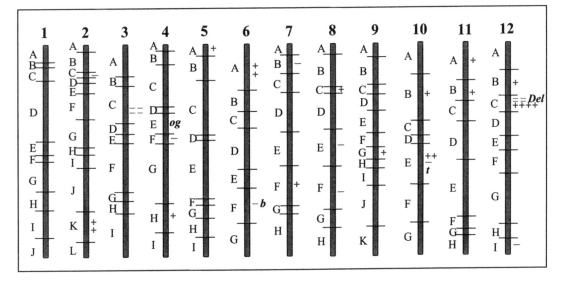

- In Figure 9.11, each vertical line represents a chromosome.
- Each dash represents a genetic **marker**.
- The letters indicate **bins**, or regions, associated with traits.
- For example, a trait found in bin 2K is on chromosome 2, between the 10th and 11th markers.

3. Each QTL is a section of DNA associated with a trait. What does the DNA contain at each QTL?

   At least one gene. (Likely a gene that influences color.) There could be more than one gene in the DNA section.

4. Look at bin 2K on the chromosome map. This bin is associated with a QTL for both color AND lycopene. Find two other locations with more than one QTL.

   Bin 3C is negatively associated with both color and lycopene levels. Bin 12C is negatively associated with lycopene and color and strongly positively associated with carotene levels. Bin 10E is associated with low color and high levels of carotene.

5. At the places with more than one QTL, might you find one gene or many genes?

   Though it is impossible to say for certain whether one or several genes have effects in these locations, it is most likely that there is one gene in these locations that impacts both characteristics (or all three characteristics). Biologists often choose the simplest explanation as their starting hypothesis. It is far simpler to expect one gene with multiple effects than to expect several genes that happen to be in the same bin and affect related characteristics.

   5a. Could one gene have an effect on more than one trait (lycopene and color, for example)? Why or why not?

   Yes, one gene can affect more than one trait. The gene makes a protein. The protein could be an enzyme in a biochemical pathway. A change in this enzyme would impact both the compounds upstream and downstream.

   Plus, color is the net effect of many biochemical compounds. Lycopene and beta-carotene are both compounds that affect color. Therefore a gene that affects lycopene levels could very easily influence color as well!

   5b. These maps have a very big scale. Is it possible to know for sure at this scale whether a bin (2K, for example) contains one gene or several genes?

   No. Given the information you have, it is not possible to rule out multiple genes. It is possible to determine this with much more genetic work like that shown in Figure 9.11. Also see number 5 above.

6. Would you expect to find the same results if you crossed a different red tomato with a different green tomato and grew them under the same environmental conditions? Why or why not?

   These results will vary from one population to another, depending on which populations are crossed and the environment in which populations are examined. The initial populations crossed determine which alleles are in the study because each will have a unique genetic composition.

7. Would you expect to find some of these same results in another population or another location? Why or why not?

   Some of the QTLs should be the same, indicating that the QTLs are important across different populations and environments.

Part II. Verification

The QTL study gives you a good idea where to look for genes affecting color in tomatoes. But what exactly are these genes and what do they do? Let's return for a moment to the biochemical pathway affecting the color pigments in tomato. Using mutants and traditional plant breeding techniques, geneticists have identified some genes involved in the pathway. The effects of some of these genes have been known for 100 years. However, scientists have not always known their precise location or their genetic sequence.

Figure 9.12. Biochemical pathway for color pigments in tomato, with mutant genes.

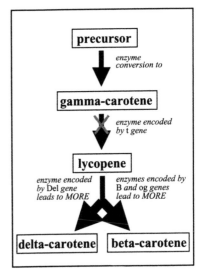

A gene called *t* (for the *t*angerine color it causes) blocks the conversion of gamma-carotene into lycopene (indicated by the X mark on Figure 9.12). Therefore it's not surprising that tomatoes with a mutant *t* gene are orange instead of red. The biochemical pathway would be blocked (probably because the mutant *t* gene codes for a defective copy of an enzyme) and plants would have lots of gamma-carotene but very little lycopene. Remember, lycopene is the pigment that makes tomatoes red. In much the same way, the *Del* gene (named for its high levels of *Del*ta-carotene) causes greater than normal conversion of lycopene into delta-carotene. Thus a plant with a *Del* gene would have high levels of delta-carotene and low levels of lycopene and would be more yellow than red. The *B* and *og* (named for high levels of *beta*-carotene and for the tomatoes *old-gold* color) lead to higher than normal conversion from lycopene into beta-carotene.

8. Using information from the QTL study, where would you predict you might find the *t* gene on the tomato genetic map? Why? (Hint: Tomatoes with the *t* phenotype would have low levels of what compound?)

   Tomatoes with the "t" tangerine phenotype would have low levels of lycopene (the downstream compound) and possibly high levels of gamma-

carotene (the upstream compound). In essence, the biochemical cascade is blocked at the t *step. Therefore, you might predict that you'd find the* t *gene somewhere associated with low levels of lycopene. Bins 3C and 12C are both strongly associated with LOW levels of lycopene.*

9. Using information from the QTL study, where would you predict you might find the *Del* gene on the tomato genetic map? Why? (Hint: Tomatoes with the *Del* phenotype would have <u>low</u> levels of what compound?)

Tomatoes with the "Del" phenotype would have low levels of lycopene (the upstream compound) and high levels of delta-carotene (the downstream compound). Therefore, you might predict that you'd find the Del *gene associated with low levels of lycopene. Bins 3C and 12C are associated with low levels of lycopene. Or, you might predict you'd find the* Del *gene associated with high levels of carotene. Bins 10E and 12C are associated with high levels of carotene.*

NOTE: The measured carotene levels include the upstream gamma-carotene, as well as the downstream delta- and beta-carotenes, so using lycopene levels is preferable to using carotene levels.

10. Using information from the QTL study, where would you predict you might find the *B* and *og* genes on the tomato genetic map? Why? (Hint: Tomatoes with the *B* or *og* phenotype would have <u>low</u> levels of what compound?)

Tomatoes with the "B" and "og" phenotypes would have low levels of lycopene (the upstream compound) and high levels of beta-carotene (the downstream compound). Therefore, you might predict that you'd find the B *and* og *genes somewhere associated with low levels of lycopene. Bins 3C and 12C are associated with low levels of lycopene. Or, you might predict you'd find the* B *and* og *genes associated with high levels of carotene. Bins 10E and 12C are associated with high levels of carotene.*

11. Table 9.3 contains the chromosomal locations for the mutant genes in the pigment pathways. Fill in table with the QTLs associated with each bin where the gene is located.

Table 9.3. Chromosome locations for genes in the color pigment pathway in tomatoes.

Gene	Chromosomal bin	Associated QTL(s)
t	10E	*– color, ++ carotene*
Del	12C	*–– color, –– lycopene, ++++ carotene*
B	6E	*– color*
og	4E	*None*

12. Record the locations of the genes in Table 9.3 on the chromosomal map. Which of the mutant genes coincide with QTLs in the color pathway?

   Interestingly, most of the genes coincide.

   Del is at 12C, a QTL associated with low red color, low lycopene, and high carotene.

   T is at 10E, a QTL associated with low red color and high carotene.

   B is at 6E, a QTL negatively associated with color.

13. Make a hypothesis (an educated guess) about what is happening at one of these QTLs.

   Students should make the connection that the bin contains a gene and the gene affects a trait (color, lycopene, or carotene) positively or negatively. Students should also provide a logical explanation of how that effect occurs. (Is it a functional copy of the gene? A defective copy of the gene?) It is critical that the students understand that at this point, <u>the connection is not proven</u>… it is only a best guess.

   For example: The Del gene, located in bin 12C, is associated with reduced color and lycopene levels, as well as high levels of carotene. Therefore, I hypothesize that bin 12C contains a functional (not defective) gene. The gene encodes the enzyme that converts lycopene into delta-carotene.

14. What would you need to do to TEST your hypothesis? (Hint: Look at the fw2.2 example in the text.)

   First you would need to find the gene in the bin. Next you would need to clone it. Then you would use genetic engineering to put the "dominant" allele into a "recessive" background to confirm that it is indeed a gene that affects tomato color.

15. Do any of the mutant genes NOT coincide with QTLs in the color pathway? If so, describe why there might not be a relationship between a mutant gene and QTL.

   The og gene does not correspond with any of the QTLs from this study. We know there's a gene in bin 4E that affects color (from the old-fashioned mutant identification of the gene). Perhaps the initial populations for this study didn't contain any variation at that gene. If the populations didn't have different alleles, it won't show up in QTL studies. That is why many QTL studies are required to fully understand a trait.

16. What can you conclude from this exercise about quantitative traits and QTL studies? (Are they useful? What can they tell you? Why do people do them?)

   QTL studies are useful because they can identify many genes involved in complex traits. However, they are time-consuming, complicated, expensive, and the results are specific to the populations and locations studied. Scientists use QTL studies to understand the genetic basis of important, complex traits like color, yield, and taste that they can't understand any other way.

Garden Genetics:

Teaching With Edible Plants

STUDENT EDITION

Garden Genetics:
Teaching With Edible Plants

ELIZABETH RICE, MARIANNE KRASNY,
AND MARGARET E. SMITH

NSTApress
National Science Teachers Association
Arlington, Virginia

NSTApress®
National Science Teachers Association

Claire Reinburg, Director
Judy Cusick, Senior Editor
J. Andrew Cocke, Associate Editor
Betty Smith, Associate Editor
Robin Allan, Book Acquisitions Coordinator

ART AND DESIGN Will Thomas, Jr., Director
PRINTING AND PRODUCTION Catherine Lorrain, Director
    Nguyet Tran, Assistant Production Manager
    Jack Parker, Electronic Prepress Technician
New Products and Services, *sci*LINKS Tyson Brown, Director
    David Anderson, Database Web and Development Coordinator

NATIONAL SCIENCE TEACHERS ASSOCIATION
Gerald F. Wheeler, Executive Director
David Beacom, Publisher

Copyright © 2006 by the National Science Teachers Association.
All rights reserved. Printed in the USA.
08 07 06 4 3 2 1

Library of Congress has cataloged the Student Edition as follows:
Rice, Elizabeth.
  Garden genetics: teaching with edible plants / Elizabeth Rice, Marianne Krasny, and Margaret Smith.
    p. cm.
  ISBN-13: 978-0-87355-274-5
  1. Plant genetics—Textbooks. I. Krasny, Marianne E. II. Smith, Margaret E., 1956- III. Title.
  QK981.R47 2006
  581.3'5—dc22
                2006006199

NSTA is committed to publishing material that promotes the best in inquiry-based science education. However, conditions of actual use may vary, and the safety procedures and practices described in this book are intended to serve only as a guide. Additional precautionary measures may be required. NSTA and the authors do not warrant or represent that the procedures and practices in this book meet any safety code or standard of federal, state, or local regulations. NSTA and the authors disclaim any liability for personal injury or damage to property arising out of or relating to the use of this book, including any of the recommendations, instructions, or materials contained therein.

Featuring *sci*Links®—connecting text and the Internet. Up-to-the-minute online content, classroom ideas, and other materials are just a click away.

This material is based on the work supported by the National Science Foundation Graduate Teaching Fellows in K–12 Education Program (DUE #0231913). Any opinions, findings, conclusions, or recommendations expressed in this material are those of the authors and do not necessarily reflect the views of the National Science Foundation.

STUDENT EDITION
Contents

SECTION 3: TOMATOES

FIGURES AND TABLES IN THE STUDENT EDITION

FIGURES

TABLES

INTRODUCTION TO GARDEN GENETICS
Student Edition

How do farmers grow the sweetest ears of corn possible? How do they grow huge red tomatoes? How do they make sure none of the cucumbers they grow are bitter? It's all genetics, and it's big business. A patent on a gene can be worth millions of dollars! *Garden Genetics* uses a series of inquiry activities and experiments to explore both traditional and cutting-edge genetics. Throughout the text and activities, you will investigate the connections between genetics, evolution, ecology, and plant biology.

With *Garden Genetics* you'll study science in the context of familiar foods. The readings and activities focus on cucumbers, corn, and tomatoes. They also address issues you hear about in the news—like the environmental and social impacts of genetically engineered food plants.

The activities in this book present genetic concepts in ways that are new and exciting. To learn about Punnett's squares, you will taste variation in bitterness of cucumber seedlings and trace these differences back to the parental generations. You'll then go on to design and conduct experiments investigating the surprising role that bitterness plays in protecting cucumber plants from insect predators. To learn about the genetics of plant breeding, you will re-enact a trial in which farmers sued seed companies to compensate for one billion dollars of U.S. corn crop losses caused by genetic uniformity! Other activities include creating geographic maps of the origin of food plants (Where did tomatoes originate? If you guessed Italy, you're wrong!); and genetic maps of economically important traits like tomato color (the redder the better, and genes control it).

The activities in this book present a unique way of looking at food and agriculture—one that applies textbook concepts in an exciting, innovative, and interesting context. We hope you will enjoy this exploration of genetics, evolution, ecology, and plant biology—along with tasty vegetables and healthy learning!

How can you avoid searching hundreds of science websites to locate the best sources of information on a given topic? SciLinks, created and maintained by the National Science Teachers Association (NSTA), has the answer.

In a SciLinked text, such as this one, you'll find a logo and keyword near a concept, a URL (*www.scilinks.org*), and a keyword code. Simply go to the SciLinks website, type in the code, and receive an annotated listing of as many as 15 web pages—all of which have gone through an extensive review process conducted by a team of science educators. SciLinks is your best source of pertinent, trustworthy internet links on subjects from astronomy to zoology.

Need more information? Take a tour—*www.scilinks.org/tour/*

SECTION 1
Cucumbers

CHAPTER 1

"IT SKIPS A GENERATION"

Traits, Genes, and Crosses

Long before they understood why the strategy worked, farmers knew how to crossbreed plants to obtain more desirable traits. Even today, a farmer who knows nothing about genetics can tell you that when a blue type of corn crosses with a yellow one, the offspring are blue. However, the farmer might add, if you cross a corn plant with small ears with a large-eared one, the offspring will have ears that are intermediate in size. Without any knowledge of genetics, the farmer has just told you a great deal about how the genes for blue color and for ear size work.

Gregor Mendel, an Austrian monk often described as the "father of genetics," worked with pea plants in the 1860s to understand how traits are passed from one generation to the next. Mendel made his discoveries by making crosses between **true-breeding** pea plant populations with different characteristics and keeping careful track of the characteristics of their offspring. Sometimes, when he transferred pollen from one tall plant to another tall plant (like in the cross shown in the F1 generation of Figure 1.1), some of the offspring were tall but some also were short. Where was this shortness coming from, if not from the parental populations?

"It skips a generation"—the shortness was coming from the grand-parental populations. Shortness, the **recessive trait**, was masked by the tall **dominant trait** in the "hybrid" or F1 generation. In essence, the shortness was hidden because of sexual recombination. Each offspring receives one copy of a gene from its mother and one from its father. In this way, gene combinations are shuffled with every generation and new types may appear.

Many of the early discoveries in genetics occurred in plants. Plants have a few special characteristics that make them ideal for studying genetics. From one known cross, many genetically similar "siblings" are produced. Pea pods, like the ones Mendel worked with, produce about five peas, and a cucumber has hundreds of seeds. Furthermore,

> A tall plant population that has all tall offspring (when crossed with itself or another tall population) is **true-breeding**.

> A **recessive trait** is not expressed unless two copies of a gene are present. A single copy of a recessive gene is "hidden" by the presence of a **dominant trait**.

SCi*L*INKS.
THE WORLD'S A CLICK AWAY

Topic: Gregor Mendel
Go to: www.sciLINKS.org
Code: GG01

Topic: Dominant and Recessive Traits
Code: GG02

Figure 1.1. Crossing generations. When plant breeders make crosses between plants, they talk about the parental (P), hybrid (F1), and segregating (F2) generations.

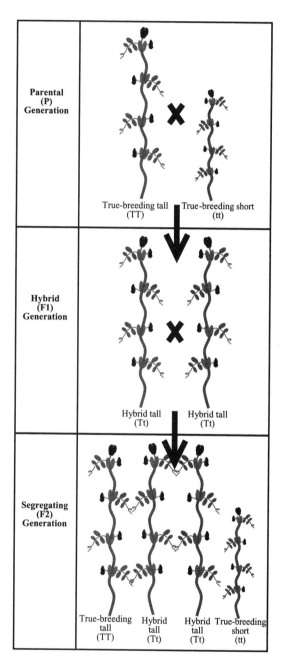

some plants (but not all) have the remarkable capability of being able to fertilize their own flowers. This means that the same plant can be both the male and female parent of a seed. Therefore, scientists can easily and naturally create whole populations of genetically identical individuals.

The cross in Figure 1.1 resulted from two true-breeding individuals. The F1 generation would have contained 5–10 seeds that were genetically identical to one another for the alleles that determine height (all had the Tt alleles). To make the F2 generation, Mendel had two options: He could self-pollinate the plants, or he could cross two different individuals of the F1 generation. Regardless of which method he used, in the F2 generation, the individuals would not all be genetically identical!

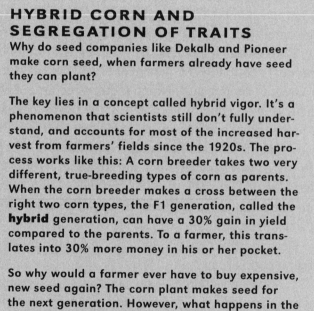

HYBRID CORN AND SEGREGATION OF TRAITS

Why do seed companies like Dekalb and Pioneer make corn seed, when farmers already have seed they can plant?

The key lies in a concept called hybrid vigor. It's a phenomenon that scientists still don't fully understand, and accounts for most of the increased harvest from farmers' fields since the 1920s. The process works like this: A corn breeder takes two very different, true-breeding types of corn as parents. When the corn breeder makes a cross between the right two corn types, the F1 generation, called the **hybrid** generation, can have a 30% gain in yield compared to the parents. To a farmer, this translates into 30% more money in his or her pocket.

So why would a farmer ever have to buy expensive, new seed again? The corn plant makes seed for the next generation. However, what happens in the F2 generation? Traits begin to segregate, meaning that at all the plant's genes, AA, aa, and Aa genotypes are possible, instead of the uniform Aa in the hybrid generation. As segregation happens, the yield advantage disappears. This can mean 30% less money in the farmer's pocket—a powerful incentive to keep buying hybrid seed.

From the company's perspective, if people are willing to keep buying seed, the company will keep producing new varieties. Thus, the segregation of traits contains the key to an entire seed industry!

Mendelian and quantitative traits

Bitterness in cucumbers is a Mendelian trait, meaning that it is controlled by a single gene—just like the traits that Mendel studied in peas (round versus wrinkled, or yellow versus green). Mendelian traits are also sometimes called **single-gene traits**, or traits under simple genetic control. With a single-gene trait, inheritance and behavior are fairly easy to understand.

Many traits, like yield, flowering time, plant height, and color, are more complex and are controlled by multiple genes. These complex traits are called **quantitative traits**. Table 1.1 has examples of both Mendelian and quantitative traits. Note that some traits like plant height can be both Mendelian and quantitative. For example, plant height in normal plants is influenced by many genes. However, in plants with dwarfing genes, plant height behaves as a Mendelian trait. In essence, a single dwarfing gene overrules the otherwise quantitative trait of plant height. Table 1.1 also shows the abbreviations that scientists often give single gene mutations, like "dw1" for a dwarfing gene or "y" for a yellow gene.

A **Mendelian** or **single-gene trait** is controlled by a single gene.

Quantitative traits are controlled by many genes.

SCiLINKS.
THE WORLD'S A CLICK AWAY

Topic: Mendel's Laws
Go to: *www.sciLINKS.org*
Code: GG03

Topic: Explore Mendelian Genetics
Code: GG04

Table 1.1. Mendelian and quantitative traits.

	Mendelian (single-gene)	**Quantitative** (multi-gene)
Cucumber	Spiny—controls the production of small spines on the fruit, producing a prickly cucumber.	
	Bushy—controls whether the plant grows as a bush or as a vine.	
Tomato		Fruit size—About 12 genes control fruit size by impacting characteristics like cell division in the fruit and growth hormones.
Corn	Dwarf (dw1)—controls the production of gibberellin, a plant hormone responsible for vertical growth.	Plant height—More than 20 genes are important in plant height in corn.
	Yellow (y)—controls whether a kernel is yellow or white.	Kernel color—Many genes modify exactly what shade of yellow a corn kernel will be, from canary yellow to a pale cream.
		Yield—The most important trait of all is influenced by dozens of genes that affect things like number of rows on an ear, number of kernels, kernel size, kernel density, and plant tolerance of competition in a field.

Questions for further thought

Evolution: What evolutionary advantage might reshuffling genes, caused by sexual reproduction, give to a new generation of plants?

What disadvantages could it have?

Genetics: When a blue type of corn crosses with a yellow type of corn, the offspring are blue. What type of trait is involved?

When a corn plant with large ears crosses with a small-eared plant, the offspring will have intermediately sized ears. What type of trait is involved?

If a true-breeding spiny cucumber plant crossed with a non-spiny cucumber always had spiny offspring, how many copies of the spiny allele would it have?

How do geneticists and plant breeders know if a plant is true-breeding?

Activity 1.

Edible Punnett's Squares—Segregation Ratios You Can Taste

Objective

To discover whether the bitter gene in cucumber plants is dominant or recessive.

Background

Cucumber plants, as well as their close relatives the squashes and melons, make a unique protein called cucurbitacin. Cucurbitacin tastes bitter to humans. Bitterness in cucumbers is caused by a single gene that has a recessive and a dominant allele. Your task in this assignment is to use your knowledge of genetics, particularly your understanding of crosses and Punnett's squares, to figure out how this bitter trait behaves. (Is bitterness dominant or recessive?) This is how scientists traditionally have learned about genes. They use populations of cucumbers or other organisms, make crosses, and use statistics to test their hypotheses about how genes behave.

SCiLINKS

THE WORLD'S A CLICK AWAY

Topic: Punnett Squares
Go to: *www.sciLINKS.org*
Code: GG05

Materials

- A population of "unknown" plants at cotyledon stage—about 10 days old
- Populations of bitter and non-bitter plants to act as taste controls—about 10 days old
- Plant tags
- Pencil
- Calculator (optional), for Part IV statistical analysis

Safety Notes

- Under normal circumstances, you should never taste anything in a biology laboratory. However, this laboratory makes an exception by asking you to taste a tiny piece of a cucumber plant's leaf.
- Students who are allergic to cucumbers, squash, melon, or zucchini should NOT taste the plants.
- If you are allergic or not comfortable tasting the plants, please ask someone else in your group to do it for you.
- You should wash your hands after handling the plants.
- You should wash your hands AGAIN at the end of the activity.

Activity

Part I. Your unknown population

1. Taste* the controls your teacher has set out. Tear a tiny piece off the edge of one of the cotyledons (see Figure 1.2). Chew the leaf between your front teeth, biting into it many times, and letting the flavor wash over your tongue. Can you tell the difference between bitter and non-bitter? Do you and your partner agree?

Figure 1.2. Tasting the cotyledons of a cucumber seedling.

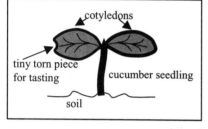

*Students who are allergic to cucumbers, squash, zucchini, or melon should not taste the plants.

2. Taste your own plants. Are they bitter? Non-bitter?

3. Once you have decided whether each of your plants is bitter or non-bitter, label that plant with a tag and place the tag in the soil next to the plant.

4. Taste your partner's plants. Are they bitter? Non-bitter?

    4a. Do your answers agree? Why or why not?

    4b. What can you do to improve your measurement?

5. Collect the totals for the class. (Sample below)

Sample calculation	Bitter	Non-bitter	Total
Number of plants			
Percentage			
Ratio			

To find the percentage, divide the number of plants in the bitter and non-bitter categories by the total number of plants. To find the ratio, divide the larger of the bitter or non-bitter number of plants by the smaller number of plants. Your results will probably not be perfect, whole numbers.

6. To figure out the genotypes of the parental generations, you need to know which genotypes go with which phenotype.

   6a. What is a phenotype? What are the phenotypes of your plants?

   6b. What is a genotype?

7. Which phenotype is there more of?

At this point we don't know which allele is dominant. But you can make a hypothesis (an educated guess) using your data. In Part IV you will test whether or not the data support this hypothesis. Right now, there isn't a "right" answer, but there are two logical ones.

8. Make a hypothesis about which trait (bitter or non-bitter) is dominant. This will be the hypothesis you test in this activity. Support your hypothesis.

9. Using your hypothesis from the last step, what symbol do you choose to represent the bitter allele? (Remember that dominant alleles are usually given a capital letter. Recessive alleles are usually given the same letter, but lowercase.)

10. What symbol do you choose to represent the non-bitter allele?

11. To summarize, fill in the table according to your hypothesis from step 8.

	Bitter	Non-bitter
Number		
Possible Genotypes		

Part II. Parents and grandparents

Figure 1.3. Pedigree representing the crosses leading to the unknown population.

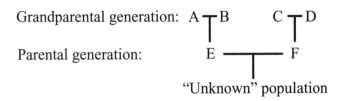

The pedigree in Figure 1.3 is a drawing that represents the crosses leading to your unknown population. Each of the letters represents a population. These are crosses between POPULATIONS, not just individuals. However, since each of the starting populations (A, B, C, and D) was genetically identical, you can think about it the same way as for individuals.

12. Describe what is happening in the pedigree.

12a. What is crossed with what to give your unknown population?

12b. Which cross led to population E?

12c. Which cross led to population F?

13. Complete the table by writing in the possible genotypes.

Population	Phenotype		Possible genotype
	% Bitter	% Non-bitter	
Grandparent Population A	100%		
Grandparent Population B		100%	
Grandparent Population C	100%		
Grandparent Population D		100%	
Parent Population E	100%		
Parent Population F	100%		

Part III. The crosses of the different generations

14. In Punnett's Square 1, what population is on the left of the square?

    14a. What is the phenotype of this population?

    14b. What are the possible genotypes of this population?

15. In Punnett's Square 1, what population is on the top of the square?

    15a. What is the phenotype of this population?

    15b. What are the possible genotypes of this population?

16. In Punnett's Square 1, what population is in the middle of the square?

    16a. What is the phenotype of this population?

    16b. What are the possible genotypes of this population?

    16c. In which other Punnett's square does this population occur again?

17. In Punnett's Square 3, what population is in the middle of the square?

    17a. What are the phenotypes of this population?

    17b. What are the possible genotypes of this population?

    17c. Where did the parents for this population come from?

18. Now you have all the information you need to test the hypothesis you made earlier about how the bitter gene works. Use the Punnett's squares on this page to work backwards to understand all the crosses that led to your population.

- Begin with what you know for sure. Which phenotype has only one possible genotype?

- Do you always know BOTH alleles for a dominant genotype?

- Do you know one of the two alleles?

Figure 1.4. Punnett's squares for activity.

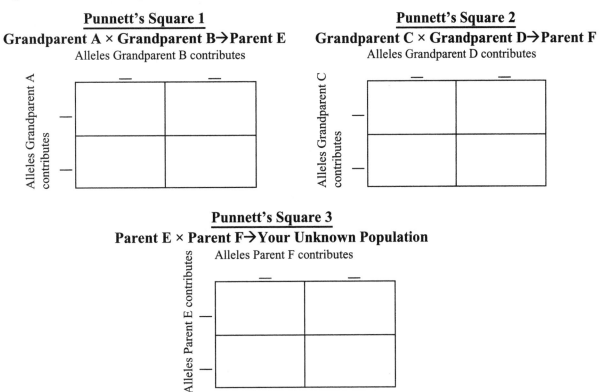

Punnett's Square 1
Grandparent A × Grandparent B→Parent E
Alleles Grandparent B contributes
Alleles Grandparent A contributes

Punnett's Square 2
Grandparent C × Grandparent D→Parent F
Alleles Grandparent D contributes
Alleles Grandparent C contributes

Punnett's Square 3
Parent E × Parent F→Your Unknown Population
Alleles Parent F contributes
Alleles Parent E contributes

Part IV. Testing your hypothesis

Statistics are the way scientists test whether or not their data fit their hypotheses.

Back at the beginning of this lab, you took a guess about whether the bitter or non-bitter trait was dominant. Now you have to evaluate whether or not that was the best guess. **Statistics** are the way scientists test whether or not their data fit their hypotheses or models. No data ever fit a model perfectly, because **random chance** also plays a role in results of an experiment.

For example, if you flip a coin, you have a 50% chance that it comes up heads. If you flip the coin twice, are you guaranteed that you'll have 1 head and 1 tail? Of course not. The second coin flip still has a 50% chance of coming up heads. Instead, we say there is a 50% chance that you will flip a head each time you flip a coin. In much the same way, you might pick a bitter or a non-bitter seed out of a bag. Each time you have a certain probability of planting a bitter seed, depending on the percent of bitter seeds in the bag. The populations you taste are only a sample of the total plants. Similar to the situation with flipping a coin, you would expect the proportion of bitter plants in your sample to be close to but not exactly the same as the true proportion of bitter plants in the population.

Given a certain set of parental genotypes, there is a probability (could be 0, 25, 50, 75, 100% chance) that offspring will have a certain genotype. You need to test if the difference between what you see and what you expect can be explained by random chance. If the difference is too large to be explained by random chance, there is probably something wrong with your hypothesis.

To determine whether or not the differences are real or due to chance, scientists use a test called a **chi-squared (χ^2) test**. This test takes the difference between the number you would *expect* and the number you *observe*, and then squares the difference to eliminate the positive or negative sign. Then you sum all the squares (in this case of the bitter and the non-bitter plants) and compare the sum to a table of probabilities.

19. Here is the data you need:

		Bitter	Non-bitter	Total
1.	Number of plants sampled			
2.	Ratio expected (from Punnett's squares)			
3.	Percentage expected (express the ratio as a percent)			
4.	Expected number of plants (line 3 × total plants)			
5.	Observed – expected number of plants (line 1 – line 4)			
6.	(Observed – expected) squared (square line 5)			
7.	(Observed – expected) 2 ÷ expected (line 6 ÷ line 4)			

The mathematical representation of what you just did in the table is:

$$\chi^2 = \frac{(\text{observed bitter} - \text{expected bitter})^2}{\text{expected bitter}} + \frac{(\text{observed non-bitter} - \text{expected non-bitter})^2}{\text{expected non-bitter}}$$

Next you compare your chi-squared total value from line 7 to the critical value in a chi-square table. In the chi-square table below, the top row of numbers indicates probabilities. You have one degree of freedom (df) for this test (number of phenotypes -1). Then you scan across the 1 df row until you find the number closest to, but smaller than, your number. In genetics, you are looking for an insignificant difference. You want your observed values to be close to your expected values.

df	Probability (p)										
	0.95	0.90	0.80	0.70	0.50	0.30	0.20	0.10	0.05	0.01	0.001
1	0.004	0.02	0.06	0.15	0.46	1.07	1.64	2.71	3.84	6.64	10.83
2	0.10	0.21	0.45	0.71	1.39	2.41	3.22	4.60	5.99	9.21	13.82
3	0.35	0.58	1.01	1.42	2.37	3.66	4.64	6.25	7.82	11.34	16.27
4	0.71	1.06	1.65	2.20	3.36	4.88	5.99	7.78	9.49	13.28	18.47
5	1.14	1.61	2.34	3.00	4.35	6.06	7.29	9.24	11.07	15.09	20.52
6	1.63	2.20	3.07	3.83	5.35	7.23	8.56	10.64	12.59	16.81	22.46
7	2.17	2.83	3.82	4.67	6.35	8.38	9.80	12.02	14.07	18.48	24.32
8	2.73	3.49	4.59	5.53	7.34	9.52	11.03	13.36	15.51	20.09	26.12
9	3.32	4.17	5.38	6.39	8.34	10.66	12.24	14.68	16.92	21.67	27.88
10	3.94	4.86	6.18	7.27	9.34	11.78	13.44	15.99	18.31	23.21	29.59
	Not significant								Significant		

20. What value do you find?

In this case, with one degree of freedom, we will use the critical cut-off value of 3.84 (5% chance that the data can be explained by random chance alone). If your value is below this, then you can conclude that the difference between observed and expected values can be explained by random chance and that your data fit your hypothesis. If the value is greater than the critical cut-off value, the difference is greater than can be explained by random chance and something is likely wrong with your hypothesis or with your experiment.

Most scientists use a threshold of 5% as an acceptable degree of uncertainty. This means that they're 95% sure that their data fit their hypothesis. Note that it's not 100% certain. Very little in science is 100% certain.

21. If the hypothesis you made in Part II about how the bitter gene behaves is not correct, you need to go back and try a new hypothesis. If your model looks good, you've solved the genetic problem.

Part V. Conclusions

22. How does the bitter gene behave? (Is it dominant or recessive?)

23. What were the genotypes of the parents of your unknown population?

24. What were the genotypes of the grandparents?

25. What were the genotypes of your unknown population?

26. What would the genotypes of the offspring be if two individuals out of your unknown population were to mate? Use a Punnett's square.

Optional Directions for Filling in the Punnett's Squares

1. Begin with what you know for sure. Which phenotype has only one possible genotype?

    Fill in the Punnett's square for all the generations you have tasted. For offspring, fill in the whole genotype in a box. For parents, the two alleles are split and go on the outside of the box. Look at the text for examples, if needed.

2. Look back at your ratio in number 5 of Part I (page 9). This should give you a clue about how many squares of your unknown population should be bitter and non-bitter.

3. Now, pick one square where you know some of the genotypes. If you know the genotype of the offspring, what does that tell you about the genotypes of the parents?

    If you know the genotypes of the parents, what does that tell you about the genotypes of the offspring?

4. At this point, you will still have some holes left in your square. Think about what you know about the populations. Were they all bitter? Were they all non-bitter? Remember, to taste a dominant phenotype there must be at least one dominant allele present.

5. At this point, you may still have some holes left in your square. You have all the tools to figure them out. If there are holes related to the parent, think about the offspring. Were they all bitter? All non-bitter? Then which alleles must the parents have had?

CHAPTER 2

BITTERNESS AND NON-BITTERNESS IN CUCUMBERS

A Story of Mutation

If you had lived in Europe in the early part of the 20th century, when you bought a cucumber in the market, you would have found a small notch cut out of its top. The notch caused problems for the cucumber. Bacteria and fungi had a quick route past the cucumber's protective skin. Thus a notched cucumber spoiled more quickly than one without a notch. Why then did cucumbers have notches cut in them?

Figure 2.1. Cucumber with notch cut for tasting.

Professional tasters cut the notches into the cucumbers (Figure 2.1). The leaves, stems, and flowers of cucumber plants are usually bitter. Sometimes, especially under the warm, moist conditions found in greenhouses, the cucumbers can become bitter too. If the top of the cucumber was not bitter—meaning the bitter protein had not made it into the top of the fruit—the rest of the cucumber was not bitter either. Therefore, cucumber growers employed professional tasters to test each cucumber before it was sold. Not surprisingly, the tasting crew was an expensive part of cucumber production.

Bitter cucumber gene history

The bitterness of cucumbers is caused by a protein called cucurbitacin, which also makes some people burp. The protein is found in the stems and leaves of many cucumber plants. Sometimes the protein can be found in the cucumber itself. This is why some people remove the skin and seeds of cucumbers before eating them.

In the 1930s, a Dutch cucumber breeder decided to make a cucumber variety that was not bitter. Before he could make such a variety, he had to find a non-bitter cucumber plant. Traditionally, a plant breeder can only use variation she or he finds in nature. This

Topic: Genetic Mutations
Go to: *www.sciLINKS.org*
Code: GG06

Topic: Seed Banks
Code: GG07

cucumber breeder contacted other cucumber breeders around the world and asked for a few seeds of their varieties. He also collected different cucumber types from **genebanks**, which are special facilities designed to preserve genetic diversity and protect seeds for future use. He then grew the different varieties in a greenhouse, under uniform, controlled conditions. Eventually, he had a crew taste thousands of cucumber plants. In an old United States variety called "Longfellow," he found the mutant, non-bitter gene.

The Longfellow variety was old and it was not patented or protected. Today, when a plant breeder creates a variety, she or he often applies for a **patent**. (Historically, plant breeders applied for a "plant variety protection" or PVP, but today breeders are more likely to use a patent.) A patent for a plant variety works just like a patent for a chemical or a machine. It lasts for 20 years and keeps other people from profiting from the "invention." The non-bitter gene was incorporated into a new Dutch variety.

Genebanks are special facilities designed to preserve genetic diversity and protect seeds for future use.

Patents are used to protect new varieties of plants. A patent means that someone must pay the plant breeder for the use of his or her "invention."

Topic: Mutations
Go to: *www.sciLINKS.org*
Code: GG08

Topic: Transcription
Code: GG09

PATENTING GENES

In recent years, many companies, researchers, and plant breeders have been applying for patents. In the United States, a patent costs about $40,000 and gives 20 years of protection for a gene, a variety, or a genetic process. Between 1985 and 2002, 914 patents were issued for plants. The vast majority of these have been issued for field corn (565 patents) and soybean (327 patents). Potato, tomato, cotton, rice, wheat, and alfalfa have all received fewer than five patents each.

Why are there so many patents for corn and soybean? They are two of the most important crops in the United States, and they have the biggest seed industries. If a company invests in producing a variety, the company wants to find a way to protect its investment. A patent is one way to do so.

Patents for plants and genes have been very controversial. To patent anything—whether it's a gene or a toothbrush—it must be novel, meaning it is something new. Is a gene novel if it already exists in nature? Is it novel if you identify it and can change it, through genetic engineering?

For years, cucumber breeders in the United States tried to gain access to the Dutch non-bitter trait (they didn't know where it had come from originally). The Dutch breeders saw no reason to share it. However, in the 1950s, the Dutch had a problem with a disease outbreak in cucumbers. A plant breeder at Michigan State University had already found a gene that gave cucumbers resistance to survive the disease. So the Dutch and American breeders made a trade—the non-bitter gene for the disease resistance gene. Since then, the non-bitter gene has been bred into many commercial varieties, which are often called "burpless" or "sweet." However, there are still many cucumber varieties available with the bitter gene. Why would plant breeders keep the bitter gene around? The gene has some positive effects on the plant's health and doesn't usually cause problems because the bitterness rarely finds its way into the fruit.

From DNA to bitterness

Bitterness in cucumbers is a trait controlled by a single gene. But what exactly is this bitter gene in cucumbers, and how does it work? The gene, as you know, is just a section of DNA that contains the genetic code for making a protein. In this case, the protein is cucurbitacin, the compound that makes cucumbers bitter.

What then is the non-bitter gene? The non-bitter gene is a mutated version of the original, which results in the plant being unable to make cucurbitacin. The gene no longer encodes the protein, and thus the plant has no way to make it.

Most **mutations** are negative for the plant's well-being. Like the non-bitter allele in cucumbers, mutations often result in the plant losing its ability to make a protein. The plant needs most of the proteins that it makes. For example, if a mutation occurs in a gene involved in producing chlorophyll—a compound that is essential to the plant's survival—the mutation is fatal. A plant cannot survive without chlorophyll. However, a cucumber plant can survive without cucurbitacin.

A bitter gene in a cucumber plant serves an important, but not essential, function. Bitterness makes cucumbers less palatable to insects and other herbivores. Therefore, a cucumber plant without bitterness might be at a disadvantage relative to other cucumber plants. On the other hand, non-bitter cucumber plants might have some less obvious competitive advantages in a field of other cucumber plants.

Mutation

A mutant isn't a monster. The word *mutation* comes from the Latin word meaning to change. That's all a mutation is—a change in the genetic code. The changes can be large or small. The smallest is a point mutation, which changes only one base in the DNA. Point mutations can be caused by mistakes in copying DNA in the cells.

Sometimes such a point mutation has no effect at all—it doesn't even change the amino acid encoded. How is that possible? Remember that the genetic code has more than one way to encode each amino acid. The code is read in codons—sets of three bases that together code for a specific amino acid.

A **mutation** is simply a genetic change.

Point mutations change only one base in the genetic code.

The codons of DNA are the template for all the proteins a body needs to make. However, a cell has a problem. The DNA can't leave the **nucleus** (Figure 2.2). Proteins are made outside of the nucleus, at the **ribosomes**. How are the instructions transferred from the DNA in the nucleus to the ribosomes? The DNA template is **transcribed** by a molecule called a **messenger RNA** (mRNA). The mRNAs then leave the nucleus and go to the ribosomes where they are "translated" into proteins.

Figure 2.3 shows the genetic code. What does cga encode? Using the table, you can see cga encodes the amino acid arginine (sometimes abbreviated with an r). A mutation that changed the c to an a would make the codon aga instead. However, aga still encodes arginine. So the mutation caused no change. This is called a **silent** mutation.

Figure 2.2. Transcription and translation.

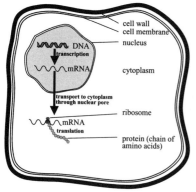

The **nucleus** of a cell is where the DNA is found.

Proteins are assembled at the **ribosomes**.

The DNA bases are **transcribed** (copied) by a molecule called **messenger RNA (mRNA)**.

A mutation that causes no change in the resulting protein is a **silent** mutation.

Figure 2.3. The genetic code.

Second letter

First letter		u	c	a	g	Third letter
u		uuu uuc } Phe(f) uua uug } Leu(l)	ucu ucc uca ucg } Ser(s)	uau uac } Tyr(y) uaa **Stop** uag **Stop**	ugu ugc } Cys(c) uga **Stop** ugg Trp(w)	u c a g
c		cuu cuc cua cug } Leu(l)	ccu ccc cca ccg } Pro(p)	cau cac } His(h) caa cag } Gln(q)	cgu cgc cga cgg } Arg(r)	u c a g
a		auu auc aua } Ile(i) aug Met(m)	acu acc aca acg } Thr(t)	aau aac } Asn(n) aaa aag } Lys(k)	agu agc } Ser(s) aga agg } Arg(r)	u c a g
g		guu guc gua gug } Val(v)	gcu gcc gca gcg } Ala(a)	gau gac } Asp(d) gaa gag } Glu(e)	ggu ggc gga ggg } Gly(g)	u c a g

Not all point mutations are silent. Let's return to our cga codon for arginine (r). If instead, the c changes to a u, we have an entirely different situation. Then uga is a stop codon. This means the end of the protein. The amino acid sequence will stop. Therefore, the protein will be very different from what it would have been without the mutation. This is called a **non-sense** mutation.

There is another type of point mutation. A **mis-sense** mutation is one that changes the function of a protein. The result is usually a protein with a slightly different shape or function, but one that still can function within the body. These mutations are one of the most important sources of variation for evolution to work upon.

Mutations that involve single changes in a codon, whether silent, non-sense, or mis-sense, are all point mutations. In contrast to these small mutations, **frame-shift** mutations are usually insertions and deletions of DNA ranging in length from one to thousands of base pairs. Because the codons are read in sets of three bases, adding or removing even one base can lead to major changes in the encoded protein. Consider the three-letter words in Figure 2.4:

Figure 2.4. Insertion and deletion.

A set of 3-letter words, like the codons of DNA:	THE CAT ATE THE FAT RAT
Suppose a deletion causes the removal of the C: Then an insertion causes the addition of an N:	THE ATA TET HEF ATR AT THE ANT ATE THE FAT RAT

In this case, the insertion counteracts the deletion and restores the reading frame with only minor differences. However, the insertion alone would have produced equally radical changes: THE CAN TAT ETH EFA TRA T. It's amazing what a difference one little base can make!

Frame-shift mutations can affect proteins in the same way that point mutations do. Very rarely are they silent. Sometimes, they cause alterations in the function of a protein (mis-sense mutation). Often, they introduce stop codons and are non-sense mutations.

A **non-sense** mutation is one that results in a stop codon and the premature end of a protein.

A **mis-sense** mutation changes the function of a protein.

A **frame-shift** mutation is caused by an insertion or a deletion of DNA and results in a different sequence of codons.

Questions for further thought

<u>Experimental Design:</u> Why did the cucumber breeder need to grow the plants in a greenhouse, under controlled, uniform conditions?

<u>Evolution:</u> Why might a cucumber be bitter?

What advantage could a bitter cucumber have over a non-bitter one?

<u>Genetic Diversity:</u> Why do we still keep the old, bitter cucumber varieties even though there are now non-bitter ones?

<u>Translation:</u> Why does Figure 2.3 have a base named u? Isn't DNA made up of a, c, g, and t?

Activity 2.

Proteins, Codons, and Mutations

Objective

Use protein and genetic sequence data to evaluate the effect of different kinds of mutations. Understand how mutation could have created a non-bitter gene in cucumbers.

Background

There are two approaches to learning about a gene. The **genetic approach** is the traditional one—a researcher finds a mutant individual and makes crosses to understand how the mutant gene or genes behave. In essence, the genetic approach studies genes by looking at their effects. This is how cucurbitacin, the bitter gene, has been studied in cucumbers.

The other way to learn about genes is to look directly at the DNA sequence—the line-up of a, c, t, and g bases. This is often part of a **genomic approach**. **Genome** means all the genes in an individual, whether it's a fish, a human, or a cucumber plant. The genomic approach looks at the sequence of many genes, often all at the same time. There have been a series of genome projects with the goal of sequencing all the genes in an individual person, mouse, bacteria, or rice plant. To do this, scientists use chemistry and instruments to read off the base pairs from one individual's DNA.

To obtain DNA for the genomic approach, scientists create **DNA libraries**. A DNA library can be obtained in one of two ways. To make a **genomic library**, all of an organism's DNA is sequenced (Figure 2.5). Reading the entire DNA sequence shows the number and location of genes, but gives no information about what they do. This approach also sequences a lot of "junk" DNA, or DNA that is not part of genes. (The chances are good that this DNA isn't "junk" at all, but we don't yet fully understand its function.) Reading this complete sequence is a good way to learn about the structure of genes, their regulation, and how they relate to one another.

Where do scientists get the DNA sequence to study cucumber plants using the genomic approach? The cucumber genome has not been sequenced. Instead, scientists use **cDNA libraries** (Figure 2.5). This method copies all the messenger RNA (mRNA) active in a cell into **cDNA** (copy DNA). Remember, **mRNAs** are the precursors to proteins. This is a more efficient way to understand the effects of genes, because mRNAs come only from the genes in a cell that are "turned on." Reading the mRNA tells you just what you want to know. Which genes are turned on in response to cold? Which genes are activated when the plant is infected by a disease?

> A **genetic approach** uses mutant individuals and crosses to understand how genes behave.
>
> A **genomic approach** looks at the sequences of many genes at the same time. A **genome** is all the genes in an organism.
>
> A genomic approach often relies on **DNA libraries**.
>
> A **genomic library** is the sequence of all the DNA in an individual's genome.
>
> A **cDNA library** is the sequence of the active genes in a cell. **cDNAs** are copies of the **mRNAs** in a cell.

Figure 2.5. cDNA and genomic sequence.

A genomic library	A cDNA library
DNA 〰️〰️ → 〰️ 〰️	mRNA 〰️
1. A genomic library cuts all the DNA in the nucleus into pieces.	1. All the mRNAs from a cell are copied into cDNAs (copy DNA) using the reverse transcriptase enzyme.
DNA pieces 〰️ → ...ATTACGCCACACGTT...	cDNA 〰️
2. The DNA pieces are sequenced.	cDNA pieces 〰️ → ...ATTACGCCACACGTT...
	2. The cDNA pieces are sequenced.
• A genomic library shows all the DNA in a genome, not just DNA in genes. • Genomic libraries are important for learning about the role of "junk" DNA. • To find genes, scientists use computers to find start codons followed by gene-length DNA sequences.	• A cDNA library represents all the DNA from each actively transcribed gene in a cell. It does not include DNA not in genes. • cDNA libraries are important for finding genes involved in a particular situation (e.g., genes activated in response to a disease).

Whether genetic sequence comes from a genomic or cDNA libary, any genetic sequence can be compared to any other genetic sequence. So knowing about the genes a plant uses for defense against a disease can teach you about the genes used by another species of plant in defense against a different disease. When scientists discover a gene, a genetic sequence, or a protein, they record it in a public database along with as much other information as possible. What does the gene or protein do? How was it discovered? What organism (plant, animal, bacteria, or fungus) did it come from?

Why do scientists bother to use these databases? Discovering a genetic sequence is time consuming and expensive. Therefore it makes sense to share information as it is gathered. With genomics, the more information that is available, the stronger the science. Today's powerful computers can easily compare millions of genetic sequences and find similarities between them. Increasingly, genetics is done in front of a computer using databases, instead of in a lab, a greenhouse, or a field!

Activity

Part I. DNA sequence

Though scientists know a lot about cucurbitacin and how it behaves, they still don't know the actual sequence of the gene that encodes it or exactly where it is located on a cucumber's chromosomes. Cucurbitacin has been studied with the genetic approach. It has not been studied with the genomic approach.

To think in detail about mutation, and how it might cause non-bitter cucumbers, we will study another example from cucumbers where the genetic sequence is known.

Some Korean researchers wanted to understand how cucumber plants respond to a disease called "target leaf spot." They compared the mRNAs from infected leaves with the mRNAs from uninfected leaves. When a cucumber leaf is infected, the gene shown in Figure 2.7 is activated. The protein made from this gene plays a role in plant defense against the disease.

Figure 2.6. The DNA sequence was created from a cucumber mRNA.

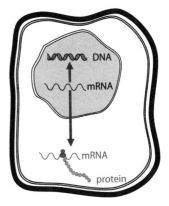

1. Where does the template for the amino acid sequence come from? In what part of the cell is the template located?

2. How do organisms move information from the DNA sequence inside the nucleus to create proteins outside the nucleus?

**Topic: DNA
Go to: *www.sciLINKS.org*
Code: GG10**

Note: GenBank uses lowercase letters in their DNA and protein sequences (See Figures 2.7 and 2.11). For consistency, we will use lowercase letters as well.

GenBank is a database for genetic sequence data (*www.ncbi.nlm.nih.gov/gquery/gquery.fcgi*). Figure 2.7 shows the sequence of GenBank entry AY365247.1. It has 855 base pairs. The numbers on the side tell you how many base pairs there are, and the letters are shown in sets. The DNA begins with base number 1 (a). Line 1 has 60 bases, ending with an a. Line 2 starts with base number 61 (t). Line 3 begins with base number 121 (a), and so on.

Figure 2.7. Cucumber DNA sequence from GenBank.

```
  1 atgggtcaag cccttggttg cattcaagtc gaccagtcaa ctgtagctat cagagaaaca
 61 tttgggagat ttgacgatgt gcttcaacct ggttgccatt gtctaccatg gtgccttggg
121 agccagatag ctggtcatct ttctttacgt ctccagcagc ttgatgttcg atgtgagaca
181 aagacaaagg acaatgtttt tgtcactgtc gttgcctcta ttcaataccg agccctagca
241 gacaaggctt cagatgcttt ttataagctt agtaatacaa gagaacagat ccaggcatat
301 gtttttgatg ttattagggc aagtgttcca aagttggacc tagattctac ttttgaacag
361 aagaatgata ttgcaaaggc ggtcgaagac gagctggaga aggccatgtc ggcttatgga
421 tacgagatag ttcaaactct aattgtggac attgagccag atgagcatgt aaagcgagca
481 atgaatgaaa taaatgcagc tgcaagactg agagttgctg caactgagaa agctgaggca
541 gagaagatat tgcagattaa gagagctgaa ggagatgccg aatccaagta tctggccggg
601 cttggtattg cacggcagcg tcaagccatt gtcgatgggc tcagagacag tgtactagca
661 tttgctgaaa acgtccctgg aacgacatct aaggatgtca tggacatggt tcttgtgact
721 caatacttcg acacgatgaa ggagattgga gcgtcatcaa agtctaattc tgtgttcatc
781 ccacatggac ctggtgcagt aaagatatt gcttcacaga tcagggatgg tcttctccaa
841 gcaagccaaa cttag
```

3. Is the sequence above DNA or RNA? How can you tell?

Figure 2.8. The cucumber mRNA.

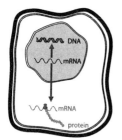

To avoid confusion, we'll convert the above sequence back into an mRNA sequence (Figure 2.9).

Figure 2.9. Converted cucumber mRNA sequence.

```
  1 augggucaag cccuugguug cauucaaguc gaccagucaa cuguagcuau cagagaaaca
 61 uuugggagau uugacgaugu gcuucaaccu gguugccauu gucuaccaug gugccuuggg
121 agccagauag cuggucaucu uucuuuacgu cuccagcagc uugauguucg augugagaca
181 aagacaaagg acaauguuuu ugucacuguc guugccucua uucaauaccg agcccuagca
241 gacaaggcuu cagaugcuuu uuauaagcuu aguaauacaa gagaacagau ccaggcauau
301 guuuuugaug uuauuagggc aaguguucca aaguuggacc uagauucuac uuuugaacag
361 aagaaugaua uugcaaaggc ggucgaagac gagcuggaga aggccauguc ggcuuaugga
421 uacgagauag uucaaacucu aauuguggac auugagccag augagcaugu aaagcgagca
481 augaaugaaa uaaaugcagc ugcaagacug agaguugcug caacugagaa agcugaggca
541 gagaagauau ugcagauuaa gagagcugaa ggagaugccg aauccaagua ucuggccggg
601 cuugguauug cacggcagcg ucaagccauu gucgaugggc ucagagacag uguacuagca
661 uuugcugaaa acgucccugg aacgacaucu aaggauguca uggacauggu ucuugugacu
721 caauacuucg acacgaugaa ggagauugga gcgucaucaa agucuaauuc uguguucauc
781 ccacauggac cuggugcagu aaagauauau gcuucacaga ucagggaugg ucuucuccaa
841 gcaagccaaa cuuag
```

Even most professional geneticists don't know the genetic code by heart. They use a table like Figure 2.3 (p. 22) to remember how the codons (sets of three bases) are translated into amino acids.

4. What are the first eight codons and amino acids of our gene? (Use Figure 2.3 to fill in the table below.)

Amino acid	Codon	Amino acid name	Number of ways it can be coded	List the different codes

5. Using Figure 2.3, determine how many different ways there are to code for each amino acid. Give a number and list the codes in the table above.

6. What might be one of the advantages of having more than one way to code for the same amino acid?

Figure 2.10. The cucumber protein.

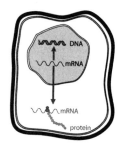

Part II. Protein sequence

The DNA sequence you decoded in Part I is linked in the database to the protein sequence, shown below.

Figure 2.11. Cucumber protein sequence from GenBank database.

```
  1 mgqalgciqv dqstvairet fgrfddvlqp gchclpwclg sqiaghlslr lqqldvrcet
 61 ktkdnvfvtv vasiqyrala dkasdafykl sntreqiqay vfdvirasvp kldldstfeq
121 kndiakaved elekamsayg yeivqtlivd iepdehvkra mneinaaarl rvaatekaea
181 ekilqikrae gdaeskylag lgiarqrqai vdglrdsvla faenvpgtts kdvmdmvlvt
241 qyfdtmkeig assksnsvfi phgpgavkdi asqirdgllq asqt
```

What does that alphabet soup mean? Each letter represents an amino acid. Proteins can be long and complex; this one has 284 amino acids. The numbers on the side tell you how many amino acids are involved and they are shown in sets of ten. Scientists use a one-letter abbreviation for each amino acid as shown in Table 2.1.

Table 2.1. Codes for the 20 amino acids common in living organisms.

1-letter abbreviation	Amino Acid	1-letter abbreviation	Amino Acid	1-letter abbreviation	Amino Acid	1-letter abbreviation	Amino Acid
a	alanine	g	glycine	m	methionine	s	serine
c	cysteine	h	histidine	n	asparagine	t	threonine
d	aspartic acid	i	isoleucine	p	proline	v	valine
e	glutamic acid	k	lysine	q	glutamine	w	tryptophan
f	phenylalanine	l	leucine	r	arginine	y	tyrosine

7. Use Table 2.1 to decode the first 10 amino acids in the sequence: mgqalgciqv.

8. The DNA sequence for this protein has 855 bases in it. The protein itself has 284 amino acids. How are the two numbers related?

9. Why are there 284 amino acids in the protein and not 285? (Hint: Look at the last codon.)

The ten amino acids you just decoded are all strung together in a line. Each amino acid has its own chemical structure, and together, they have chemical interactions that cause the string to fold up into a unique 3-D structure. During the folding process, many amino acids are folded into the center of the protein or made chemically inactive because of bonds to other amino acids. A few remain in active sites—these are the sites that can bind to proteins and are where chemistry occurs.

Part III. Mutation

So, now we've seen that proteins come from amino acids, and amino acids come from genetic code. Let's see what happens if there are mutations in the genetic code.

Scenario 1

10. Let's start with the first glycine from our protein, encoded "ggu." What is its abbreviation?

11. What are the different ways to code for glycine?

12. What sequence occurs if a one-base mutation changes the last letter to an a?

13. What does that codon encode?

14. Describe the mutation:

   14a. How does it affect the DNA? (point or frame-shift mutation)

   14b. How does it affect the protein? (silent, non-sense, or mis-sense)

15. What would that mean for our protein?

Scenario 2

16. Let's start with a cysteine from our protein. What is its abbreviation?

17. What are the different ways to code for cysteine?

18. What sequence occurs if a one-base mutation changes the last letter to an a?

19. What does that codon encode?

20. Describe the mutation:

    20a. How does it affect the DNA? (point or frame-shift mutation)

    20b. How does it affect the protein? (silent, non-sense, or mis-sense)

21. What would that mean for our protein?

Scenario 3

22. Let's return to the first 15 bases of the sequence in Figure 2.7: `atg ggt caa gcc ctt`. What is the sequence of the amino acids it encodes?

23. A mutation causes a deletion of the first g to give: `atg gtc aag ccc ttg`. Circle where the change occurred.

24. Now, what is the sequence of the amino acids it encodes?

25. Describe the mutation:

    25a. How does it affect the DNA? (point or frame-shift mutation)

    25b. How does it affect the protein? (silent, non-sense, or mis-sense)

26. What would that mean for our protein?

Scenario 4

27. Let's return to the first 15 bases of the sequence in Figure 2.7 again—atg ggt caa gcc ctt. What is the sequence of the amino acids it encodes?

28. A mutation causes an insertion of two t's to give: atg ggt cat tag ccc. Circle where the change occurred.

29. Now, what is the sequence of the amino acids it encodes?

30. Describe the mutation:

    30a. How does it affect the DNA? (point or frame-shift mutation)

    30b. How does it affect the protein? (silent, non-sense, or mis-sense)

31. What would that mean for our protein?

Part IV. Mutation of the bitterness gene

We don't know the sequence for cucurbitacin (the bitterness gene) in cucumbers. But we do know of cucumber plants with a mutant gene that cannot make cucurbitacin.

32. What type of mutation would lead to a dysfunctional copy of the bitterness gene? Be specific.

33. How could you design an experiment to find the sequence for the bitter gene? Assume you have all the same tools as the Korean researchers investigating target leaf spot disease in cucumbers.

    What would you compare?

    Once you found a difference, what would you do?

The end result: a "candidate" gene for bitterness in cucumber plants. You wouldn't be sure that the gene caused bitterness until you put it into a non-bitter plant (using genetic engineering) and turned that plant bitter.

Why are some genes sequenced and others not sequenced? There are vast numbers of important genes in the world, and genetic sequencing and genomic approaches are still relatively new. The first genes to be sequenced are ones that have important consequences for major global problems. For example, scientists have sequenced genes that influence diseases like breast cancer in humans. In food plants, sequencing has focused on genes that improve yield and genes that are critical for food plants' response to diseases. Bitterness in cucumbers is not an important enough problem for scientists to have invested time and money in sequencing the bitter gene. Scientists can already solve any "bitterness problems" they have in their cucumbers with old-fashioned crosses and genes they've known about for a long time. They can use the genetic rather than genomic approach to bitterness in cucumbers.

CHAPTER 3

Figure 3.1. A thistle's spines are part of its physical defenses.

SURVIVAL STRATEGIES

How does a plant defend itself? It can't run away or turn and fight like many animals can. Instead, plants employ a variety of **chemical and physical defenses**. Chemical defenses are compounds in or on the plant like the "poison" of poison ivy. Plant structures like a thistle's spines or a tree's bark are physical defenses. Both chemical and physical defenses are encoded in a plant's genes and have been selected over evolutionary time because they give the plant some sort of advantage.

Plant chemical defense strategies

Plants are part of complex ecosystems. They must defend themselves from predators. They also must compete with other plants for light, soil, nutrients, and water. Over time, plants have evolved many strategies for defense and competition. Sometimes, the same strategy is effective for both.

Consider the strategy of a walnut tree. Its genes encode proteins called tannins. Tannins are familiar natural acids—they make the bitter taste in black tea. Because the walnut tree and its nutshells taste so unpleasant, many **herbivores** simply aren't interested in them—an effective plant chemical defense strategy.

Interestingly, this strategy also reduces competition with other plants. When the walnut tree drops its leaves and nuts, they decay into the soil, releasing acidic tannins and making the soil inhospitable for other plants to grow. So while a walnut tree can't move away from predators, its chemical defenses force herbivores to go elsewhere. And while a tree can't move away from another plant that competes for the same sunlight, water, and nutrients, it can create an environment where it is difficult for that competitor to survive.

Herbivores, predators, and prey

How do the walnut tree's tannins help it, from an evolutionary perspective? Think about the walnut's strategy from an herbivore's point of view. Presented with a forest full of trees, why would you choose to

Chemical and **physical defenses** are the way plants defend themselves. The "poison" of poison ivy is a **chemical defense**. Cactus spines are a **physical defense**.

Herbivores are organisms that eat plants. Herbivory is a form of predation, but herbivores rarely kill their prey (plants).

Topic: Plant Adaptations
Go to: www.sciLINKS.org
Code: GG11

Generalist herbivores can eat many different plants.

Specialist herbivores specialize in one or a few plants that are usually unpalatable to generalists.

eat the bitter one, if you could choose one that tasted better and from which you could digest more nutrients? On the other hand, if many other herbivores are eating the non-bitter trees, you might get more food (and therefore have a better chance of passing your genes on to the next generation) if you ate the bitter trees that no one else wanted.

Thus, insect herbivores have evolved many different strategies. Some, like mites, grasshoppers, and locusts, are **generalists** and feed on a variety of plants. Plant chemical defenses, such as capsaicin that makes hot peppers hot (Figure 3.2), and tannins that make tea and walnuts bitter, are usually effective against generalist herbivores.

Other herbivores have evolved to specialize on particular species of plants or particular compounds produced by these plants. These herbivores are called specialists. For many specialists, chemical defense compounds like capsaicin or tannins are actually attractants. Specialists have evolved the ability to recognize these compounds and to either digest them or sequester them inside their bodies. An insect with bitter tannins in its body will taste bitter to its own predators. Most specialists retain their ability to eat other plants, though they prefer their specific plant. A few specialists go to the extreme of specialization and will eat only their specific plant—without it, they will starve.

Figure 3.2. Generalist predators are usually deterred by capsaicin, the compound that makes hot peppers hot.

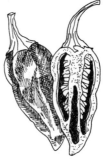

Figure 3.3. A cucumber plant food web.

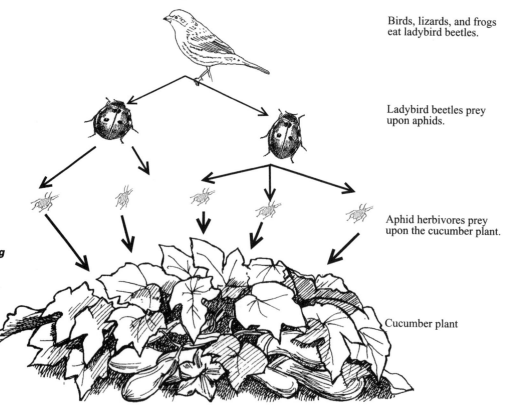

Birds, lizards, and frogs eat ladybird beetles.

Ladybird beetles prey upon aphids.

Aphid herbivores prey upon the cucumber plant.

Cucumber plant

Topic: Food Webs
Go to: *www.sciLINKS.org*
Code: GG12

The opposite of predator is prey, of course. However, in real-life food webs many organisms are both predator and prey (Figure 3.3). Consider the case of a cucumber plant. The cucumber plant is prey for aphids. The aphid, therefore, is the predator (also known as an herbivore, or plant predator). Aphids are major pests on agricultural crops. Ladybird beetles, also known as ladybugs, are predators of aphids. Often farmers use ladybird beetles to protect crops. By keeping aphid populations under control, these beetles can reduce the need for pesticides. The ladybugs in turn may be eaten by birds, lizards, and frogs. Thus, aphids and ladybugs are both predator and prey in agricultural ecosystems.

Questions for further thought

<u>Evolution</u>: What might be one evolutionary advantage and one disadvantage to being a specialist?

<u>Ecology</u>: Can an organism be both a generalist and a specialist? Explain your answer.

Figure 3.4. Do cucumber plants have physical defenses?

<u>Ecology and evolution</u>: What are the defense mechanisms of cucumber plants? (Hint: Look at Figure 3.4 and think about cucumber plants you may have touched or tasted.)

Activity 3.
Insect Predation and Plant Genes

Objective
Design and conduct an experiment to learn about the biology of cucumber beetles.

Background
There are two species of cucumber beetles—striped and spotted (see Figure 3.5). Both have similar bodies and both feed on cucumber plants. Your task is to discover more about their ecology and food preferences. Are these beetles generalists that feed on many different species of plants? Are they specialists that focus only on cucumbers? Are they intermediate between a generalist and a specialist, with some of the characteristics of each? Do they eat only certain types of cucumbers? Do the two species have the same food preferences?

sciLINKS.
THE WORLD'S A CLICK AWAY

Topic: Predator/Prey
Go to: *www.sciLINKS.org*
Code: GG13

Figure 3.5. Striped and spotted cucumber beetles.

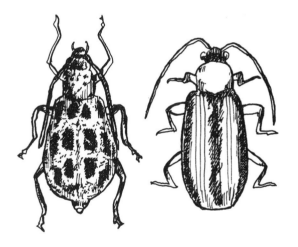

One of the cucumber plant's defenses is a bitter compound called cucurbitacin. This protein is produced in the stems, leaves, and fruit (yes, cucumbers are fruit) of cucumber plants. Though it's not harmful to humans, cucurbitacin makes the plants taste bitter. What effect does this compound have on the beetles? If the beetles are generalists, the cucurbitacin will likely deter them. If the beetles are specialists, the bitterness might actually attract them.

Materials
- Seedlings: bitter cucumbers, non-bitter cucumbers, corn
- Soil and containers
- Water source
- Area with light to grow plants
- Striped and/or spotted cucumber beetles
- Insect cage
- Rulers

Safety Notes
- This activity uses cucumber beetles. They are insects that naturally occur in most parts of the United States. If they escape from their cage, they will not cause harm to houseplants.
- Do not eat the cucumber beetles.
- Students who are allergic to cucumbers, squash, melon, or zucchini should NOT handle the plants.
- If you are allergic or not comfortable handling the plants, please ask someone else in your group to do it for you.
- You should wash your hands after handling the plants.
- You should wash your hands AGAIN at the end of the activity.

Activity

Part I. Design your experiment

1. Your objective is to investigate the effect of bitter and non-bitter cucumber genes on cucumber beetles. Formulate a hypothesis. A hypothesis is a possible explanation or an educated guess about what you will find. It is a starting point for your experiment.

2. How will you plan your experiment to investigate your hypothesis?

    2a. What do you plan to do?

    2b. What supplies will you need? How will you get any that are not already available in the classroom?

2c. How do you plan to schedule the project?

2d. How will you measure your results?

3. Evaluate your experiment.
   3a. Does your experiment test the effect of cucumber bitter and non-bitter genes on cucumber beetles?

   3b. Does your experiment frame a clear question?

   3c. Does your hypothesis propose a possible answer to the clearly stated question?

   3d. Is the proposed experiment feasible given the time and materials at hand?

   3e. What are your controls?

Part II. Data and results

4. Initial description of your plants. Do they look the same? Are they the same size, shape, and color?

5. Use this space to record your raw data:

6. Make a table here to summarize your data. Include calculations such as averages for amounts of predation.

7. Graph your data.

Part III. Conclusions

8. What conclusions can you reach? (What did you learn from your experiment? Was your hypothesis correct? Can you think of any other possible explanations for your results?)

9. Did you have any unexpected results? What were they and why do you think they happened?

10. How could you improve your experimental design? (Are there ways your experiment could be improved to better answer the initial question? Did you come up with questions you can't answer using your data?)

11. Based on what you know about generalists and specialists, are there other questions you would like to investigate with the techniques you developed in this experiment?

Part IV. Applying what you've learned

12. What does your experiment tell you about bitterness in cucumbers?

13. What does your experiment tell you about the behavior of cucumber beetles? Are they generalists or specialists?

SECTION 2
Corn

CHAPTER 4

DOMESTICATION

Evolving Toward Home

How did dogs become our companions? Once they were wolves, roaming in packs. What did that first wolf that left the pack to join a human group look like? People probably found the wolf-dogs useful for keeping the true wolves away from human camps and helpful for hunting. Humans saw the value of these animals and began to feed them. People and their dogs have been inseparable ever since.

It's easy to see the evolution from wild wolf to docile dog as **domestication**. The wolf lives in the wild and feeds itself. The dog lives with humans and is fed by them. Imagine a Chihuahua trying to survive on its own in the wild! The dog has joined the circle of a human home. The word *domestication* comes from the Latin word *domus,* meaning home. Domestication is literally the process of bringing an organism, animal or plant, into the home. A domesticated plant is one that is dependent on humans for its survival. In turn, we humans couldn't survive very long without our domesticated plants.

A **domesticated** plant or animal is dependent on humans for its survival.

SCI*L*INKS.

Topic: Crop Pollination
Go to: www.sciLINKS.org
Code: GG14

The changes of domestication

What makes a domesticated plant? Something about the wild plant has to change. Think about a field of wild grasses. When you walk through a field of wild grass, you come home with different kinds of seeds or grain stuck to your legs. When you touch some heads of grain, they explode or shatter, tossing their seeds to the ground. These are dispersal mechanisms—ways to distribute seeds for the next generation (Figure 4.1). Nothing happens when you walk through a field of

Figure 4.1. Some plant dispersal mechanisms.

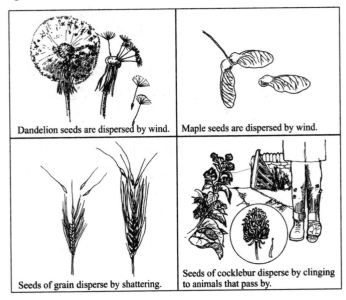

Dandelion seeds are dispersed by wind.

Maple seeds are dispersed by wind.

Seeds of grain disperse by shattering.

Seeds of cocklebur disperse by clinging to animals that pass by.

wheat or corn (both domesticated grasses). No grain sticks to your pant legs; no seeds are thrown to the ground. How then could a wheat or corn plant disperse the seeds that will become the next generation? Wheat and corn are dependent on humans to collect the seeds and plant them—a dispersal mechanism of a different kind.

Domestication is really a form of **evolution**. Instead of changes being driven by **natural selection**, the changes of domestication are driven by **artificial selection**—meaning selection done by humans, toward human goals. Domestication almost always involves reproductive changes. Strategies that work well in nature are often inconvenient for farmers and other human caretakers. In nature, if a head of grain does not shatter, the seeds remain on the head. They don't reach the ground. They don't germinate. They don't become part of the next plant generation. In fact, natural selection would eliminate non-shattering heads of grain.

However, when humans found a plant with a mutation that meant the heads of grain didn't shatter, more of that plant's seed ended up in the harvest. More of it was planted for the next generation because the farmer was able to collect the non-shattering seeds more easily. Each generation, more and more of the non-shattering grain ended up in the harvest. Eventually, all the plants in a field were non-shattering, and the shattering types of plants disappeared from farmers' fields. Thus artificial selection often drives plants in different directions than natural selection.

Artificial selection and human preference change plants in consistent ways. Fruits become larger. Flavors become sweeter. Grains and fruits remain on the plant longer. Plants flower and mature at the same time, making harvests easier and more productive. Natural selection, on the other hand, is not directional and does not lead to a progression toward an ideal or goal. (An example of artificial selection is diagramed in Figure 4.3.)

Targets of domestication

Considering the hundreds of thousands of plants that exist in nature, it is remarkable that we are dependent on just a handful of domesticated plants for most of our food. Figure 4.2 shows the 32 crops for which more than 25 million metric tons were harvested around the world in 2004. Four crops—wheat, rice, corn, and potatoes—represent the majority of the harvest. Why are we dependent on so few crops, when there were so many to start with? The answer begins with which plants can be easily domesticated, as well as with taste, yield, and ease of growing.

Topic: Natural Selection
Go to: www.sciLINKS.org
Code: GG15

Evolution is driven by **natural selection**—a process that results in the most fit individuals having the most offspring.

Domestication is driven by **artificial selection**—human decisions toward human goals.

Figure 4.2. World production (millions of metric tons) for 2004 (from FAOSTAT database).

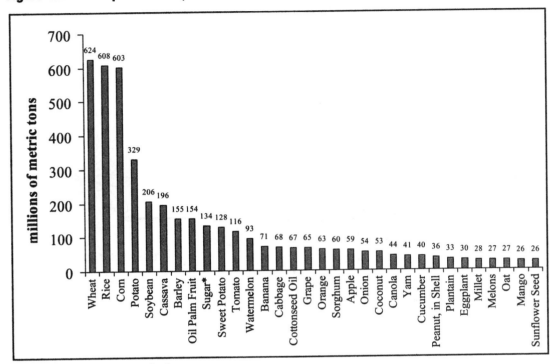

*2002 refined sugar equivalent

Not all plants are easily domesticated. For example, wild almonds and acorns suffer from the same major problem (from the human perspective). Their fruits are full of bitter, toxic compounds, which the plants use for defense and which interfere with human digestion. So why has the almond been domesticated while the oak has not? Both were eaten extensively by prehistoric people. Non-bitter forms of both trees exist in nature. But in almonds, bitterness is largely under the control of one gene. So the offspring of a non-bitter almond tree are likely to be non-bitter. Thus non-bitter almonds are relatively easy to select. On the other hand, many genes play a role in controlling the bitterness of acorns. When the acorns from non-bitter oaks are planted, the new generation still has bitter acorns. The critical trait that influences oak domestication is too genetically complex for non-bitter oaks to be easily domesticated.

THE POWER OF ARTIFICIAL SELECTION

Artificial selection is a powerful tool. The pressure of human selection has produced many different vegetables from the same plant, *Brassica oleracea*.

The original *Brassica* plant probably looked like a wild mustard plant. Broccoli, cauliflower, kohlrabi, brussels sprouts, cabbage, and kale are all modifications of the leaf, shoot, flower, or root system.

Figure 4.3. Artificial selection has produced many vegetables from the same wild mustard ancestor.

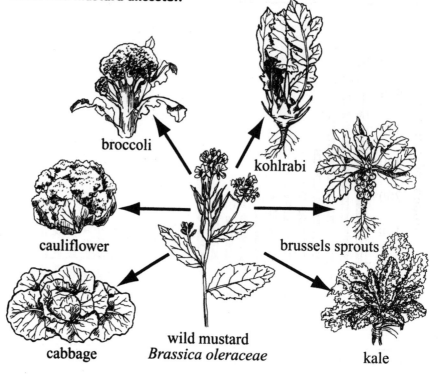

broccoli

kohlrabi

cauliflower

brussels sprouts

cabbage

wild mustard
Brassica oleraceae

kale

Timescale of change

How fast does domestication occur? Beginning with Darwin, people proposed that domestication, like all evolution, was the accumulation of small changes over time. This theory is often called **gradualism**. Many small, advantageous mutations would be selected for, and species would change slowly. More recently, people have proposed that evolution and domestication might occur with short bursts of radical change followed by periods of relative stability. This theory is called **punctuated equilibrium**. Domestication could also involve both kinds of change—rapid changes followed by slow changes or vice versa.

The process of domestication was different for each species. No one knows exactly how fast domestication of a species occurred because it happened a long time ago. However, the archeological and genetic records provide important clues. Prehistoric ears of corn and corncobs are visual evidence of how corn was domesticated. But how does genetic information help us understand domestication?

Corn: A genetic case study

The changes of domestication are genetic changes. For over a century, people studied, debated, and speculated about origins of corn. There was no obvious wild relative—nothing looked like the corn

Gradualism is the accumulation of small changes over time. It leads to slow, gradual evolution.

Evolution by **punctuated equilibrium** has bursts of change followed by periods of stability. It leads to much faster evolution.

plants people knew. Eventually, scientists began to suspect that grassy weeds called teosinte, growing in cornfields, might be related to corn. Initially teosinte was considered a separate species. Further studies identified this grass, shown in Figure 4.4, as corn's nearest wild relative. Even though they look different, they have the same number of chromosomes and can cross in the field. They are now considered to be part of the same species. Genetic studies have shown that corn was domesticated from teosinte about 9,000 years ago.

Figure 4.4. Teosinte and corn.

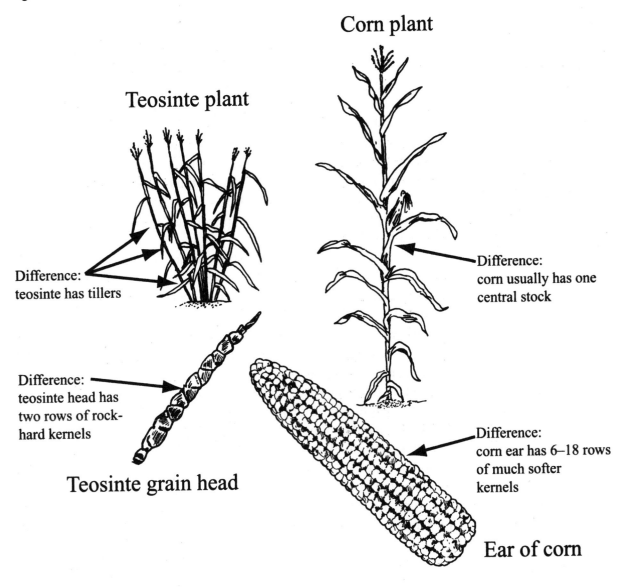

Corn plant

Teosinte plant

Difference: teosinte has tillers

Difference: corn usually has one central stock

Difference: teosinte head has two rows of rock-hard kernels

Teosinte grain head

Difference: corn ear has 6–18 rows of much softer kernels

Ear of corn

How, genetically, was the wild grass teosinte transformed into corn? Teosinte heads have two rows of rock-hard triangular seeds. Corn seeds or grains are softer and occur on cobs, sometimes with more than 20 rows. Teosinte has many tillers, or stems, growing from the same root base. Corn rarely has more than one main stalk.

Corn and teosinte seed heads or cobs are so physically different from one another that most people thought that many gradual changes over a long time must have been required for the domestication of corn (gradualism). They simply couldn't think of a few changes (really a few genes) that could result in such a different plant. To study the genetic basis for the differences, a group of scientists headed by John Doebley made crosses between teosinte and corn. Then they used a set of genetic tools called a QTL (quantitative trait locus) analysis to understand which genes were involved in domestication. (More on quantitative traits and QTL studies in Chapter 9.)

To everyone's surprise, Doebley's group found that the differences between corn and teosinte are controlled by a handful of genes (only five to ten). One of these genes accounted for a whopping 40% of the variation between corn and teosinte. Instead of finding support for slow change over a long time (gradualism), they found genetic evidence for a few genes with dramatic effects. The changes to so few genes could have happened very quickly (punctuated equilibrium)—possibly within a few generations.

How could rapid changes in the teosinte plant be caused by differences in a few genes? Most changes to genes (usually mutations) inactivate or disable a protein that the plant makes. (See Chapter 2 for details.) The plant needs most of the proteins it makes. Therefore, losing the ability to make a protein (like chlorophyll) is often fatal. In other words, most mutations are bad for the plant. Only occasionally do positive mutations occur. Therefore people thought that it would take a long time to build up the many small, positive mutations of gradualism. The Doebley teosinte study was exciting because the changes in phenotype resulted from as few as five positive mutations—this number of mutations is small and so the changes could have occurred in a short period of time. Thus, the teosinte study provided genetic evidence for the theory of punctuated equilibrium. With so few mutations being responsible for so large a change, people could envision the genetic basis for punctuated equilibrium's burst of rapid evolution.

Questions for further thought

Evolution: What is the definition of species? How could teosinte originally be considered a different species from corn if it is now considered the same species? What sort of information would be required to change a species classification?

Genetics: The radical difference between the grass-like teosinte and corn is thought to be controlled by as few as five or ten genes. Is each of these genes likely to have single effects (one for shattering, another for tillering, and still another for multi-rowed ears)? Or are they likely to be genes that have multiple effects (one gene affects both tillering and multi-rowed ears)?

How could a gene have multiple effects?

Activity 4.
Corn and the Archeological Record

Topic: Food Crops
Go to: www.sciLINKS.org
Code: GG16

Objective
Use predictions, genetic evidence, and the archeological record to determine a history of domestication for corn.

Background
Domestication (like evolution) can occur rapidly or slowly or with some alternation of the two rates. Genetic evidence tells us corn was domesticated about 9,000 years ago. Figure 4.5 shows actual sized illustrations of corn and teosinte, its wild relative.

Figure 4.5. Actual size drawings of teosinte and corn.

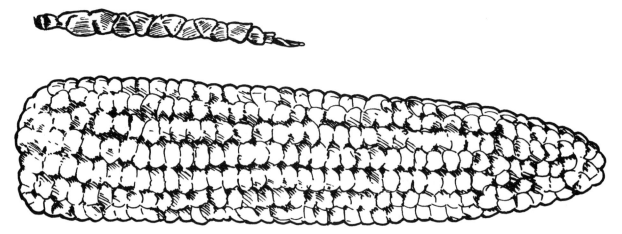

Activity

Part I. Predictions
Draw teosinte grain heads and corn ears on the timeline below to predict how corn might change if domestication occurred in the following ways.

1. Slow evolution, with small changes.

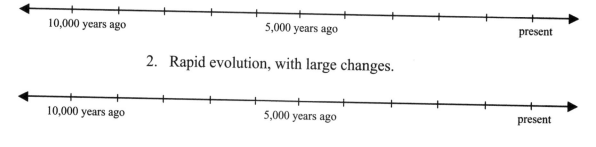

10,000 years ago   5,000 years ago   present

2. Rapid evolution, with large changes.

10,000 years ago   5,000 years ago   present

3. Slow evolution followed by rapid evolution.

10,000 years ago   5,000 years ago   present

4. Rapid evolution followed by slow evolution.

10,000 years ago   5,000 years ago   present

Part II. Evidence of domestication—genetic

There are two important lines of evidence to help us understand the domestication of corn: the archeological record and the genetic record. The chapter text reviews some of the recent genetic evidence.

5. Did scientists expect to find the effects of many genes (each providing small changes) or few genes (each providing large changes)? What about corn and teosinte led them to that expectation?

6. What did John Doebley's genetic experiments show?

7. How is this genetic evidence interpreted in regard to rate of domestication?

8. How long ago did the domestication events occur? Draw them on a timeline.

```
◄──┼───┼───┼───┼───┼───┼───┼───┼───┼───┼──►
  10,000 years ago        5,000 years ago              present
```

Part III. Evidence of domestication— archeological

The archeological record provides physical evidence of the past. However, the archeological record has some limitations. Without an appropriate site and prehistoric corn or cobs, there is nothing to examine. If you have ever thrown an ear of corn onto a compost pile, it will be obvious that unusual circumstances are required to preserve corn kernels for thousands of years. Most importantly, the ear must be kept dry. Some of the most important archeological sites are caves, because the contents have been well protected from weather.

Furthermore, the archeologist is limited to studying the parts of the plant that remain behind. In the case of corn, the cob is the most durable part. Though whole ears with kernels thousands of years old have been found, most archeological corn samples are cobs or pieces of cob. Additionally, the story told by archeological evidence from one site is unique. A different site might yield different evidence.

In 1960, with the help of some local students, archeologist Richard MacNeish found several caves in the valley of Tehuacan, in the state of Mexico. MacNeish began digging (very carefully!) and within a week, found corn. From 1960 to 1963, archeologists and scientists came to Tehuacan to study the domestication and evolution not just of corn, but also of beans, squash, cotton, hunted animals, and the humans who lived there for thousands of years.

In the five caves of the Tehuacan valley, archeologists found 24,186 corn specimens. More than half (12,860) were whole or almost whole cobs. The corn specimens were deposited in layers, as various groups of people used the caves as shelter, over thousands of years. Each generation piled their garbage on top of that from the generation before, leaving a time sequence of the evolution of corn in the Tehuacan valley.

Each picture on pages 79 and 80 is a subset of the cobs found at a different level in the San Marcos cave in Tehuacan. The dates are provided for you from the original study. **The photos are actual size. Please determine the average size of the ears in each photo.**

Figure 4.6. Actual size photos of archeological corn from Tehuacan cave layers A and B.

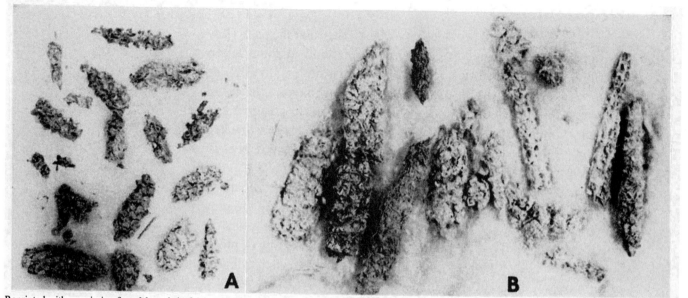

Reprinted with permission from Mangelsdorf, MacNeish, and Galinat. 1964. Domestication of corn. *Science* 143: 538–545. Copyright AAAS.

9. A   age: 7,200 to 5,400 years old   average size:

10. B   age: 5,400 to 4,300 years old   average size:

Figure 4.7. Actual size photos of archeological corn from Tehuacan cave layer C.

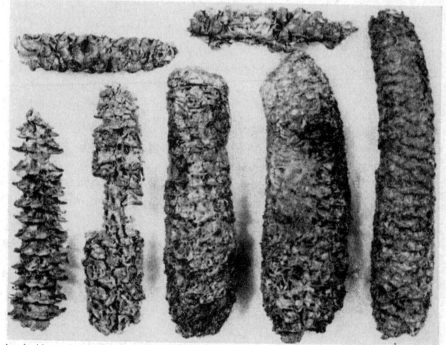

Reprinted with permission from Mangelsdorf, MacNeish, and Galinat. 1964. Domestication of corn. *Science* 143: 538–545. Copyright AAAS.

11. C   age: 3,500 to 2,900 years old   average size:

Figure 4.8. Actual size photos of archeological corn from Tehuacan cave layer D.

Reprinted with permission from Mangelsdorf, MacNeish, and Galinat. 1964. Domestication of corn. *Science* 143: 538–545. Copyright AAAS.

12. D   age: 2,700 to 2,200 years old   average size:

13. On your timeline, first show the changes suggested by the genetic evidence. (This is what you did in question 8.) Next, show on your timeline how the archeological evidence would influence the changes from teosinte to corn.

```
◄———┼———┼———┼———┼———┼———┼———┼———┼———┼———┼———►
     10,000 years ago         5,000 years ago           present
```

Part IV. Putting the evidence together

14. Given the genetic and archeological evidence, how would you describe the domestication of corn? Was it fast? Was it slow? Was it a combination of the two?

15. Does your timeline based on evidence agree with any of your predicted timelines? Why or why not?

A final note: You have just told a credible story of corn domestication (and evolution) based on two different kinds of evidence. In the last century, hundreds of studies were conducted to learn about the evolution of corn, but they did not all agree with one another. Like any scientist, you've drawn the best conclusions you can, given the evidence you have. This evidence reflects our current best knowledge about corn domestication. However, if you were given more evidence, like any scientist, you might have to adjust your conclusions.

16. How would you adjust your conclusions if a new archeological study found corn that looks like corn we eat today in a South American cave from 15,000 years ago?

17. How would you adjust your conclusions if a recent genetic study showed large blocks of DNA in modern day corn that were similar to an entirely different species called *Tripsacum dactyloides*?

The evidence in questions 1–15 represents the current majority opinion about the origins of corn, but some scientists disagree. All conclusions are interpretations of the data. No one really knows exactly how corn was domesticated. Questions 16 and 17 are included to illustrate that there has been a hundred years of debate on the origins of corn. New evidence requires new interpretation. Though the "evidence" presented is fictional, the questions represent real debates that have occurred.

THE RISKS OF IMPROVEMENT

Genetic Uniformity and an Epidemic

In the Mexican state of Jalisco, Don Paulo grows different kinds of corn (Figure 5.1). Mexico is the homeland for corn—the "Center of Diversity"—a place rich in corn genes and genetic diversity. Don Paulo's cornfields have short plants and tall plants, plants that mature quickly and plants that mature slowly, plants with large starchy kernels and others with small hard kernels. Yields are low, and the corn ripens at different times. Don Paulo harvests the corn by hand, so it doesn't matter if it matures at different times. His fields are on steep hillsides; he couldn't use a tractor even if he had one. The genetic diversity in his field is a good insurance policy—if a corn disease outbreak occurs, or a big storm blows through, some plants in his field are likely to survive. Don Paulo's yields are likely to be low even in a good year. But there will almost always be something to harvest, even in a bad year.

Topic: Plant Propagation
Go to: *www.sciLINKS.org*
Code: GG17

Crop improvement is driven by **artificial selection** in which humans make decisions about what kinds of plants they want.

The power of selection

Every year, Don Paulo saves the best seed from his harvest to plant again. This is a form of selection. He chooses seeds from plants that have characteristics he favors, such as large white grains, straight rows, and large ears.

Like Don Paulo, plant breeders select desirable traits in the plant populations they work with. Plant breeders select the best of a population of plants and use it as the parents of the next generation (Figure 5.2). By continuing to select the best, a plant breeder increases the frequency of those desirable genotypes. This is **artificial selection**.

Figure 5.1. Don Paulo in a Mexican cornfield.

Artificial selection differs from natural selection because humans do the selecting, instead of "nature" selecting the "fittest."

Selection improves whatever characteristic the breeder is working on, for example, ear size, yield, or resistance to a disease. Figure 5.2 shows that selection also results in genetic narrowing. Selection improves crops by eliminating the "undesirable" genotypes—the smaller ears, the lower yielding, or less disease resistant. This means that genetic diversity is lost with each round of improvement.

Figure 5.2. Effects of selection.

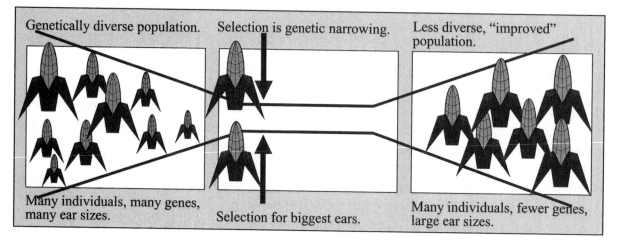

Genetically diverse population. Selection is genetic narrowing. Less diverse, "improved" population.

Many individuals, many genes, many ear sizes. Selection for biggest ears. Many individuals, fewer genes, large ear sizes.

The downside of diversity

Is genetic diversity always a good thing? To Don Paulo, it is. But to farmers with rich, flat land, like in the midwestern United States, diversity has some drawbacks. Having different varieties in the same field may mean lower yields, plants that ripen at different times, and difficulty using tractors because the plants are too variable.

Farmers care about yield. Yield means money in their pockets. Without high yield, many farmers can't afford to stay in business. Therefore, when a new variety arrives that is better than the old varieties, farmers want to plant it. Figure 5.3 shows how much area in the United States was planted with the six most popular varieties of corn, cotton, soy, and wheat. In 1970, more than 70% of the corn-growing area in the United States was planted with only six corn varieties. What does this mean, when huge areas of land are planted to exactly the same variety? (Notice that by 1980, the area planted with the six most popular varieties had decreased to 43%—meaning that farmers were planting more different varieties. Something happened between 1970 and 1980 that made farmers realize the value of more diversity in the varieties they plant. More about this in Activity 5.)

Figure 5.3. Percent area planted with 6 most popular varieties of important crops, 1970 and 1980.

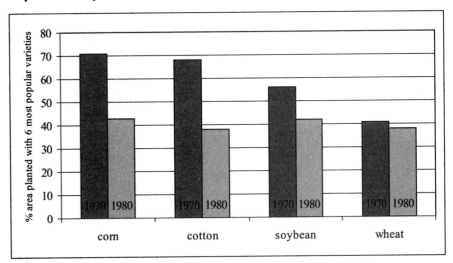

Pressure

Imagine a new variety of corn is created that is resistant to rust, a disease caused by a fungus. Farmers want to plant the variety because rust causes major losses in their crops. Suddenly, huge areas are planted with this variety.

Next try to predict what happens to the rust fungus. At the beginning, most of the rust-causing fungi die because they have no host plant and therefore no food source. However, there are a few fungi with a mutation or an adaptation that allows them to survive. Those few become the parents of the next generation of rust-causing fungi, many of which can survive on the new corn variety. Within a few generations there is a population of rust-causing fungi that can attack the corn that was bred to resist them. Thus, lack of diversity, or planting large areas of the same variety, has some major drawbacks when it comes to disease. It can create powerful natural selection pressure on insects, diseases, and other pests to change to forms that can survive on the new variety.

Corn hybrids

Hybrids take advantage of one of corn's unique traits: Corn can be pollinated by its own pollen (**selfed**) or by pollen from another plant (**crossed**). Making a hybrid requires both types of pollination. First a line of corn is selfed for many generations until it is homozygous, meaning it has two identical copies of the same allele at all of its loci. Then, two homozygous lines, called inbred lines, are crossed with each other. The resulting hybrid generation of plants will be heterozygous (one allele from each line). No one fully understands why, but that hybrid generation has about a 30% boost in yield. The yield gain disappears again in

A **hybrid** is a cross between two different things. A hybrid car is half gas, half electric. A hybrid plant results from a cross between two different parents. It has two different alleles at its loci, one from each parent.

Selfing is when a plant is pollinated by itself. In corn, pollen from the tassel of one plant is used to pollinate the ear of the same plant.

Crossing uses pollen from one plant to pollinate a different plant.

the next generation of plants, so farmers have a big incentive to keep buying new hybrid seed. (See figure 5.4)

So it seems easy. You take pollen from inbred plant B and use it to pollinate inbred plant A (Figure 5.5). But how do you keep the pollen from plant A from landing on the flowers of plant A and "contaminating" it?

Figure 5.4. Impact of hybrid varieties on historical U.S. corn yield.

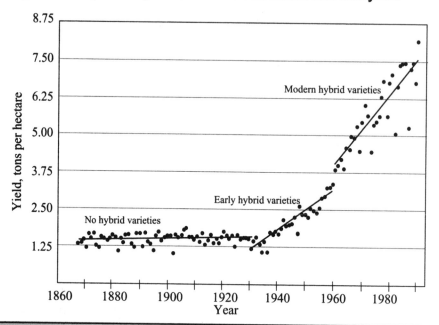

GREEN REVOLUTION

New crop varieties, fertilizers, pesticides, irrigation, and mechanization all contributed to increasing corn yield in the United States during the 21st century. The Green Revolution attempted to eliminate hunger worldwide by using similar methods to increase crop yields of other crops, like rice and wheat.

Green Revolution rice and wheat varieties have shorter stalks that can support large heads of grain without falling over. This new plant architecture is caused by one or a few mutations called dwarfing genes. When grown with fertilizers, these "dwarf" plants produce much higher yields.

The Green Revolution brought tremendous benefits in feeding a hungry world. In addition, with higher yields from existing farmland, less new land needed to be cultivated. This meant saving rain forests and other important ecosystems. However, the Green Revolution was not without problems. Crops were more uniform genetically and thus more subject to disease. Farmers became dependent on fertilizers and pesticides to produce high yields. And unfortunately, the benefits were not equally distributed across nations or socioeconomic groups; often only wealthier farmers were able to access the Green Revolution crops, fertilizers, and other technologies.

Figure 5.5. Hybrid production.

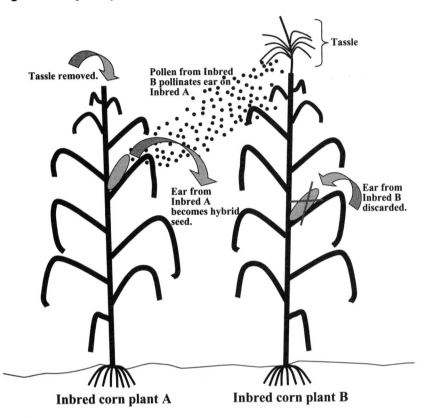

Inbred corn plant A   Inbred corn plant B

To prevent this, plant breeders **detassel**. As the word suggests, they remove the tassel from plant A, so its pollen can't contaminate the ear. This means that seed companies employed many young people, usually students, during the summer to detassel corn. It's hot, sticky work in the cornfields, and it was a major expense for seed companies.

You can imagine how excited seed companies would be to find a way to eliminate detasseling. In the 1950s, a mutant type of corn was found in Texas. It produced sterile pollen.

Think about that for a second. A plant that produces sterile pollen doesn't have to be detasseled! Male sterility is a very rare mutation in "nature." A plant that cannot produce pollen cannot be a male parent and is quickly eliminated from the gene pool. But corn breeders discovered the sterile pollen mutation and quickly bred it into their inbred lines. The mutation saved the seed companies lots of money and made hybrid production more reliable. By 1970, 85% of the corn planted in the United States had this single male-sterility gene, called T-cytoplasm.

What do you think happened? There have been plenty of other cases where large geographic areas have been planted with similar gene-types, and nothing happened. But in this case…(Activity 5 will explore what happened to T-cytoplasm corn in the United States).

Questions for further thought

<u>Variation:</u> Figure 5.2 shows changes that can occur with selection. Why is there still variability in yield after selection? If only a few individuals are selected, shouldn't the population that results from those individuals have very little yield variability?

<u>Genetics:</u> Why does selfing make populations homozygous? (Hint: Use Punnett's squares to cross individuals with themselves and see what happens.)

Activity 5.
Trial

Objective

Recreate the courtroom trial in which U.S. Farmers sued seed companies for crop losses in 1970 caused by the southern corn leaf blight (SCLB) epidemic.

Background

In 1970, an epidemic swept through the corn crop in the United States. After an unusually warm, wet spring, a previously rare disease, southern corn leaf blight (SCLB), began to cause problems in farmers' cornfields in the southern part of the United States. In Florida, Georgia, Alabama, and Mississippi, many farmers lost most of their corn crop. As the warm weather moved north toward the major corn producing states, the disease moved with it.

The plants vulnerable to SCLB had the male sterile gene known as T-cytoplasm. More than 80% of the U.S. corn crop in 1970 had this gene. Ultimately, the epidemic caused the loss of 15% of the United States corn crop—a loss worth more than one billion dollars.

Within a few short years, lawsuits were filed in the states of Indiana and Iowa against seed companies. They were class action lawsuits on the behalf of many individual farmers who were harmed by the crop losses of 1970. The farmers alleged that the seed companies had behaved irresponsibly in releasing corn varieties that all had the same gene for T-cytoplasm, and therefore should be financially responsible for the farmers' loss.

Activity

Part I. Trial format

You will reconstruct the class action trial against the seed companies. Everyone will have a role to play. Using the materials provided on pages 96–107, and any others you care to supplement from your own research, each "witness" will present part of the story. The class will act as the jury. At the end of the trial, you, as a juror, will present your opinion in the case as a 2–3 page paper. Be sure you address the importance of genetic diversity and the consequences of genetic uniformity in the paper.

In a trial, both sides have time to present their cases. The trial begins with opening statements from the lawyers. Then the prosecution, arguing on behalf of the farmers, will call all their witnesses, in an order to be determined by the lawyers. After the prosecution is done, the defense will call all their witnesses. Then the trial ends with the closing arguments from the lawyers.

Witnesses should speak briefly, answering the questions they are asked in their own words. If they don't know the answer to a question, they should say so. Whenever possible, they should use visual aids (pictures, tables, graphs, charts) in presenting their information.

Part II. Roles and overview

Table 5.1 shows an overview of the roles in the trial. Following the table you will find the specific information for each individual witness's testimony. Witnesses are responsible for learning the material for their own testimony. Lawyers will also read the information and will ask questions of the witnesses to elicit the information. Witnesses should present this information in their own words and can supplement it with their own research or with visual aids like drawings, charts, and graphs.

Please look up underlined terms if you do not already know what they mean and answer the underlined questions in your testimony.

Table 5.1. Overview of roles and responsibilities for trial.

Prosecution (arguing on behalf of the farmers)		
Student	Role	Responsibility
	Prosecution lawyer(s)	Responsible for opening statement, closing statement, organization of the prosecution witnesses, cross-examination of defense witnesses (if applicable).
	Farmer 1	Describe crop losses—personal and national.
	Expert witness: pathologist 1	Describe how southern corn leaf blight (SCLB) occurs in the field.
	Expert witness: pathologist 2	What causes SCLB? Describe the different races of blight before and after 1970.
	Expert witness: nursery manager from Florida	Noticed that T-cytoplasm hybrids had problems with SCLB but the few varieties without T-cytoplasm did not.
	Expert witness: Philippine scientist	Published two papers in late 1960s detailing a possible connection between T-cytoplasm and vulnerability to a new strain of SCLB.
	Expert witness: geneticist	What is T-cytoplasm? What is mitochondrial DNA? How does it work?
	Expert witness: corn breeder	What is a hybrid? How do corn breeders make them? Why is T-cytoplasm used? Are there alternatives to T-cytoplasm?
	Expert witness: seed store manager	Describe varieties available. How many of them had T-cytoplasm in 1970? What percentage of the corn area in the United States was planted with T-cytoplasm?
	Expert witness: trader in corn futures	Describe how corn is traded and what corn futures are. Describe the effect of SCLB epidemic on corn futures.
Defense (arguing on behalf of the seed companies)		
Student	Role	Responsibility
	Defense lawyer(s)	Responsible for opening statement, closing statement, organization of defense witnesses, cross-examination of prosecution witnesses (if applicable).
	Seed company president	What is the goal of a seed company? (Produce high-quality seed at a reasonable price.) How do you do it?
	Seed company corn breeder 1	No known problems with T-cytoplasm. No known vulnerabilities.
	Seed company corn breeder 2	Few, if any, people in the United States knew about the Philippine papers. Those who knew discounted them.
	Expert witness: pathologist	Race T of SCLB was virtually unknown before 1970.
	Seed company executive	Reaction to the problem. Eliminate T-cytoplasm from seed stocks at tremendous cost to the companies.

Part III. Roles and material

Farmer 1: Overview of crop losses—personal and national

Internet search terms: Southern corn leaf blight 1970 epidemic "crop loss"

In the spring and summer of 1970, SCLB began to show up in farmers' fields in Florida, Georgia, Alabama, and Mississippi. By June, we knew it was an epidemic that was spreading to Louisiana and Texas. Losses in the Gulf region of the South were commonly 50% or more in fields with T-cytoplasm. People became very worried when they realized that more than 80% of the U.S. corn crop was susceptible (because it had T-cytoplasm).

Weather patterns favored the spread of the disease. The weather was warm and wet, with northerly winds blowing spores up into Kentucky, Ohio, Indiana, and Illinois (where 85% of U.S. corn is grown) by late June and July. In August, there were reports of SCLB in Wisconsin, Minnesota, and Canada.

People worried. How much of the crop would be lost? Would there be enough to meet U.S. food needs? Would there be enough to feed all the animals in the United States that eat corn? Would there be enough for the industries that use corn? Would there be a similar or worse epidemic next year? Could anything be done to stop the disease? If resistance to the disease could be found, how many years would it take before that resistance made it into new seed? Rumors began that the corn grain and plants were toxic to humans and animals. The rumors were false, but frightening. The states with early disease problems immediately began experiments feeding SCLB-infected grain to animals that showed the infected grain was undesirable, but safe to eat.

The United States keeps stocks of grain in silos around the country to buffer just such a crisis. In 1970, the reserves were adequate to make up for the shortfall. But would they be adequate if such a problem occurred in 1971 and 1972 as well? There probably would have been enough to survive two years of bad blight.

Prices of corn and corn products rose. Prices of meat and other grains rose as well.

Epidemic Facts

July 1970 estimate of U.S. corn crop: 4.82 billion bushels.
December 1970 estimate of U.S. corn crop: 4.11 billion bushels.
Market price = $1.50/ bushel.
Loss (710 million bushels × $1.50) = about 1 billion dollars in crop losses because of disease.

Average U.S. yield in 1969: 83.9 bushels/acre.
Average U.S. yield in 1970: 71.7 bushels/acre.
Some southern states lost more than 50% of their corn crop (though those states do not count for much of the national production).

Expert witness—Pathologist 1: How SCLB occurs in the field.

Internet search terms: Southern corn leaf blight "in the field," southern corn leaf blight symptoms, southern corn leaf blight description

Moisture is critical for development of an outbreak of SCLB. For the disease to enter the plant, only a thin film of moisture on the leaves, stalks, or husks is necessary. The fungus enters through the <u>stomata</u> and produces a toxin that attacks the <u>mitochondria</u>. This destroys the cell's ability to utilize energy from glucose. (Why?) Within 24 hours, tan, cigar-shaped spots called lesions begin to appear on leaves. By passing spores from one plant to another, the disease can wipe out a field in 10 days.

Under optimal conditions (20–30 degrees C and damp weather), the fungus can begin reproducing itself within 60 hours of landing on a plant and thus can complete a generation in 3 days. The spores can survive temperatures of 28 degrees C below zero, meaning they can survive winter in the field. In some cases, the disease can also penetrate seed, causing the seed to produce diseased seedlings or to not germinate at all.

Weather plays a critical role in the spread of SCLB. Cool, dry weather stops the spread of the disease.

Expert witness—Pathologist 2: What causes SCLB? Describe the different races of blight before and after 1970.

Internet search terms: Southern corn leaf blight "race T," southern corn leaf blight "race O," *Bipolaris maydis* "race T," *Bipolaris maydis* "race O"

SCLB is caused by a fungus with the Latin name *Bipolaris maydis*. Historically, the disease was of only minor significance, causing average crop yield losses of about 1 to 2.3% in the United States. Hybrids were relatively resistant to the common strain of SCLB. Different strains of SCLB are referred to as "races." In 1970, race T of SCLB caused a 15% loss of the national corn crop.

Infection of corn depends on the amount of the different types of the fungus, the genetic background of the plant, and the reproductive rates of both the fungus and the plant. When a new plant variety is introduced, the balance shifts. Diseases to which the new variety is resistant are suppressed. Diseases to which the new variety is susceptible will thrive and multiply. Often, it is impossible to know exactly how the balance will shift until after the variety has been released and is planted on thousands and thousands of hectares.

What happened to corn is similar to what happened to wheat in the 1950s. In 1953, a wheat stem rust race called 15B destroyed 65% of the U.S. durum wheat crop and 25% of the bread wheat crop. In 1954, the same race of rust destroyed 75% of the durum wheat crop and 25% of the bread wheat crop. Race 15B was found in surveys of wheat rusts in very low frequencies from 1942 to 1953. During these years, it adapted, changed, and accumulated the genetic traits it needed to become an epidemic.

Before 1970, SCLB caused only minor losses in corn. Prior to 1970, SCLB was caused by "race O" of the fungus, and it left relatively small brown areas on plant leaves. The epidemic in 1970 was caused by "race T," which was previously unknown. Race T produced a stronger infection with longer, browner spots on leaves. It could also infect stems and ears.

Expert witness—Nursery manager from Florida: Noticed that T-cytoplasm hybrids had problems with SCLB but the few varieties without T-cytoplasm did not.

In 1968, about 100,000 kg of seed were infected with SCLB on seed farms in Iowa and Illinois. Seed farms produce the seed corn that farmers will plant the next year. (This is where hybrids are made.) At the time, seed farmers called SCLB "ear rot" because SCLB was not known to infect ears of corn before this. Instead, they thought the "ear rot" might be a combination of two other familiar diseases. In fact, this was probably the first strike of the new strain of the disease. The losses were small, however, and people discounted them as part of normal fluctuations in diseases.

In 1969, farm managers on the same midwestern seed farms noticed much more severe problems. Ears rotted inside their husks, leaves had ugly brown lesions spreading on them, and stalks fell over. Nursery managers in Florida (where winter crops of seed corn are planted to help produce seed corn faster) noticed more SCLB in the corn plants. They knew the disease was caused by a fungus, but that was all they knew. It didn't behave like other familiar diseases (even the types of SCLB with which that they were familiar).

By 1970, the problem was obvious in cornfields. The Florida fields have narrow plots of different varieties planted right next to each other. You could look down the row and see which plants had T-cytoplasm by looking for the blight. Those that had T-cytoplasm were infected. Those that didn't have T-cytoplasm were healthy.

Further tests in the greenhouse that took the fungus from infected fields and exposed plants in otherwise disease-free environments showed that SCLB was the culprit! And it was causing heavy losses in plants with T-cytoplasm.

Expert witness—Philippine scientist: Published two papers in the 1960s detailing a possible connection between T-cytoplasm and vulnerability to a new strain of SCLB.

Internet search terms: southern corn leaf blight epidemic "Philippine plant breeders"

As early as 1961, two Philippine scientists reported that corn with T-cytoplasm was more likely to become infected with SCLB. In 1965, Philippine scientists showed stronger proof of the vulnerability. Both articles were published in the journal *Philippine Agronomy*, which was not read by many scientists in the United States. However, some people argue that the seed companies should have read these studies and seen the dangers that might lie ahead.

A 1972 study by the National Academy of Sciences in the United States dismissed these reports noting that the scientists from the Philippines did not warn of an epidemic. The report also pointed out that scientists are trained NOT to extrapolate from local data to worldwide epidemics. The fact that the problems were noticed in a tropical environment made it easy for scientists to dismiss the results as a local, tropical problem, unlikely to occur in the United States.

Expert witness—Geneticist: What is T-cytoplasm? What is mitochondrial DNA? How does it work?

Internet search terms: cytoplasmic inheritance T-cytoplasm, maternal inheritance T-cytoplasm, mitochondrial DNA

T-cytoplasm was first described in 1952. It was found in Texas (accounting for the "T" in T-cytoplasm) in a line of corn called Golden June. Geneticists and breeders were immediately intrigued by the sterile male flowers it produced. Male sterility can be caused by genes in the nucleus or by genes found in the cytoplasm (more specifically in the mitochondria or the chloroplasts, which are found in the cytoplasm). Nuclear genes are the ones we usually study. An individual has two copies of each nuclear gene—one from the mother and one from the father. Mitochondrial genes, like T-cytoplasmic male sterility, are inherited only from the mother. Maternal inheritance means the genes are passed from mother to offspring in the cytoplasm of the egg cell, without contribution from the father.

The people making hybrids have a fundamental problem. To make hybrid crosses, they want plants without pollen (so the hybrid crosses aren't self-contaminated—see Chapter 5 text). But to make hybrid seed, plants must make pollen. A corn variety that doesn't make pollen can't pollinate the ears around it, and those ears then won't make seed. If there is no seed in a field, a farmer has nothing to harvest. Obviously, that would make for a very bad variety!

As the name suggests, cytoplasmic male sterility is caused by a gene (called tcms) found in the cytoplasm (really in the mitochondrial DNA). The intriguing thing about the tcms gene is that the expression of its phenotype (sterile or not sterile) is controlled by genes in the nucleus, even though the gene is found in the mitochondria. This gives plant breeders a "switch" that can be turned on and off. This way, corn breeders can make hybrids with the pollen "switched off." Then, in the next generation, they can "switch" the pollen back on. These nuclear genes, the "switches," are called fertility restorers. The fertility restorer genes suppress the male sterile genes, allowing the plant to make functional pollen again. Therefore the fertility-restored hybrid will have no problems making pollen or grain.

Expert witness—Corn breeder: What is a hybrid? How do corn breeders make them? Why was T-cytoplasm used?

Internet search terms: USDA timeline corn hybrid, detasseling hybrid production, hybrid corn production

Advantages of T-cytoplasm:
- Avoids the substantial cost of detasseling, whether manual or mechanical.
  - Manual, summer detasseling crew costs: finding, training, paying, and supervising detasselers. (At the peak, more than 125,000 people/day detasseled corn in hybrid production fields in the United States!)
  - Mechanical costs: machinery, maintenance, and operational costs.
- Greater precision because human error can lead to missed tassels and contamination.
- Works even during poor weather conditions when detasseling is not effective.

These cost savings could be passed along to the farmer, through the cost of seed.

In 1970, at least 80% of the United States corn crop contained T-cytoplasm.

Expert witness—Seed store manager: Describe varieties available. How many of them had T-cytoplasm in 1970? What percentage of the corn area in the United States was planted with T-cytoplasm?

In 1970, more than 80% of the United States corn crop had T-cytoplasm. Nearly all commercial varieties had T-cytoplasm. In fact, the problem even extended beyond the United States.

No one knew it before 1970, but SCLB could enter the corn seed, not just the corn plant. This raised worries that the blight was being exported to other countries in seed exports. In 1971, SCLB was reported in Latin America, Africa, Japan, and the Philippines. At the time the United States was exporting 46.8 million pounds of seed, worth about $5 million a year. But no one could prove whether or not the blight was being exported, since no one was checking the seed. By the time people knew to check seed, the problem (presence of the tcms gene in seeds) had largely been eliminated.

Prices for corn seed jumped because of the blight. Seed without the tcms gene was scarce and therefore more expensive. In 1969, the U.S. price for hybrid corn seed was $13.70/bushel. By 1974, the price was $25.00/bushel. (Part of the increase was caused by high inflation rates in the United States.)

Expert witness—Trader in corn futures: Describe how corn is traded and what corn futures are. Describe the effect of SCLB epidemic on corn futures.

Blight developed in the high corn production areas of the Midwest in July and August 1970. People began to fear that the harvest plus our national reserves would not be adequate to meet demand. (Did you know that we keep national reserves of important commodities like corn and oil that we might need in an emergency?)

Stocks from previous years: 999 million bushels. The 1970 crop fell 700–800 million bushels short of expectation, and therefore, prices rose. High corn prices spilled over into other grains, like sorghum, barley, oats, and wheat, which could be used instead of corn as animal feed.

News stories about the spread of the disease began to scare investors. The price of "corn futures" on the Chicago Board of Trade began to rise steeply. Corn futures are the price for a contract for a bushel of corn at the *future* harvest. People began to trade corn futures madly. Volumes of trade increased and so did prices. When the blight was confirmed to be in midwestern states, panic struck. At the peak, 193 million bushels of corn were traded in one day, topping a record that had stood for 122 years. The Dow Jones index for commodity futures had its highest one-day advance in 19 years. Prices of other grains and livestock soared as well. The blight boosted the price of corn 20% (increased $0.30 on a price of $1.50/ bushel).

Seed company president: What is the goal of a seed company? How is it accomplished?

Goal: to produce and sell high-quality seed at a reasonable price.

To do so, seed companies employ corn breeders, entomologists, agronomists, geneticists, pathologists, field workers, salespeople, and many others!

- Corn breeders: make crosses, design varieties, and invest years in developing varieties with new and/or improved traits.
- Entomologists: study insect interactions with the crops.
- Agronomists: study how to best manage the crop for high yield, high quality, and resistance to diseases.
- Geneticists: use the latest techniques to understand corn genetics. Which genes are involved in important traits like yield and disease resistance?
- Pathologists: study corn diseases and help look for new resistant genes.
- Field workers: plant, weed, water, harvest, and otherwise take care of the thousands of hectares of fields required to produce our hybrid seeds.

Producing a hybrid variety takes an average of eight years, large areas of land, and millions of dollars of investment. For example, seed companies start with 50,000 to 60,000 new experimental hybrids every year. They select the best 10% of the hybrids to continue working with each year. Of the 50,000 hybrids they start with, fewer than 10 will be released as commercial varieties. That's roughly 1 of every 5,000 hybrid varieties the companies try. All of that means seed companies make large investments in people, land, and time for every hybrid released.

Seed company corn breeder 1: No known problems with T-cytoplasm. No known vulnerabilities.

In 1965, to everyone's best knowledge, there were no disease-related differences between T-cytoplasm and regular cytoplasm corn varieties in the United States. Seed companies even tested T-cytoplasm varieties against known variants of SCLB, but they didn't test with Race T of the SCLB, because they didn't know about Race T.

By early 1970, someone had isolated, identified, and reported Race T. Reports in 1970, using data from the new strain of SCLB, warned of epidemic possibilities, but by then the epidemic was already underway. Simply put, seed companies were unaware of the problem in time to warn their customers. The seed sold in 1970 was produced in 1969 and parent stocks were produced in 1968.

Genetic sameness may mean vulnerability to disease. However, for years, breeding programs have been managing this vulnerability without major problems. To do this, they keep a steady stream of new varieties coming out, so no one genotype dominates the entire production area. There is always a new variety ready should an old one become susceptible to disease. Corn breeders all over the world are in contact with one another as they keep tabs on the disease problems and pressures in their area.

Historically, corn has been less susceptible to disease than other crops like wheat and oats. This is probably because it is out-crossing (meaning that a corn crosses with another corn plant, as opposed to crops like wheat and rice where a plant must pollinate itself) and it has a wealth of genetic diversity. However, hybrid varieties are not as diverse as "wild" corn and have some of the same problems as crops that do not out-cross.

Seed company corn breeder 2: Few if any people in the United States knew about the Philippine papers; those who knew discounted them.

Seed company scientists believed that the susceptibility to SCLB in the Philippine studies was caused by the tropical environment. The studies were small-scale and in a very different environment than the United States. Tropical areas have more problems with disease than the United States because warm temperatures incubate disease-causing agents, especially fungal ones like SCLB. Simply put, scientists didn't think problems in the Philippines would apply to the United States.

Tropical environments have no winter. Winter plays an important role in killing off pathogens. In non-tropical areas like the United States, to survive winter, pathogens end up synchronizing their life cycles. Therefore, pests in a place with winter, like the United States, are much easier to control, because they are all vulnerable at once. This is another reason scientists expected SCLB in the United States to be different from SCLB in the Philippines.

Expert witness—Pathologist: Race T of SCLB was virtually unknown before 1970.

The pathogen responsible for the epidemic of SCLB we call Race T, because it only caused disease on plants with T-cytoplasm. Race T was virtually unknown before the epidemic. Scientists were surprised and shaken at the strength of the outbreak. Presumably Race T existed, but at levels that were difficult to detect. Furthermore, there was no way to detect it without the plants on which its unique symptoms appear (T-cytoplasm plants). It's a circular problem—scientists couldn't see Race T until they had plants that were susceptible to it. But until they had plants that were susceptible, they didn't even know Race T existed.

Before this case, there was no evidence of susceptibility to disease being caused by cytoplasmic genes. Understanding of the genetic basis for resistance and susceptibility to disease was based on genes in the nucleus. Immediately after 1970, a great deal of research was launched to better understand cytoplasmic genetics and inheritance.

Rapid reproduction rates of pathogens mean their population can grow fast when conditions (environment and genetics of the host plant, like corn) are favorable. This can happen with little or no warning signs beforehand.

Seed company executive: Reaction to the problem. Eliminate T-cytoplasm from seed stocks at tremendous cost to the companies.

By 1970, when the epidemic began, seed companies understood that the problem was caused by T-cytoplasm. At the time, most seed was grown during the summer in the Midwest. In 1970, seed production had already begun to shift away from heavy reliance on T-cytoplasm and back to manual detasseling. Seed produced in the traditional way, by detasseling, is resistant to the T race of SCLB. In the winter of 1970/1971 (after the epidemic), seed companies had plantings everywhere they possibly could, including Florida, Hawaii, Argentina, and Mexico. Their goal was to increase non-T-cytoplasm seed stocks so there would be enough non-T-cytoplasm seed for the 1971 planting. (These plantings were very expensive, especially because of the short notice.) In some cases, 1971 seed was 20–30% lower yielding than 1970 seed. However, the lower yield was preferable to the risk from seed that resulted in a 50% loss from some fields.

In 1971, there was only enough non-T-cytoplasm seed to plant 23% of the nation's corn crop. Most of that seed went to the South, where disease pressures were most intense and damage had been most severe. The idea was to create a buffer zone to block progression of the disease north. Seed companies also sold mixtures of 50% susceptible and 50% resistant seed. Some farmers complained damage was still high in their fields.

In 1971, much of the United States was planted to susceptible varieties of corn, and the infestation of SCLB was light. The weather helped the situation—1971, unlike 1970, had a cool, dry spring and somewhat drier summer conditions. There were some local outbreaks, but overall, the national crop had only minimal losses in 1971. By 1972, susceptible seed had been eliminated from the system and detasseling was back in style!

Certainly farmers, scientists, and seed companies learned their lesson. Look back at Figure 5.3. In 1970, more than 70% of the corn-growing area in the United States was planted with only six corn varieties. By 1980, the area planted with the top six varieties had decreased to 43%—meaning that farmers were planting far more varieties. And those six varieties didn't share a gene for cytoplasmic male sterility!

Part IV. Optional extra role and material

Optional extra expert witness for the prosecution—Geneticist: Details of how T-cytoplasm works.

How does this work? The cytoplasmic gene has two alleles: male sterile (MS) or normal (N) (Figure 5.6). All plants with N cytoplasm will always be "male fertile," meaning they make viable (normal) pollen. If a plant has N cytoplasm, it doesn't matter what fertility restoring genes it has in the nucleus (Rf genes), it will always make normal pollen.

Plants with MS cytoplasm can either have normal (male fertile) or sterile pollen. Male sterile plants, those where fertility is "switched off," must also have two recessive alleles of the nuclear gene rf. If a plant with male sterile cytoplasm has even one of the dominant fertility restoring nuclear alleles, Rf, then it too will be able to produce pollen.

Figure 5.6. Interactions of genes in cytoplasm and nucleus to produce male sterility.

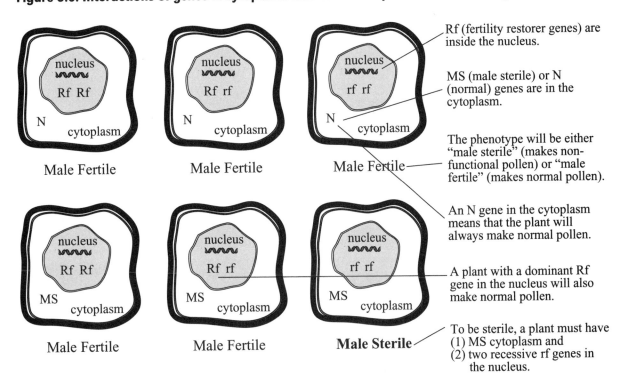

Rf (fertility restorer genes) are inside the nucleus.

MS (male sterile) or N (normal) genes are in the cytoplasm.

The phenotype will be either "male sterile" (makes nonfunctional pollen) or "male fertile" (makes normal pollen).

An N gene in the cytoplasm means that the plant will always make normal pollen.

A plant with a dominant Rf gene in the nucleus will also make normal pollen.

To be sterile, a plant must have (1) MS cytoplasm and (2) two recessive rf genes in the nucleus.

GENETIC ENGINEERING

Do you eat genetically engineered foods? Though you might not know it, the answer is probably yes. Recent studies estimated that about 60% of food products in grocery stores in the United States contain ingredients from genetically engineered plants. How is that possible? Are all the plants we eat genetically engineered?

Interestingly enough, genetically engineered varieties of only 12 crops have been approved for commercial production. The three most important of those plants—corn, soybean, and canola—account for almost all of the genetically engineered food we eat. Genetically engineered foods aren't labeled in the United States, so how do you know whether or not you're eating them?

As a rule of thumb, anytime you're eating something that contains corn, soy, or canola, you can assume that some of it is genetically engineered. The systems for moving crops from farmers to processing plants do not keep genetically engineered crops separate from non-genetically engineered crops—so anything containing corn can be assumed to have some genetically engineered corn in it. However, very little sweet corn (only 3–5%) is genetically engineered, and there are no genetically engineered popcorns on the market. The box on page 110 shows a partial list of products that are made from corn and soy.

Focus on genetically engineered corn

Since genetically engineered corn was introduced in 1996, farmers have been planting more and more of it. Figure 6.2 shows that in 2003, 40% of the corn area in the United States had genetically engineered varieties.

Why do farmers plant genetically engineered varieties? They have to pay quite a lot for the seed, so there must be a reason they want it. Most of the genetically engineered corn in the United States and other countries has one of two characteristics to address one of two problems: The varieties are either **herbicide resistant** to combat weeds or they contain **Bt genes** to combat some insect predators.

Herbicide resistance involves inserting a gene that makes plants immune to herbicide.

Bt genes make bacterial proteins that are toxic to many insect predators.

SCi*L*INKS.
THE WORLD'S A CLICK AWAY

Topic: Genetic Engineering
Go to: *www.sciLINKS.org*
Code: GG19

PRODUCTS MADE FROM CORN AND SOY

Where do you find corn and soy products? Nearly everywhere! And in many places you might not suspect. The following list contains some (not all) of the products made from corn, soy, or both. Corn and soy are the source of many of the unpronounceable ingredients in your food!

ascorbate (vitamin C)	aspartame	beta-carotene (vitamin A)	caramel
carotenoids	cellulose	cobalamin (vitamin B12)	corn flour
corn masa	corn meal	corn oil	corn starch
corn syrup	cystein	dextrin	dextrose
fructose	glucose	glutamate	gluten
hemicellulose	high fructose corn syrup	inositol	invert sugars
lactoflavin	lactose	lecithin	leucine
lysine	maltose	methionine	modified starch
mono- and diglycerides	monosodium glutamate (MSG)	niacin	phenylalanine
riboflavin (vitamin B2)	sorbitol	soy flour	soy isoflavones
soy isolate	soy lecithin	soy oil	soy protein (vitamin E)
textured vegetable protein (TVP)	threonine	tocopherol	tryptophan
vanilla extract (contains corn syrup)	vegetable oil	xanthan gum	zein

FIGURE 6.1. LABEL WITH CORN AND SOY PRODUCTS.

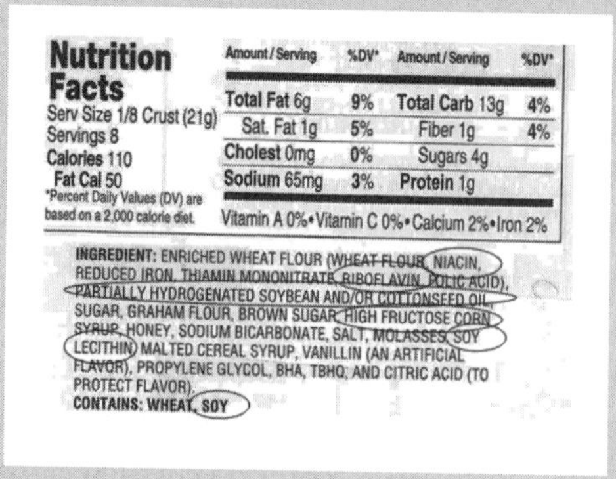

Nutrition Facts
Serv Size 1/8 Crust (21g)
Servings 8
Calories 110
Fat Cal 50
*Percent Daily Values (DV) are based on a 2,000 calorie diet.

Amount / Serving	%DV*	Amount / Serving	%DV*
Total Fat 6g	9%	Total Carb 13g	4%
Sat. Fat 1g	5%	Fiber 1g	4%
Cholest 0mg	0%	Sugars 4g	
Sodium 65mg	3%	Protein 1g	

Vitamin A 0%•Vitamin C 0%•Calcium 2%•Iron 2%

INGREDIENT: ENRICHED WHEAT FLOUR (WHEAT FLOUR, NIACIN, REDUCED IRON, THIAMIN MONONITRATE, RIBOFLAVIN, FOLIC ACID), PARTIALLY HYDROGENATED SOYBEAN AND/OR COTTONSEED OIL, SUGAR, GRAHAM FLOUR, BROWN SUGAR, HIGH FRUCTOSE CORN SYRUP, HONEY, SODIUM BICARBONATE, SALT, MOLASSES, SOY (LECITHIN) MALTED CEREAL SYRUP, VANILLIN (AN ARTIFICIAL FLAVOR), PROPYLENE GLYCOL, BHA, TBHQ; AND CITRIC ACID (TO PROTECT FLAVOR).
CONTAINS: WHEAT, SOY

Figure 6.2. Percent of U.S. corn area planted with genetically engineered corn varieties. (The dip in 2000 was due to the rejection of genetically engineered foods by the European countries. Farmers feared they would not be able to sell their genetically engineered crops.)

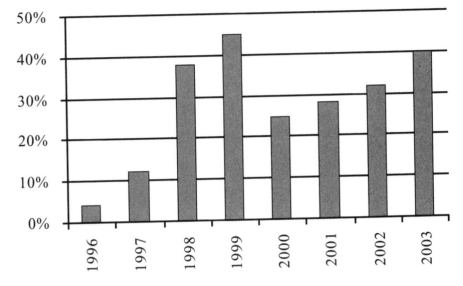

In herbicide-resistant corn, a gene is inserted that makes corn immune to the effects of herbicides like Roundup. A farmer can spray an herbicide-resistant field and know she'll kill all the weeds in her fields, but she won't kill her crop. This means less work for the farmer.

Insect protection: A plant that makes its own pesticide?

Bt genes come from a common type of soil bacteria called *Bacillus thuringiensis*. The bacteria produce a protein toxic to insects. The protein ingested by insects is actually harmless, but it is quickly cut by an enzyme in their guts to a smaller, deadly form. The small pieces bind to receptors in the insect digestive system. These bound proteins disrupt the insect's digestive system, ultimately killing it. There are many different Bt toxins that exist in nature, and each affects a different group of insects. The Bt genes commonly used in genetically engineered crops today affect moths, butterflies, beetles, and their larvae. For many years, organic farmers have used bacteria that produce the Bt protein as an organic insecticide to protect their crops.

A plant engineered to express Bt genes often produces the toxin, in essence a pesticide, in all its tissues—leaves, stems, roots, grain, and pollen. That means that the chances are high that humans are eating the pesticide. However, the toxin is not considered to be harmful to humans because our digestive systems lack the toxin receptors that insects have. Furthermore, the Bt protein is quickly broken down to harmless components in *our* digestive systems.

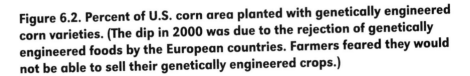

Topic: Biological Pests
Go to: *www.sciLINKS.org*
Code: GG20

**Topic: Biological
Pest Control
Code: GG21**

Bacteria genes in a corn plant?

The **DNA** of all organisms is made up of the same bases (A, C, G, and T), whether it comes from bacteria, fish, or corn plants. Therefore, a segment of DNA from bacteria, if inserted properly into a corn plant, will lead to production of the same proteins it encoded in bacteria.

By carefully choosing and carefully inserting the gene from the bacteria that encoded the Bt toxin, scientists were able to "engineer" a plant that produced a bacterial toxin. Genetic engineering is time-consuming and expensive but many seed companies and farmers think it is worth the costs. Many plant breeders see genetic engineering as simply another tool for creating new and improved crop varieties.

Unintended consequences?

What happens when the pollen from the genetically engineered corn plant blows in the wind? The pollen has the Bt toxin (though recent varieties have much less of the toxin than early Bt corn varieties had). At pollination time, corn pollen is everywhere—the puddles around cornfields have a yellow pollen layer on top of them, and so does everything else. What happens to something like the larvae of the monarch butterfly? In some places, monarch larvae are looking for milkweed to eat at the time that corn plants are producing all that pollen. The pollen is deposited on milkweed too. The larvae only feed on milkweed, but if there's corn pollen on it, they'll eat the pollen as well (Figure 6.3).

Studies in 1999 showed that Bt pollen can be toxic to monarch butterfly larvae. This came as a terrible surprise to some people who argued that Bt genes would not have impacts beyond the cornfield.

Further studies published in 2001 concluded that most tested Bt corn varieties didn't cause problems for monarch butterfly larvae. Rain quickly washes pollen off milkweed leaves. In many places the time when the monarch larvae are eating milkweed does not overlap with the time when corn pollen is being dispersed. Bt genes from genetically engineered corn seem to have far smaller impacts on monarch larvae than a single application of pesticide to the same field. On the other hand, field corn is not often sprayed for the pests that Bt corn varieties control, because the pests eat their way into the center of the corn stalk where pesticides do not penetrate well.

Regardless of the conclusions about Bt effects on monarch larvae, the studies raise the important issue of unintended consequences of genetically engineered plants. No new technology is without risks. And people are concerned that the risks of genetically engineered plants could be high.

DNA (deoxyribonucleic acid) is the double-stranded series of bases (A, C, G, and T) that compose genes and encode proteins.

Figure 6.3. Monarch butterfly larvae eating corn pollen on a milkweed plant.

Who is in charge?

In the United States, a number of government agencies regulate food, plants, pesticides, and agriculture. The Food and Drug Administration (FDA) regulates food. The Environmental Protection Agency (EPA) regulates pesticides. The U.S. Department of Agriculture (USDA) regulates agriculture. Who regulates a plant that makes its own pesticide? Is it a plant? Is it a pesticide? Who decides if the food from it is safe? You will find your own answers to these questions in the activity that follows.

Genetically engineered crops cross boundaries that traditional crops do not. Thus, these crops pose new and challenging regulatory issues.

Question for further thought

Ecology: For years, organic farmers have used organic pesticides containing Bt bacteria. "Organic" in this case means pesticides that occur in nature and are not created from chemicals. How might the widespread use of genetically engineered Bt crops impact the effectiveness of these organic Bt bacteria pesticides? Think about ecology and resistance.

Activity 6.

*Congressional Hearing on Genetic Engineering**

Objective

Hold a Congressional hearing to determine whether or not genetic engineering of food plants should be banned.

Activity

Part I. Congressional hearing

A Congressional hearing is one of the ways lawmakers seek information to help inform the laws they make. A series of experts are called to give their opinions about a list of subjects the Congressional committee wants to learn about.

In this case, you will be the experts called before Congress. Each of you will be responsible for learning about a certain aspect of genetic engineering and then presenting your findings. As an expert, you're not necessarily arguing for or against genetic engineering. Your job is to present balanced information as accurately as you can.

When you are called to speak in front of "Congress" you will have four minutes. Be sure your information is organized and concise. Please use visual aids (pictures, graphs, tables) whenever possible.

The class (with you as a part of it) will also serve as Congress. At the end of the hearing, you will be asked to submit your informed opinion in the form of a paper.

SCI LINKS.
THE WORLD'S A CLICK AWAY

Topic: Food Safety
Go to: *www.sciLINKS.org*
Code: GG22

---

* This activity was created in collaboration with Nicole Bernati at Ithaca High School.

Part II. Roles

Person	Topic	Resources
Organizational Unit: Background		
	What are the GE foods on the market?	http://geo-pie.cornell.edu/crops/eating.html
	In what food products do corn and soy appear? What percentage of corn and soy products is genetically engineered?	http://geo-pie.cornell.edu/crops/ingredients.html http://geo-pie.cornell.edu/crops/soybeans.html http://geo-pie.cornell.edu/crops/corn.html
	What are the GE crops NOT in the marketplace?	http://geo-pie.cornell.edu/crops/eating.html#eating http://geo-pie.cornell.edu/traits/traits.html
	Please explain why many people see GE as an extension of plant breeding. What is the major difference between traditional plant breeding and GE?	http://beyonddiscovery.org/content/view.page.asp?I=171 http://beyonddiscovery.org/content/view.page.asp?I=187
	How are genetically engineered foods labeled? How are GE foods labeled in other countries?	http://geo-pie.cornell.edu/issues/labeling.html http://geo-pie.cornell.edu/regulation/FDA.html#labeling http://geo-pie.cornell.edu/issues/intllabeling.html http://geo-pie.cornell.edu/issues/ANZlabels.html
Organizational Unit: Regulation and Distribution		
	Does our food distribution system have a way to keep GE separate from non-GE foods? (Starlink case study.)	http://geo-pie.cornell.edu/issues/starlink.html
	What is the FDA? What is the role of the FDA in regulating GE foods and crops? Are there differences in GE requirements for human food versus animal feed?	http://geo-pie.cornell.edu/regulation/reg.html http://geo-pie.cornell.edu/regulation/FDA.html http://vm.cfsan.fda.gov/%7Elrd/biocon.html
	What is the EPA? What is the role of the EPA in regulating GE foods and crops? Who regulates a plant that produces its own pesticide? Is it a plant or a pesticide? Which agencies are responsible for regulating each?	http://geo-pie.cornell.edu/regulation/reg.html http://geo-pie.cornell.edu/regulation/EPA.html
	What is the USDA? What is the role of the USDA in regulating GE foods and crops?	http://geo-pie.cornell.edu/regulation/reg.html http://geo-pie.cornell.edu/regulation/APHIS.html
Organizational Unit: Potential Risks		
	What is "horizontal gene transfer"? What are the risks it poses? How can it be controlled? Does GE increase the chances that a crop may "escape" the field and become a weed? How likely is it? What are the risks associated with "weedy" crops?	http://geo-pie.cornell.edu/issues/hgt.html http://geo-pie.cornell.edu/issues/pollenbio.html http://geo-pie.cornell.edu/issues/gmofree.html http://geo-pie.cornell.edu/issues/triple.html http://geo-pie.cornell.edu/issues/weeds.html

	What are the risks of GE foods to people with food allergies? Who regulates and tests for allergic food qualities? Are these tests stringent and effective?	*http://geo-pie.cornell.edu/issues/allergy.html* *http://geo-pie.cornell.edu/issues/brazilnut.html* *http://geo-pie.cornell.edu/issues/convallergy.html*
	What are the risks of GE plants producing toxic substances? Do conventional crops have toxins in them? Please describe.	*http://geo-pie.cornell.edu/issues/toxins.html* *http://geo-pie.cornell.edu/issues/convtoxins.html* *http://geo-pie.cornell.edu/issues/pusztai.html*
	What are some of the potential risks from antibiotic resistance? What methods are available to deal with these risks?	*http://geo-pie.cornell.edu/issues/antibiotic.html*
	What are the potential effects of GE on non-target insects? Have any cases been documented?	*http://geo-pie.cornell.edu/issues/monarchs.html*
	Has enough research about GE foods been done? Has the research asked the right questions?	*http://geo-pie.cornell.edu/issues/science121500.html*

Organizational Unit: Current and Potential Benefits

	What are the current benefits of GE use of Bt genes? What are the potential problems in terms of evolution of insect resistance to over-used pesticides like Bt? How does the use of GE Bt impact organic farmers who have used Bt on their crops for many years?	*http://geo-pie.cornell.edu/traits/traits.html* *http://geo-pie.cornell.edu/traits/bt.html*
	What is herbicide resistance? What are the current benefits from GE use of herbicide resistance?	*http://geo-pie.cornell.edu/traits/traits.html* *http://geo-pie.cornell.edu/traits/herbres.html*
	What are the current and potential benefits of GE in reducing pesticide use? Please give an example where GE has reduced pesticide use, and another example where GE is associated with increased pesticide use.	*http://geo-pie.cornell.edu/issues/pesticide.html* *http://geo-pie.cornell.edu/issues/pestnum.html* *http://geo-pie.cornell.edu/issues/glyphosate.html*
	What are the potential benefits of GE in terms of resistance to viral diseases that have no other cure? Please give an example.	*http://geo-pie.cornell.edu/traits/virusres.html*
	How can GE alter plant nutritional qualities? What is altered oil content? What are the current benefits from GE use of altered oil content?	*http://geo-pie.cornell.edu/crops/rice.html* *http://geo-pie.cornell.edu/crops/canola.html* *http://geo-pie.cornell.edu/traits/altoil.html*
	How can GE eliminate chemicals known to be harmful? Describe the case of nicotine-free cigarettes.	*http://geo-pie.cornell.edu/crops/tobacco.html*
	What are the potential benefits in solving problems like plant growth in drought or salt conditions? Please give an example.	*http://advance.uconn.edu/2001/011119/01111912.htm*
	What are the potential benefits of GE in terms of plant-based vaccines? Please describe an example.	*www.nature.com/nsu/020715/020715-16.html*

Part III. Notes

Use this form to take notes on the arguments presented about various topics. You will use this information to write your paper, so your notes are important!

Person	Topic	Arguments
Organizational Unit: Background		

Organizational Unit: Regulation and Distribution

Organizational Unit: Potential Risks

Organizational Unit: Current and Potential Benefits

Part IV. Opinion paper

At the end of the hearing, you will be asked to submit your informed opinion as a member of Congress about genetic engineering, in the form of a paper.

The paper will be 2–3 pages long, double spaced, and will present what you think are the two strongest arguments for genetic engineering and the two strongest arguments against genetic engineering. The paper will conclude with your opinion about whether or not genetic engineering of food plants should be banned. Make sure your opinion is well supported by arguments. Be sure you take notes during the hearing so you will remember the information you have heard.

SWEET GENES IN CORN

One of the joys of summer is sweet, fresh, crisp corn on the cob. Little did you know, this corn contains a puzzle. Most corn is starchy—just think of tortilla chips, which are made of corn. Usually, corn doesn't taste sweet. In fact, more than 75% of the weight of a kernel of popcorn is starch. Why isn't corn on the cob starchy? What makes sweet corn sweet?

Leaves: A sugar factory

In all plants, sugar comes from **photosynthesis**. The leaves of a plant are like a factory for capturing the energy of the Sun and converting it into sugar. Plants make the sugar **glucose** ($C_6H_{12}O_6$) using carbon dioxide (CO_2) from the air, water (H_2O) from the soil, and energy from the Sun. The Sun's energy is captured by light-absorbing chloroplasts inside the plant's cells. Through a variety of chemical reactions, the captured energy ends up stored in the bonds between the atoms of the sugar glucose.

Inside a cell, sugar can be changed into a variety of forms. All sugars have a similar chemical structure. They are made up of rings of carbon atoms. Changes between different types of sugars are simply a matter of joining and separating carbon rings. For example, corn makes the sugar glucose. A corn plant also contains **fructose**, a different type of simple sugar often found in fruits and juices. The corn plant transports sugar in the form of **sucrose** from the leaves where it is produced to the other plant parts. Sucrose, also known as table sugar, is made up of one glucose molecule plus one fructose molecule. **Enzymes** are the agents within the cell that convert one carbohydrate form into another by connecting or disconnecting the sugar groups.

Starches are long chains of sugars. The sugar chains can be straight or branched (see Figure 7.1). Starches are assembled from sugars by enzymes that join sugar groups together. Starches can easily be broken back into sugars by a different set of enzymes. Together, the sugars and

Photosynthesis is the process of taking the Sun's energy, in combination with water and carbon dioxide from the air, to make sugars, oxygen, and water.

Topic: Photosynthesis
Go to: **www.sciLINKS.org**
Code: GG23

Carbohydrates are sugars and starches made up of carbon, hydrogen, and oxygen. Carbohydrates are converted from one form to another by **enzymes**. **Glucose**, **fructose**, and **sucrose** are all sugars.

starches are called **carbohydrates**. (The name comes from the fact that they are a combination of carbon, hydrogen, and oxygen.) The starch in a corn kernel is roughly 75% amylopectin and about 25% amylose.

Figure 7.1. Common carbohydrate forms within plant cells.

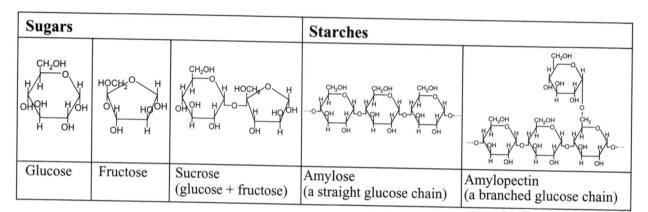

Sugars			Starches	
Glucose	Fructose	Sucrose (glucose + fructose)	Amylose (a straight glucose chain)	Amylopectin (a branched glucose chain)

The sugar shuffle

Why does the plant need all these different forms of carbohydrates? It seems more complicated than necessary. The plant's basic job is to reproduce itself. The seed is its way of doing so. In essence, the seed is the plant's "lifeboat." The plant puts all the resources necessary for survival into this lifeboat and then casts it loose. The most essential thing the plant puts into the lifeboat is enough food to nourish the seedling until it can produce its own food. That food is carbohydrate. So for many plants, the point of photosynthesis is to load carbohydrate into the seed.

Why not just send sugar to the seed? Sugar is water soluble. When you put a spoonful of sugar (sucrose) into water, it dissolves. So moving sugar around the plant is not much more difficult than moving water. In fact, sugar (sucrose) is the form of carbohydrate that is most easily transported in the plant. Sugar moves out of the leaf, where it is highly concentrated, by **diffusion**. The sugar moves down a **concentration gradient** from an area of high sugar concentration to an area of lower sugar concentration.

After diffusion, the sugar concentration would be the same inside and outside the seed, and the sugar solution would stop moving. Therefore, no more sugar would enter the seed. How then do seeds manage to capture sugars at concentrations greater than in other parts of the plant? (Remember, loading that seed "lifeboat" up with carbohydrate is critically important to the survival of the next generation!)

The corn plant has two solutions to the problem of building up sugar in its seeds. First, the corn plant can *actively* pump sugar out of the leaf and into the seed using **ATP energy**. Second, the seed is full of

The movement of molecules of a substance down a **concentration gradient** (from an area of high concentration to an area of lower concentration) is called **diffusion**.

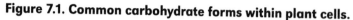

SciLINKS.
THE WORLD'S A CLICK AWAY

Topic: Diffusion
Go to: *www.sciLINKS.org*
Code: GG24

an enzyme, called starch synthase, which turns sugar into starch. Thus, the plant can pack the seed full of sugar, which in turn is transformed into starch. In starchy corn, starch synthase converts sugars into starch, and the plant can keep packing carbohydrate into the "lifeboat."

A sweet treat

All of that explains why a corn kernel is starchy. Why then is sweet corn sweet? Sweet corn is not the same *genetically* as starchy field corn. Sweet corn contains a gene, called su1 (for "sugary"), that blocks the conversion of sugar to starch in the kernel. The su1 gene encodes a defective copy of the enzyme needed to convert sugar into starch. Therefore at the immature, corn-on-the-cob stage, sweet corn's kernels are full of sugar and water—creating the sweet taste of summer corn. However, if that same sweet kernel is left to reach full maturity, it dries and shrivels up. Sweet corn seeds become shriveled because they have very low starch reserves to fill the endosperm in the center of the seed (see Figure 7.2). Without the water that fills the kernel at the corn-on-the-cob stage, the sugars have very little bulk to fill the seed.

ATP is the **energy** that organisms use to fuel life processes. An **active** process requires energy. A **passive** process (like diffusion) does not require energy.

Figure 7.2. Kernel profiles of starchy and sweet corn.

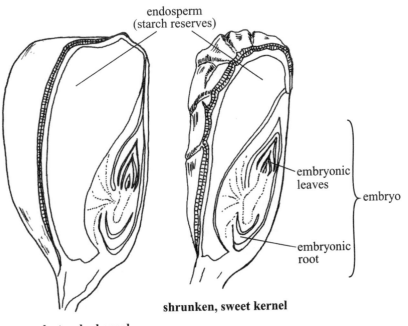

The sweet mutation was first described in 1901, and was one of the first mutations in corn to be officially described. Since then, plant breeders and farmers have been breeding it into their sweet corn varieties, which are eaten fresh, canned, or frozen. For years, sweet corn was a local crop—people ate it in areas very close to where it was grown. It had to be eaten quickly before the ears lost their sweetness. The ears lose their sweetness because sugars in the kernel are slowly converted into starch after the ears are picked. In the 1950s, sweet corn breeders began looking for a different genetic system that would hold its sweetness longer. They turned their attention to a different gene, called sh2 ("shrunken" because of its shriveled appearance).

Corn breeders had known about sh2 for a long time. They knew it produced even sweeter corn than the su1 gene. However, they considered it impractical for making sweet corn varieties because sh2 seed had terrible problems. It was so shrunken and shriveled that the plants could barely get started. Remember that the amount of carbohydrate in the seed lifeboat plays an important biological role. Plants grown from the sh2 gene grew slowly and had problems with mold and disease. Basically, the sh2 gene left its seed with so few reserves that it couldn't produce plants with good ears of corn.

The sweet corn breeders, however, were persistent. For years, they worked with the natural variation in other genes and eventually selected plants with the sh2 gene that could also compete and produce good ears. These varieties are now sold under the names " super-sweet" and "x-tra sweet." Because these varieties are sweeter, and the sugars last longer, farmers in Florida and California can now produce sweet corn that can be transported long distances. So if you see sweet corn in the grocery story in New York in February, you can bet that it has the sh2 gene and that it has had a long journey!

sci LINKS.
THE WORLD'S A CLICK AWAY

Topic: Biochemical Processes
Go to: www.sciLINKS.org
Code: GG25

XENIA—POLLEN PAINTING

When you read the planting instructions for sweet corn, they recommend you plant it more than 150 m from other corn. Why?

Corn has an interesting phenomenon called **xenia** (pronounced "zeen-eeya"). The pollen "paints" the seed with the pollen plant's characteristics. Seed from white corn pollinated by blue corn will be blue. Seed from sweet corn pollinated by starchy corn will be starchy.

How does it work? Before fertilization, the endosperm of what will become the seed has two sets of chromosomes from the female parent (2n). Once the kernel is fertilized, it gains a third set of chromosomes from the male parent (n): 2n + n = 3n. This means the endosperm has three sets of chromosomes. Therefore kernels reflect the male parent's genes too! And if the male parent is starchy, the sweet corn won't be as sweet.

The two sweet mutations occur at different genes. A sweet su1 variety has starchy alleles at the sh2 locus, and vice versa. Since they are both recessive genes, neighboring corn, even if it is sweet, might not have the same sweet recessive mutation. Therefore even sweet corn can make other sweet corn starchy.

How do su1 and sh2 work?

Both the sugary (su1) gene and the super-sweet gene (sh2) block steps in the same **biochemical pathway**. Biologists often talk about biochemical pathways as the "route" that one substance, like sugar, takes in order to become another substance, like starch. Each of the "steps" in the pathway, shown as an arrow in Figure 7.3, is really a chemical reaction controlled by a particular **enzyme**. A gene that blocks a step in the pathway is really a mutant, defective gene that leads to a dysfunctional version of the enzyme (see Chapter 2 for details). If a plant lacks the enzyme that executes a step in the pathway, the whole pathway is blocked.

Each step in the pathway converts one type of carbohydrate into another (shown in bold print). Each conversion is done by a different enzyme (shown as an arrow). The su1 and sh2 genes encode defective copies of enzymes needed to perform a conversion. Therefore, the plant accumulates glucose, instead of starch.

The plant transports sugar as sucrose. In the cells of the seed, the sucrose is first broken down to one form of glucose. A second enzyme that is defective in sh2 plants then converts the first form of glucose into a second form of glucose (Figure 7.3). The two glucoses have slightly different chemical structures. The second form of glucose is then chained together to make the starches amylose and amylopectin. (See Figure 7.1 to remind yourself how the glucose and starches look.) The su1 gene makes a defective copy of an enzyme that converts glucose into amylopectin. If a plant has the su1 gene, it will have glucose, and the starch amylose, but no amylopectin. Remember that in a normal kernel of corn, about 75% of the starch is amylopectin. This is why old-fashioned su1 sweet corn tastes sweet. But it is also why su1 sweet corn loses its sweetness over time. The sugars in su1 sweet corn are slowly converted into amylose. Sh2 sweet corn stays sweet longer because it can't make either amylose or amylopectin.

Amylose is a straight chain starch that plays a role in the firmness of cooked foods (Figure 7.1). Amylopectin is a branched glucose chain that has an important role in thickening starchy foods. Amylopectin is also important because it affects the ability of starchy foods to hold fat and protein molecules that lead to better texture and flavor. Tortillas made with higher levels of amylopectin are softer. Therefore neither sh2 nor su1 sweet corn would make very soft tortillas!

A **biochemical pathway** is a way to describe the series of chemical reactions required to convert one compound (like sucrose) into another compound (like starch). Each of the "steps," shown by arrows in Figure 7.3, is performed by a different **enzyme**.

Figure 7.3. Biochemical pathway for creation of starch from sugar (sucrose).

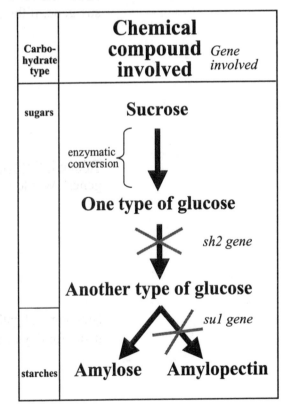

Questions for further thought

Experimental Design: Scientists have used the xenia effect to study how pollen moves in cornfields. Can you describe how they might do so? (Hint: They use blue corn and white corn. Blue is dominant over white.)

Evolution: What would happen to the su1 or sh2 gene in nature?

Genetic Diversity: Why do farmers keep growing sweet corn with the su1 gene, if the sh2 gene is sweeter?

Taking it further: Why don't varieties have BOTH the sh2 and the su1 genes? Wouldn't they be sweetest of all?

Biochemical pathways: Why does su1 sweet corn lose its sweetness if it sits for days without being eaten?

Activity 7.
Sweet Seeds

Objective

Design an experiment to test the effects of the su1 and sh2 genes on seed germination.

Background

Seeds contain all the material necessary to start the next generation off properly. The genetic material contains all the instructions the plant will need for growth. The endosperm has the nutrients the seed will need until it can begin producing its own food through photosynthesis. The seed coat protects the seed from bacteria, fungi, mold, and other threats.

What does a seed need to germinate or sprout? Primarily it needs water, air, and suitable temperatures. If the environment is too cold or too hot, the seed will not germinate. Temperature and water requirements help the seed to germinate under circumstances that give it a good chance of surviving. Germinating in the middle of winter, or under the Sun in the desert, would not give most seedlings a good chance to survive.

Does a seed require light? Most seeds germinate under the soil, in the dark, so light is not essential. Shortly after germinating, the part of the embryo that will become the root, called the radicle, grows down. The coleoptile, the part of the embryo that will become the leaves, grows up. Until the plant reaches the light and unrolls its first leaf, all the energy for the growing plant comes from the starch reserves in the endosperm (see Figure 7.4).

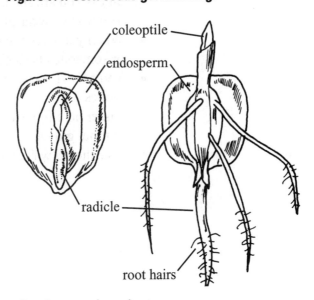

Figure 7.4. Corn seeds germinating.

coleoptile

endosperm

radicle

root hairs

Normally, corn is planted a few centimeters deep. For the seed to grow, the soil must be moist. Some varieties of corn planted by Native Americans in the southwestern United States grow more than 40 cm before they reach the light. The seeds are planted deep where the soil is moist. Just think of the amount of energy reserved in the endosperm that is required for the seedling to grow up to the soil surface!

What happens to sweet corn seeds with their shrunken, shriveled endosperms that lack sufficient reserves to get the seed started? You will design your own experiment to test the effects of the sweet genes on germination.

Materials
- Gloves
- 3 types of corn seeds: sh2, su, and starchy
- Paper towels
- Soil and containers
- Water source
- Dark location
- Ruler
- Scale (optional)

Safety Notes
- Many corn seeds are sold already treated with a fungicide to improve germination in cold soils. The fungicide is toxic. If your seed is pink, green, or blue, it has definitely been treated with fungicide. If your seed is not colored, assume that it has been treated unless you are specifically told otherwise.
- You MUST wear gloves when handling seeds.
- When you have the gloves on, do not touch your face, your skin, or someone else's skin.
- You MUST wash your hands immediately after taking off the gloves.
- Under no circumstances should you taste a seed, or touch a seed without gloves.
- You should wash your hands AGAIN after the activity.

Activity

Part I. Design your experiment

Sweet corn seeds have smaller amounts of starchy reserves to start seedlings. You will design your own experiment to see how much the different seeds will grow with the starch reserves they have.

1. Formulate a hypothesis about how corn seedlings from kernels with starch, sweet, and super-sweet genes will grow. A hypothesis is a possible explanation or an educated guess about what you will find. It is a starting point for your experiment.

2. How will you plan your experiment to investigate your hypothesis?

   2a. What do you plan to do?

   2b. What supplies will you need? How will you get any that are not already available in the classroom?

2c. How do you plan to schedule the project?

2d. How will you measure your results?

3. Evaluate your experiment.

    3a. Does your experiment test the effect of seed reserves on the seedling growth?

    3b. Does your experiment frame a clear question?

    3c. Does your hypothesis answer the clear question?

    3d. Is the proposed experiment feasible given the time and materials at hand?

    3e. What are your controls?

3f. Be sure you have considered the following review questions. Do you need to re-evaluate your experiment after answering these?

- Where does the energy for plant growth come from once the plant's leaves reach light?

- Where does the energy for plant growth come from BEFORE the plant reaches the light?

- Therefore, if you want to test the effects of the energy contained within seeds on seedling growth, what variable must you eliminate from your experiment?

Part II. Data and results

4. You need to document initial differences between the seed types. Do they have the same mass? Do they look the same?

Characteristic	Starchy corn	su1 gene corn	sh2 gene corn

5. Use this space to record your data.

6. Make a table here to summarize your data. Include calculations such as averages for length measurements.

7. Graph your data.

Part III. Conclusions

8. What conclusions can you reach? (What did you learn from your experiment? Was your hypothesis correct? Can you think of any other possible explanations for your results?)

9. Did you have any unexpected results? What were they and why do you think they happened?

10. How could you improve your experimental design? (Are there ways your experiment could be improved to better answer the initial question? Did you come up with questions you can't answer using your data?)

11. Based on what you know about seed reserves and sweet genes in corn, are there other questions you would like to investigate with the techniques you developed in this experiment?

Part IV. Applying what you've learned

12. What does your experiment tell you about the effect of sweet genes (compared with starchy genes) on germination?

13. Are there differences in germination ability between the su1 gene and the sh2 gene? If so, describe. If not, why do you think they don't differ?

14. What do you think would happen if sweet corn breeders tried to make a variety with both the su1 gene and the sh2 gene in it?

SECTION 3
Tomatoes

CHAPTER 8

CENTERS OF DIVERSITY

What country do you think of when you think about a tomato? For most people, Italy immediately springs to mind. Red pasta sauce, red pizza sauce— it's hard to imagine Italian food without the tomato. How long do you think the tomato has been in Italy, given how widespread it is in Italian cooking?

Interestingly, the tomato is a relative newcomer to Italy. Originally, the tomato came from the Americas. It didn't arrive in Europe until the 1500s. The Spanish explorers found it in Central America and brought seeds back to Spain. The tomato is first mentioned in print in Europe in 1544, roughly 50 years after Columbus set sail for the New World.

Even after the tomato arrived in Europe, it was regarded mostly as a curiosity. People grew the plants because they were novel and interesting to look at. It never occurred to people to *eat* the red fruits! (Botanically, the tomato is a fruit because it is the structure that contains the plant's seeds.) In fact, it seemed wise *not* to eat the tomato, since it is a member of the nightshade plant family, which includes many poisonous plants. It wasn't until 1692, 200 years after Columbus headed for the New World, that the tomato first appeared in a European cookbook. Even then, recipes called for sparing use, only for flavoring.

In the 1600s and 1700s, the Pilgrims bound for North America carried the tomato back to the New World. However, suspicions about it persisted. In 1820, Colonel Robert Gibbon Johnson decided to put an end to all the suspicion. He declared that he would eat an entire bushel of these "nonpoisonous" fruits. People came from far away to watch his death by poisoning. You can imagine how surprised they were when he lived! Within a few short years, the tomato became increasingly popular, appearing in gardens, seed catalogues, and foods throughout the New World.

It is surprising that we think of Italy when we think of tomatoes, given that Italians have only eaten tomatoes for about 300 years, while South Americans have grown and eaten tomatoes for thousands of years!

Figure 8.1. What country do you think is the origin of the tomato?

Geographic patterns

It's difficult to imagine how different the world must have been, even just 100 years ago. Transportation was time-consuming and difficult. People rarely traveled far from home. People's diet was limited to foods that grew locally and that were in season. An orange in the middle of winter was a rare luxury rather than a common occurrence.

Explorers have always recorded the plants they saw in journals and brought seeds home. But it wasn't until the early 1900s that botanists began systematically traveling around the world to collect edible plants. A Russian named Nikolai Vavilov was one of these collectors.

From 1916 to 1940, Vavilov made many trips around the world, collecting thousands of plants. He and his colleagues carefully catalogued and transported the plants to storage facilities in Russia.

Vavilov was interested in collecting plants from places with the most genetic diversity. He realized that crop plants exhibited amazing diversity in some regions, while other regions had very little diversity. From these observations, he came up with the theory of the **center of origin**. A center of origin is the place where a food plant was **domesticated** from its wild relatives. He concluded that a place like Peru, which has the highest diversity of tomatoes, was likely the site of domestication of the tomato. In other words, Vavilov proposed the idea that the center of origin for tomato is the same as its **center of diversity**.

Vavilov noticed that the same places had high diversity not just in one food plant, but in many different crops. For example, where he found many tomato varieties, he also found many potato varieties. Thus he concluded that there were a few of these centers of origin for all of agriculture—each of them giving rise to many food plants. He described seven centers: Central Asia (including China), South Asia (including India), the Middle East, the Mediterranean, Africa, Central America, and Andean South America. These were the places, he argued, where agriculture arose (Figure 8.2).

Changes to Vavilov's centers of origin ideas

Vavilov's ideas about agricultural centers of origin are still important today, and the basic concept is still accepted. However, detailed genetic and geographic studies have given us some important modifications of his theory.

Many crops, like wheat and barley, have a clear center of origin. However, others, like yam and cotton, do not. Yam appears to have been domesticated separately in Africa, Asia, and South America. Cotton seems to have been domesticated separately in Mexico, South America, Africa, and India.

Vavilov first suggested that the geographic center of diversity of a plant is also likely its center of origin.

Domestication is the change from a wild to a cultivated plant. A domesticated plant is dependent on humans for its survival.

Figure 8.2. Vavilov's proposed centers of origin.

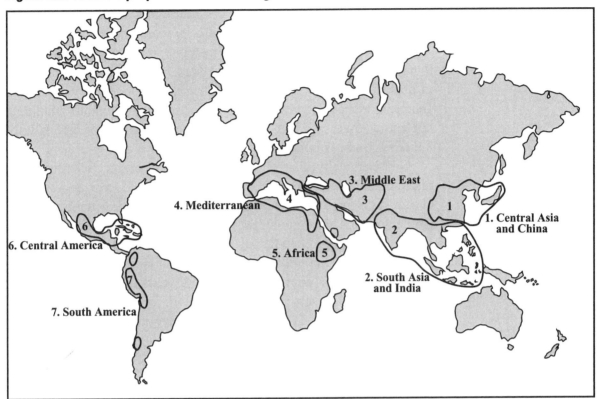

INTERSECTION OF SCIENCE AND POLITICS: NIKOLAI VAVILOV'S LIFE

In 1916, Vavilov began his worldwide plant collection trips. What happened in Russia in 1917? The Communist Revolution overthrew the tsar. This was the beginning of the Soviet Union.

Scientists faced a new, difficult political reality. Scientists were educated, elite people under the old regime. Under the communist government, educated, elite people often were put in work camps in Siberia to be "re-educated." Very few returned alive. However, scientists like Vavilov were in an unusual position. The Soviet Union needed their skills to increase crop yields in order to feed its people. Therefore, Vavilov was able to continue working on genetic diversity and crop breeding through the 1920s and 1930s.

However, by the late 1930s the political climate had changed. Science, like all other aspects of life in the Soviet Union, had become politicized. Genetics and heredity were rejected as "elitist." Vavilov became the object of a slander campaign by one of his former students, Trofim Lysenko.

In 1940, Vavilov was arrested, interrogated for 11 months, and eventually sentenced to death for political crimes. In 1943, he died in a Stalinist prison cell. Ironically, after devoting a life to plant breeding and fighting hunger, he died of malnutrition-related disease while in prison.

Other crops, like corn and tomato, have clear centers of origin and two (or more) centers of diversity. Centers of diversity can arise independently in the original center of origin and in a secondary site to which a crop was transported. For example, most people believe that tomatoes were domesticated in the Andes of South America, probably in present-day Peru. The Peru hypothesis is supported by fossil and genetic evidence. However, a very rich diversity of tomatoes is found in Central America. Thus, Central America is a center of diversity for tomatoes but not a center of origin.

Geographically, what constitutes a center of origin? Scientists have discovered that crops do not always come from the same area within a center of origin, such as the Andean region of South America. For example, tomatoes may come from the coastal areas near the base of the Peruvian Andes, while potatoes appear to come from higher altitudes within the Andes mountains. In this case, both potatoes and tomatoes are from the South American center of origin, though their source areas are not exactly the same.

The central idea of Vavilov's theory, that the center of origin of a crop is likely to be found at its center of diversity, remains the starting point for research on crop origins. In many cases, his theory holds true. In other cases, the center of origin is not in the same place as the center of diversity. Regardless, Vavilov's ideas give us an important starting point for understanding the geographic distribution of diversity.

Activity 8.
Where Does It Come From?

Objective
Use tables and graphs to understand the relationship between food plants and the biomes they originated in. Use tables and maps to understand the geographic origins of food plants.

Background
Plant centers of origin are related to the ecology of geographic regions. Which **biomes**, or environments with characteristic climates and communities of plants and animals, are most important for agriculture?

Some biomes are inhospitable for agriculture even today. The Arctic tundra is too cold and dry for farming. Reindeer were domesticated there by native people, and there is some forestry, but no farming. It would be an unlikely origin for agricultural plants.

A **biome** is an environment with a characteristic climate and biotic community of plants and animals.

Activity

Part I. Biomes and food plants
1. Table 8.1 shows which biomes contributed which of the most important foods consumed worldwide. Graph the food contributions that originated in each biome.

SCiLINKS.
THE WORLD'S A CLICK AWAY

Topic: Biomes
Go to: *www.sciLINKS.org*
Code: GG26

Table 8.1. Source biomes for common food plants (from FAOSTAT database and Harlan 1992). (MT= millions of metric tons, or megatons.)

Source Biome	Crop	2004 world production (MT)	Plant part consumed	Annual or perennial?
Costal areas				
	Tomato	108.5	fruit	annual
	Cabbage	62.5	leaves	annual
	Coconut	49.6	seed	perennial
	Sugar Beet	24.6	tuber	annual
Dry shrubland				
	Wheat	572.9	seed	annual
	Barley	132.2	seed	annual
	Canola	33.2	seed	annual
	Oat	25.5	seed	annual
	Rye	21.2	seed	annual
	Onion	51.9	bulb	annual
Prairie				
	Sunflower	23.9	seed	annual
				(continued on p. 126)

(continued from p. 125)

Source Biome	Crop	2004 world production (MT)	Plant part consumed	Annual or perennial?
Savanna				
	Maize	602.6	seed	annual
	Rice	576.3	seed	annual
	Cassava	184.9	tuber	perennial
	Sweet Potato	136.1	tuber	annual
	Watermelon	81.8	fruit	annual
	Sorghum	54.5	seed	annual
	Cottonseed Oil	53.7	seed	annual
	Yam	39.6	tuber	annual
	Peanut	34.1	seed	annual
	Millet	23.3	seed	annual
	Beans	18.3	seed	annual
	Triticale	11.0	seed	annual
Temperate forest				
	Soybean	179.9	seed	annual
	Grape	61.0	fruit	perennial
	Apple	57.1	fruit	perennial
Tropical mountains				
	Potato	307.4	tuber	annual
Tropical rain forest				
	Sugar Cane	142.9	stem	perennial
	Banana	69.8	fruit	perennial
	Orange	64.1	fruit	perennial
	Plantain	32.2	fruit	perennial
	Mango	25.8	fruit	perennial
	Coffee	7.4	seed	perennial
Total		3,898.9		

Graph the food contributions that originated in each biome in the box above.

2. Which two biomes are the origin for the largest quantity of food?

3. What do the climates of these two biomes have in common? (Use Table 8.2.)

Table 8.2. Climate descriptions of agricultural biomes.

Biome	Water availability	Temperature
Coastal areas	wet	varies
Dry shrubland	dry summer, wet winter	hot summer, cool winter
Prairie	dry summer, wet winter	hot summer, cold (below-freezing) winter
Savanna	wet season, dry season	always hot
Temperate forest	wet	cool season and warm season
Tropical mountains	wet	cold season and warm season
Tropical rain forest	very wet	always warm

4. Do any other biomes share these same features? If so, which?

5. How much of world food production comes from crops that originated in the biome(s) of question 4?

6. In what part of the year does plant growth occur in the biomes of questions 2 and 4? (Use Table 8.2 and think about both temperature and water. How well do plants grow when temperatures are below freezing? How well do plants grow when the climate is hot and dry?)

7. What relationship do you see between growing season and the number of plants each biome has contributed?

An **annual** plant completes its entire life cycle within one year. The life of a **perennial** plant lasts more than one year.

Water is critical for plant survival. In drought-prone biomes, many plants transfer energy into a seed, which can survive the drought inside its protective seed coat. The more energy the plant packages into the seed, the better the chance that the seed will germinate successfully the following season. Grains, such as wheat and corn, share this strategy. An **annual** plant is one that completes its entire life cycle—from seed to plant to seed again—within a year. Another successful drought strategy is to transfer all the plant's resources belowground to a tuber, root, or bulb. Potatoes, carrots, and onions share this "annual" strategy. Technically, potatoes and onions aren't annuals because the same plant can grow again from the tuber in the next wet season. However, from an agricultural perspective, they are annuals since they can be harvested and planted anew each year. Thus, the parts of these annual plants where sugars are stored so that plants survive from one year to the next—seeds, roots, and tubers—have high energy reserves and have become important sources of food for humans.

Perennial plants, like trees and shrubs, live much longer than one year. Some produce an annual crop of fruits or nuts that we harvest.

8. Table 8.1 shows whether agricultural plants are annual or perennial. Graph the amount of food produced by annual plants versus perennial plants in the box below.

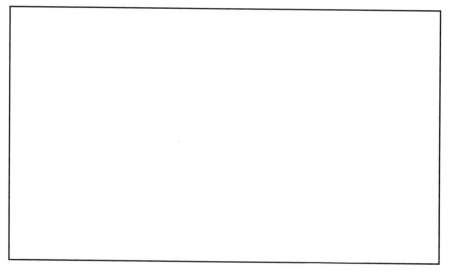

9. Which plant strategy is more important for agricultural production?

10. Which biomes have been the most important sources for annual plants? (Refer to Table 8.1.)

11. What important climate feature do these biomes share? (Refer to Table 8.2.)

12. Why is climate important for producing annual plants? (Think about how plants survive until the next generation.)

13. Which biomes have been the most important sources for perennial plants? (Refer to Table 8.1.)

14. What important climate feature do these biomes share? (Refer to Table 8.2.)

15. What part do we eat of the perennial plants from these biomes? (Refer to Table 8.1.)

Perennial plants typically do not face the biological challenge of severe drought. Therefore they can make a long-term investment in woody growth and can drop leaves to survive cold winters. The perennial plants' "problem" is dispersal. How does an apple tree move its seeds far from itself so the new seedlings don't compete with the parent tree and with each other? Many of the food plants from this biome have solved their dispersal problems in the same way. They focus their energy on making their fruits attractive to animals that might help in dispersal. Humans and other animals eat the fruits and help transport the seeds to new locations.

16. In conclusion, which biomes have been the most important source of agricultural food plants and why?

Part II. Centers of origin and food plants

17. Use Table 8.3 (p. 133) to fill in the geographic region of origin for the following food plants:

Food plant	Plant part consumed	Annual or perennial?	Source biome	Geographic center of origin
apple	fruit	perennial	temperate forest	
avocado	fruit	perennial	tropical rain forest	
bean	seed	annual	savanna	
beet	root	annual	coastal	
cabbage	leaves	annual	coastal	
carrot	root	annual	dry shrubland	
chocolate (cacao)	seed	perennial	tropical rain forest	
coffee	seed	perennial	tropical mountains	
corn	seed	annual	savanna	
cranberry	fruit	perennial	wetland	
okra	fruit	annual	savanna	
orange	fruit	perennial	tropical rain forest	
peach	fruit	perennial	woodland	
potato	tuber	annual	tropical mountains	
raspberry	fruit	perennial	temperate forest	
rice	seed	annual	savanna	
spinach	leaves	annual	unknown	
sugar cane	stem	perennial	tropical rain forest	
sunflower	seed	annual	grasslands	
tomato	fruit	annual	coastal	
vanilla	seed	perennial	tropical rain forest	
walnut	seed	perennial	temperate forest	
watermelon	fruit	annual	savanna	
wheat	seed	annual	dry shrubland	
yam	tuber	annual	savanna	

18. Give two examples of food origins that surprised you. Explain why.

19. Several of the food plants listed in Table 8.3 have more than one center of origin. Find five plants with multiple centers of origin.

Food plant	First area of geographic origin	Second area of geographic origin

20. What do you notice about the two centers of origin, geographically? (Are they isolated from one another? Close to one another?)

21. How can a plant have two centers of origin? Explain.

22. Map the crops of Table 8.3 onto Figure 8.3. Connect the crop pictures to their regions of origin and add the names of food plants from the table if they are not already pictured on the map.

Table 8.3. Geographic centers of origin for various food plants (From Harlan 1992).

| Geographic center of origin | Crop | | | | | | |
	Cereals	Legumes	Roots and tubers	Oil crops	Fruits and nuts	Vegetables and spices	Stimulants
Central America	corn	bean	sweet potato, cassava, jicama	cotton	papaya, guava, avocado, pineapple, prickly pear	pepper, squash, tomato, vanilla	cacao
North America			Jerusalem artichoke	sunflower	strawberry, raspberry, grape, cranberry, pecan		tobacco
South America		peanut, bean, lupine, inga, jack bean	arracacha, achira, yam, cassava, jicama, potato, oca, anu, ullucu	peanut, cotton	cashew, pineapple, guanábana, chirimoya, Brazil nut, papaya, guava avocado	pepper, squash, tomato	coca, mate
India, Indochina, Pacific Islands	Asian rice	pigeon pea, jack bean, winged bean, moth bean, rice bean	yam, arrowroot, taro	coconut	bread fruit, orange, lime, tangerine, grapefruit, mango, banana	cucumber, nutmeg, eggplant, plantain	
China	Asian rice, proso, foxtail millet	soybean, adzuki bean	turnip, yam	canola	chestnut, quince, persimmon, lychee, apricot, peach	Chinese cabbage, ginger	tea, ginseng, camphor
Africa	African rice, pearl millet, sorghum, teff, fonio	cowpea, hyacinth bean, groundnuts (Bambara, Kersting's)	yam	oil palm, castor bean	watermelon, melon, baobab	okra	coffee
Middle East	wheat, barley, rye, oat	pea, chickpea (garbanzo), lentil, lupine	turnip, carrot, radish, beet	canola, safflower, flax, olive	fig, hazelnut, walnut, pistachio, date palm, almond, grape, apple, pear, plum, melon	onion, leek, garlic, lettuce, saffron, parsley	poppy, digitalis, belladonna, licorice

Figure 8.3. Map of geographic origins of some food plants.

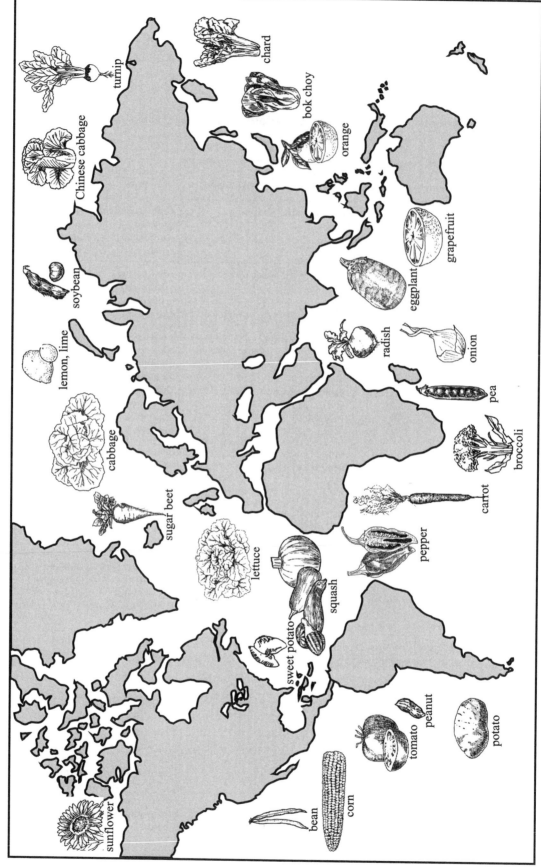

QUANTITATIVE TRAITS

Our world holds an astonishing array of diversity. Everyone knows about red tomatoes. Many people are also familiar with the orange and yellow tomato varieties. But few of us have seen the little known varieties that are green, purple-black, blue, and even white when they are ripe. Some tomatoes look like peaches, complete with fuzzy skin and peachy color. The sausage tomato is a long, red cylinder. The yellow pear variety is bite-sized and shaped like a pear. There are tomatoes named for peaches, pears, cherries, plums, and currants. Some have ridges like pumpkins. Others are perfectly smooth. Many of these varieties have been around for more than a century. Their seeds are sold as "heirloom" tomatoes. Gardeners all over the world grow them for their intriguing looks and novel flavors. Look at the different types of tomatoes to the right in Figure 9.1.

With all this variety in color, shape, and size, it's no wonder that these traits are controlled by more than one gene. Most of the traits that people care about in plants (like yield, color, and flavor) are complex. They are not controlled by a single gene, like Mendel's wrinkled peas or the bitterness gene in cucumbers. Instead, these complex traits are controlled by many genes, each having a small effect. Nowhere can you find a color gene that has red, orange, green, yellow, and purple alleles. Instead color is influenced by dozens of different genes, making dozens of proteins. Each of those proteins has a small effect on color.

Gene hunting

It's easy to understand why plant breeders would want to discover the genes involved in yield, fruit size, or flavor. People have been improving crops for these complex traits for centuries. Until recently, though, we did not have the right tools to isolate the effect of specific genes on a complex trait like yield.

Traditionally, to understand the behavior of traits and genes, plant breeders made crosses between mutant and normal **phenotypes** and

Figure 9.1. Diversity in tomato shape.

SCiLINKS.
THE WORLD'S A CLICK AWAY

Topic: Observing Traits Molecularly
Go to: *www.sciLINKS.org*
Code: GG27

A **phenotype** is the physical expression (often visible) of an individual's genes.

Figure 9.2. Crosses and behavior of single-gene and multiple-gene traits.

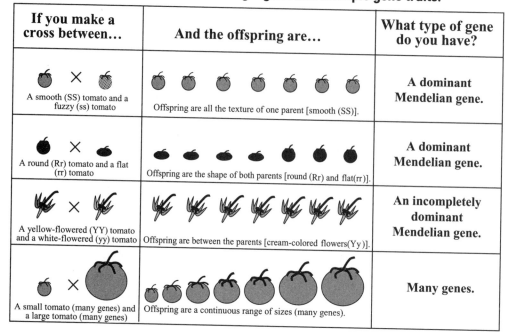

If you make a cross between...	And the offspring are...	What type of gene do you have?
A smooth (SS) tomato and a fuzzy (ss) tomato	Offspring are all the texture of one parent [smooth (SS)].	A dominant Mendelian gene.
A round (Rr) tomato and a flat (rr) tomato	Offspring are the shape of both parents [round (Rr) and flat(rr)].	A dominant Mendelian gene.
A yellow-flowered (YY) tomato and a white-flowered (yy) tomato	Offspring are between the parents [cream-colored flowers(Yy)].	An incompletely dominant Mendelian gene.
A small tomato (many genes) and a large tomato (many genes)	Offspring are a continuous range of sizes (many genes).	Many genes.

A **Mendelian trait** is controlled by a single gene. Mendelian traits can be **dominant**, **recessive**, or **incompletely dominant**.

Quantitative traits are controlled by many genes.

Sci**LINKS**.
THE WORLD'S A CLICK AWAY

Topic: Genome Research
Go to: *www.sciLINKS.org*
Code: GG28

looked at the offspring. This approach worked well with single-gene, **Mendelian traits**. For example in Figure 9.2, when a mutant fuzzy-skinned tomato crossed with a normal smooth-skinned tomato, and all the offspring have the smooth-skinned phenotype of one parent, it is a clear case of **dominance**. If a mutant flattened tomato is crossed with a normal round tomato and the offspring have both the flat and round phenotypes of the parents, the situation is equally clear, and also indicates a dominant gene. A third single-gene scenario, **incomplete dominance**, allows for three phenotypes: the parental yellow-flowered and white-flowered as well as cream-flower offspring.

However, things are not always so simple! What happens when a cross of a small tomato and a large tomato gives offspring that range in size from small to large, with many sizes in between? The situation can no longer be explained by one gene. Suddenly, plant breeders are trying to understand the behavior of many genes, all acting together to create one phenotype. Until quite recently, plant breeders and scientists didn't have the tools to find the different genes involved and separate the effects of each.

New techniques

Why can't plant breeders simply look at a plant's DNA to find the multiple genes involved in quantitative traits? Unfortunately, DNA is not something we can see easily. With a microscope, you can sometimes see chromosomes, but not genes or DNA. Even if you could see DNA, what would a gene look like? DNA is just a sequence of base pairs. There is no visible information in those base pairs about which sections of DNA are coded into proteins and which are not. Only 28% of a tomato's total DNA, or **genome**, is actually in genes. The rest is **non-coding** DNA that we don't understand well. Some people call it "junk" DNA, though it likely serves an unknown purpose.

Furthermore, there is a lot of DNA! A tomato has 637 million base pairs. Compared to other organisms in Table 9.1, like corn or humans, that is a small genome. However, it would still take years to carefully examine every gene.

So scientists have come up with a short cut. They use **genetic markers** (also called molecular markers) to focus in on sections of DNA, instead of trying to look at every base pair. These markers are the equivalent of bookmarks placed throughout the plant's genome. They are short (50–500 base pairs) sequences of DNA, usually at known places on the plant's chromosomes. Markers allow scientists to narrow down the locations of genes.

Table 9.1. Genome size.

Organism	Genome size
bean	637 Mb
tomato	**953 Mb**
chicken	1,130 Mb
corn	**2,671 Mb**
peanut	2,800 Mb
mouse	3,010 Mb
human	**3,190 Mb**
pea	4,000 Mb
grasshopper	13,400 Mb
wheat	16,979 Mb
lily	124,852 Mb

Some DNA **codes** for genes that make proteins. Other DNA is **non-coding**.

A **genome** is an organism's complete DNA, including both genes and non-coding DNA.

Genetic markers are short sequences of DNA in an organism's genome.

Topic: Genes and Chromosomes
Go to: *www.sciLINKS.org*
Code: GG29

WHY ARE GENETIC MARKERS CALLED MARKERS?

Historically, plant breeders used visible phenotypes, like purple-colored leaves, to "mark" desirable invisible phenotypes, like resistance to a disease. These "markers" were rare—occurring, for example, only when the genes for purple-colored leaves and disease resistance were located close together on the chromosomes.

Genetic markers also mark phenotypes, but in this case, the marker does not cause a phenotype of its own. It is just a section of DNA, probably not in a gene, chosen because the sequence of its end points and its location are known (Figure 9.3). Instead of looking at all of the roughly 79 million base pairs of DNA on a chromosome, researchers can look at short sections of about 500 base pairs of DNA in 10 marker locations. Because the genetic markers are DNA, at the marker location, an individual will have an "allele." The individual could have one of up to four alleles—up to two from the mother and up to two from the father. The roughly 7 million unknown base pairs of DNA in between markers are called bins.

Figure 9.3. Tomato genetic markers.

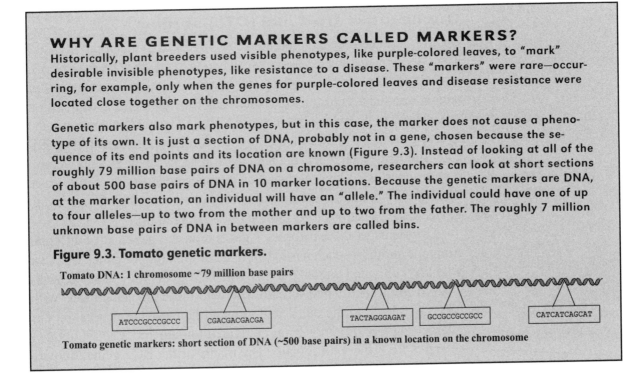

Tomato DNA: 1 chromosome ~79 million base pairs

| ATCCCGCCCGCCC | CGACGACGACGA | | TACTAGGGAGAT | GCCGCCGCCGCC | CATCATCAGCAT |

Tomato genetic markers: short section of DNA (~500 base pairs) in a known location on the chromosome

The area between genetic markers is called a **bin**.

Chromosomes are long strands of DNA. Tomatoes have 12 pairs of chromosomes, corn has 10 pairs, and humans have 23 pairs.

Tomatoes have 12 **chromosomes**, shown on the map in Figure 9.4. Chromosome 1 shows nine markers, labelled m1 through m9, and represented by a bar across the chromosome. Between the markers are unknown areas of DNA called **bins**. Markers can have several alleles, just like genes have alleles. The alleles are slightly different lengths of DNA found at the same location. It is these differences at the same location that allow researchers to do quantitative trait loci or QTL studies.

Figure 9.4. Tomato chromosome map with bins. Markers are only labeled on the first chromosome. Unlabeled markers are represented by bars on other chromosomes.

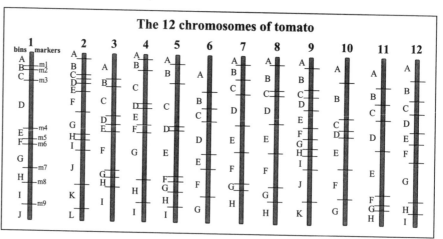

Quantitative trait loci (QTL) studies

So how do plant breeders find the genes involved in quantitative traits? They begin by making a cross between two very different types of plants. For example, researchers interested in genes involved in tomato fruit weight crossed a wild tomato (which has tiny, green tomatoes) with a cultivated tomato (which has large, red fruits) The next generation is the hybrid generation (also called F1 generation), where plants are genetically similar to each other (but not identical, because the parents weren't homozygous at all loci) and similar in appearance to the wild tomato. The hybrid generation is then crossed back to a cultivated tomato again to create the backcross 1 generation (BC1 generation).

The plants of the backcross 1 generation are genetically different from one another—each has a different combination of genes from the wild and cultivated tomato parents. The BC1 generation is again backcrossed to the cultivated tomato to create the BC2 generation. With each cross back to the cultivated tomato, the resulting generation has a larger number of genes from cultivated tomato and a small number of genes from the wild tomato. The plants of the BC2 generation are each genetically distinct and will show differences in fruit weight, as well as in many other characteristics. The BC2 generation will be more physically and genetically similar to the cultivated tomato than to the wild tomato (see Figure 9.5).

Figure 9.5. QTL study to find tomato fruit size genes.

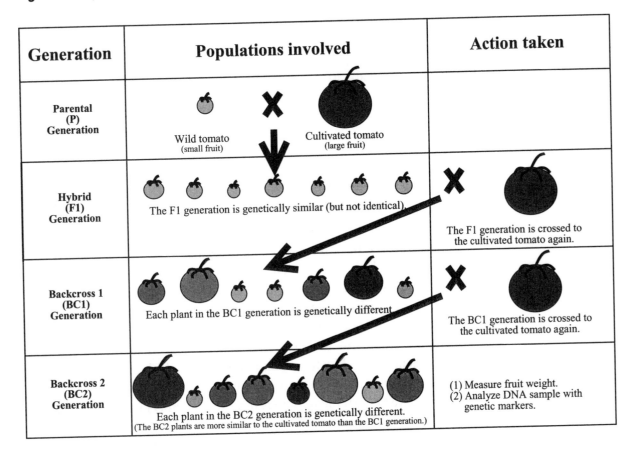

From each plant in the BC2 generation, the researchers take both a measurement of fruit weight and a DNA sample (Figure 9.6). The genetic markers shown in Figure 9.4 are used on the DNA sample from each plant. By comparing each plant's markers and fruit weight, the researchers are able to pinpoint areas of the genome that are associated with fruit weight. In Figure 9.6, markers 1 and 2 always have allele A in heavy tomatoes and always have allele B in light tomatoes. Therefore there is a QTL for fruit weight in the bin between markers 1 and 2. Because there are 107 markers, finding these associations requires powerful computers and complicated statistics. (Another reason these studies couldn't be done until recently!)

Figure 9.6. Measurements and DNA analysis on BC2 generation.

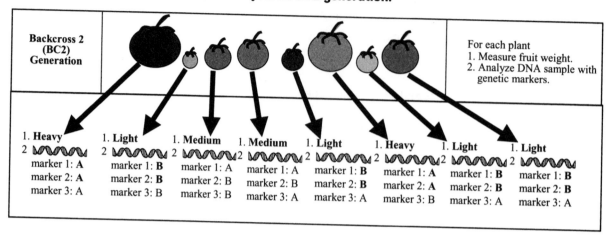

The relationship between marker and fruit weight is only an association—genetic variation near that marker coincides with variation in tomato weight. The markers don't *cause* the variation, but a gene near the marker might.

The results from these quantitative trait locus (QTL) studies are highly specific because they depend on the alleles present in the parents, the markers used to detect them, and the environment in which the plants were grown. In a different tomato population or environment, other genes might be involved. To control for the highly specific results, scientists compare plants grown in different environments or compare studies to look for bins that have been identified multiple times as having QTLs for a trait like fruit size. If the same QTL shows up in multiple studies, it is more likely to be important.

Scientists studying tomatoes have looked at QTLs for fruit weight, fruit shape, and fruit color, as well as flavor and sweetness (Table 9.2). In all cases, many genes are involved. For example, 28 different QTLs were associated with fruit weight in at least two studies.

Table 9.2. Examples of QTL studies in tomato.

Trait	QTLs appearing in more than two studies	Major QTLs (>20% in at least one study)
Fruit weight	28 QTLs	6 major QTLs
Fruit shape	11 QTLs	5 major QTLs
Fruit color (lycopene)	8 QTLs	1 major QTL

Figure 9.7. QTLs, variation, and QTLs of major effect.

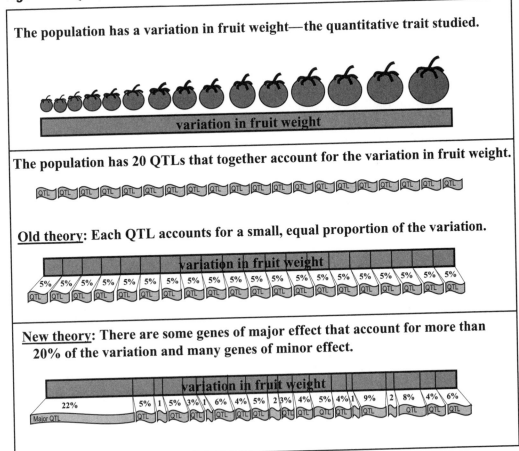

Genes of major effect

Historically, scientists believed that quantitative traits were controlled by many genes, all contributing equally to the phenotype (Figure 9.7). Data from QTL studies show that most QTLs do not account for more than 20% of the variation in a trait. However, it is common to discover one or two QTLs that account for larger amounts of the variation (up to 70%). These QTLs are called **major QTLs**. Six of the fruit weight QTLs in Table 9.2 are major in at least one study. That means that though there may be many genes involved in a trait like fruit weight, some genes have greater effects than others. How? Researchers are only beginning to understand the function of the proteins that these genes encode and how they interact with one another to produce quantitative traits.

In the case of tomato fruit weight, one major QTL, called fw2.2, accounts for about 30% of the variation. All large-fruited tomato varieties have one version, while all small-fruited varieties have a different version of the QTL. When crossed, the small-fruit allele was

A major QTL accounts for more than 20% of the variation in a trait.

Topic: Genome Mapping
Go to: www.sciLINKS.org
Code: GG30

somewhat dominant (remember there are lots of other genes involved also) to the large-fruit allele. When you consider that dozens of QTLs are involved, 30% is a very big proportion! If each of the 28 QTLs from Table 9.2 accounted for an equal proportion of the variation in fruit weight, each would contribute 3.6% of the variation. Therefore, a QTL that accounts for 30% of the variation indicates the presence of an important gene.

Naturally, people wanted to know how this important gene worked. But first they had to find it. The early QTL studies located fw2.2 in bin B on chromosome 2. But that bin contained millions of DNA base pairs. Further studies zoomed in closer and closer (Figure 9.8) until researchers could identify "Candidate gene A," a 1.8 kb (1,800 base pairs) section of DNA. But how could they be sure that this was the important fruit weight gene?

To prove they had found the gene, scientists did something very clever. They copied the "small-fruit-causing" version of the gene and used genetic engineering to insert it into a "large-fruit-type" tomato plant. When the previously large-fruit-type plants grew only small fruit (under identical conditions) the researchers knew they had found the fruit weight gene they were looking for!

Figure 9.8. Fine mapping studies zoom in on the region with the major fw2.2 gene or genes for fruit weight.

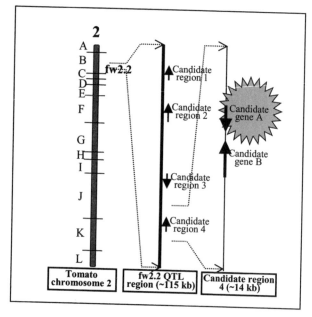

Genetic sequence is the reading of base pairs in a section of DNA (for example, ACGGG...).

Fw2.2 does *what*?

At that point, researchers knew the DNA sequence of the gene. Using powerful databases, they were able to compare fw2.2 to other **genetic sequences** from plants and animals (see Activity 2 for more details). One sequence in the database matched fw2.2 closely. To everyone's surprise, the matching gene was a gene involved in human cancer. How could that be possible? It seemed ridiculous until people compared the effects of both genes.

The small-fruit allele appears to be a protein that regulates cell division. In small tomatoes, the gene switches cell division in the fruit on and off. Evolutionarily, this makes sense. The small fruits are large enough to contain hundreds of seeds, and small enough to be transported by birds or rodents. From the tomato's perspective, there is no reason to invest in making larger fruits. Especially if further investment makes the fruits too big to be transported by birds and rodents!

The large-fruit allele disables the protein that stops cell division. In other words, large tomatoes have many more cell divisions than small ones. Cancer is also often the result of unregulated cell division. It's remarkable that a similar process can have such different effects!

The fw2.2 gene has importance beyond just tomato weight. Remember that one of the important differences between wild tomatoes and the domesticated tomatoes that grow in our gardens is fruit size. When humans began to select wild tomatoes for characteristics that appeal to us, fruit size was at the top of the list! Remember that all large tomatoes have one version of fw2.2 while all small tomatoes have another. In other words, fw2.2 is an important gene in the evolution and domestication of cultivated tomatoes.

Review

The interesting and important gene fw2.2 was discovered through a QTL study. QTL studies are a way of investigating quantitative traits, where many genes have an effect on a trait. Until recently, it was difficult to pinpoint the genes involved in quantitative traits. With powerful computers and DNA markers, QTL studies are now possible. The fw2.2 gene accounts for 30% of the variation in fruit weight. That's a large amount considering the dozens of genes involved in controlling fruit weight. However, that still leaves 70% of the variation controlled by the many other genes.

Questions for further thought

<u>Mendelian genetics:</u> What would happen if a true-breeding fuzzy, flat tomato was crossed with a true-breeding smooth, round tomato (see Figure 9.2)?

<u>Quantitative genetics:</u> When researchers were testing to be sure they had found fw2.2, why did they take the small-fruit-causing gene and put it into a large-fruit plant? (Remember that the small-fruit allele was somewhat dominant to the large-fruit allele.)

Activity 9.
Mapping Tomato Color

Objective
To map the results from a QTL study of color in tomato in order to understand the genetics of tomato color.

Materials
- Colored pens or pencils

Background
The study of color in plants is more important than you might think! Plant pigments have impacts on human health, as well as on the plant's ability to capture sunlight and protect its tissues. In tomatoes, as in many other plants, color is determined by a group of pigments called carotenoids. Carotenoids are familiar to us as vitamins and nutritional supplements. Beta-carotene, a carotenoid, is a precursor to Vitamin A and is responsible for yellow color in carrots, squash, and sweet potatoes. Lycopene is the carotenoid pigment that makes tomatoes red. Lycopene has recently been in the news for its antioxidant properties, which may be important for healthy hearts.

Color pigments also play an important role in plants. Chlorophyll, which captures the Sun's energy to convert carbon dioxide (CO_2) into sugars, is one such pigment. Other pigments help protect the plant from damage caused by the Sun's light—sunlight can harm plant tissues just like it can harm human skin.

Because of the importance of carotenoids to humans and plants, scientists have studied the biochemical pathways involved in making them. Figure 9.9 shows the tomato carotenoid biochemical pathway. The arrows represent enzymes—the actors within the cell that convert one pigment into the next. An enzyme converts phytoene into gamma-carotene. Another enzyme is responsible for converting that into lycopene.

Many pigments and enzymes are involved in determining tomato color. And many genes are involved in making those pigments and enzymes. (Pigments and enzymes are just proteins, after all. And genes encode proteins.) Therefore, it is not surprising that color in tomatoes is a quantitative trait.

Figure 9.9. Biochemical pathway for color pigments phytoene, gamma-carotene, lycopene, delta-carotene, and beta-carotene.

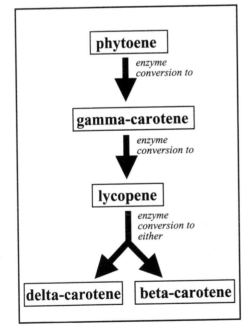

Activity

Part I. QTL study

Since color is an important trait, it's not surprising that plant breeders were interested in understanding where the many color genes could be found in the tomato genome. To find the color genes, plant breeders did a QTL study.

1. The first step was to make a cross. Since this study was about color, what important difference must have existed between the two parents they crossed?

Figure 9.10. QTL study to find tomato color genes.

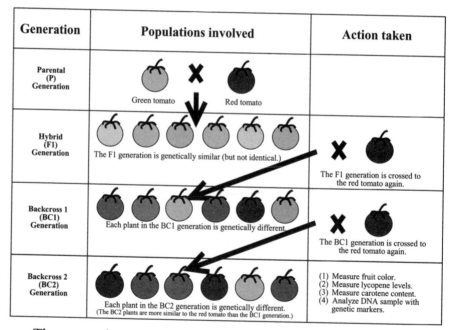

Generation	Populations involved	Action taken
Parental (P) Generation	Green tomato ✗ Red tomato	
Hybrid (F1) Generation	The F1 generation is genetically similar (but not identical.)	The F1 generation is crossed to the red tomato again.
Backcross 1 (BC1) Generation	Each plant in the BC1 generation is genetically different.	The BC1 generation is crossed to the red tomato again.
Backcross 2 (BC2) Generation	Each plant in the BC2 generation is genetically different. (The BC2 plants are more similar to the red tomato than the BC1 generation.)	(1) Measure fruit color. (2) Measure lycopene levels. (3) Measure carotene content. (4) Analyze DNA sample with genetic markers.

A **spectrophotometer** measures light intensity and color (or more specifically, the wavelength of light).

The researchers crossed a wild tomato relative with green fruits and a commercial tomato variety called M82 with red fruits (Figure 9.10). Interestingly, wild relatives have useful genes to improve characteristics like color, even though their own color is not desirable in commercial tomatoes. The researchers grew the F1 and BC1 generations, making the crosses shown in Figure 9.10 until they reached the BC2 generation.

Next, the researchers needed to measure the BC2 generation for color, lycopene content, and carotene content—the traits of interest in this study. Lycopene and carotene are measured by grinding up the tomato, separating the compounds chemically, and measuring lycopene and carotene content with a **spectrophotometer**. To measure color, they used a scale from 1 to 5 where 1 = yellow, 2 = orange, 3 = light red, 4 = red, and 5 = dark red.

- A + sign indicates the QTL is associated with redder color, more lycopene, or more carotene.

- A − sign indicates the QTL is associated with less color, less lycopene, or less carotene.

- Multiple + or − signs (+++, or −−) indicate a stronger association.

Chromosomal bin locations for:		
Color	**Lycopene**	**Carotene**
2C (−)	2K (+)	10E (++)
2K (+)	3C (−−)	12C (++++)
3C (−−)	5A (+)	
4F (−)	6A (+)	
4H (+)	11A (+)	
6A (+)	12B (+)	
6E (−)	12C (−−)	
7B (−)		
7F (+)		
8C (+)		
8E (−)		
8F (−)		
9G (+)		
10B (+)		
10E (−)		
11B (+)		
12C (−−)		
12H (−)		

The next step was to look for QTLs associated with tomato color, lycopene, and carotene levels. The list to the right shows the locations on the tomato chromosome map (QTLs) that are associated with color, lycopene, and carotene levels in the tomato crosses. The QTLs can be associated with positive values for the trait (redder color, more lycopene, or more carotene) or negative values for the trait (less red color, lower lycopene or carotene levels). Some associations are stronger than others. In the list, stronger association between QTL and trait are shown with more + or − signs.

2. Use the list and the map of tomato's 12 chromosomes in Figure 9.11 to map QTLs for color, lycopene, and carotene. Draw the color QTLs in red, lycopene QTLs in green, and carotene QTLs in blue on the map. Use multiple + or − signs to show strength of the association.

Figure 9.11. Chromosome map for exercise: Student Version

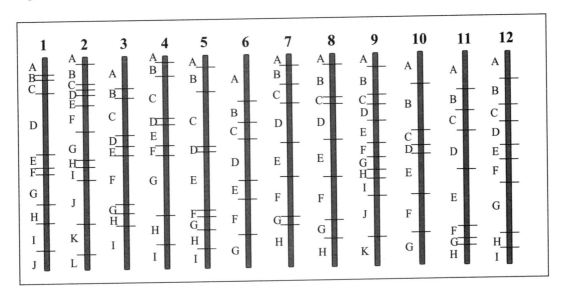

- In Figure 9.11, each vertical line represents a chromosome.
- Each dash represents a genetic **marker**.
- The letters indicate **bins**, or regions, associated with traits.
- For example, a trait found in bin 2K is on chromosome 2, between the 10th and 11th markers.

3. Each QTL is a section of DNA associated with a trait. What does the DNA contain at each QTL?

4. Look at bin 2K on the chromosome map. This bin is associated with a QTL for both color AND lycopene. Find two other locations with more than one QTL.

5. At the places with more than one QTL, might you find one gene or many genes?

   5a. Could one gene have an effect on more than one trait (lycopene and color, for example)? Why or why not?

   5b. These maps have a very big scale. Is it possible to know for sure at this scale whether a bin (2K, for example) contains one gene or several genes?

6. Would you expect to find the same results if you crossed a different red tomato with a different green tomato and grew them under the same environmental conditions? Why or why not?

7. Would you expect to find some of these same results in another population or another location? Why or why not?

Part II. Verification

The QTL study gives you a good idea where to look for genes affecting color in tomatoes. But what exactly are these genes and what do they do? Let's return for a moment to the biochemical pathway affecting the color pigments in tomato. Using mutants and traditional plant breeding techniques, geneticists have identified some genes involved in the pathway. The effects of some of these genes have been known for 100 years. However, scientists have not always known their precise location or their genetic sequence.

Figure 9.12. Biochemical pathway for color pigments in tomato, with mutant genes.

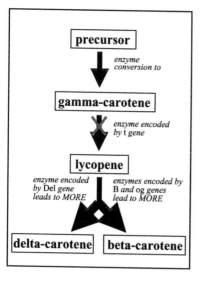

A gene called *t* (for the *t*angerine color it causes) blocks the conversion of gamma-carotene into lycopene (indicated by the X mark on Figure 9.12). Therefore it's not surprising that tomatoes with a mutant *t* gene are orange instead of red. The biochemical pathway would be blocked (probably because the mutant *t* gene codes for a defective copy of an enzyme) and plants would have lots of gamma-carotene but very little lycopene. Remember, lycopene is the pigment that makes tomatoes red. In much the same way, the *Del* gene (named for its high levels of *Del*ta-carotene) causes greater than normal conversion of lycopene into delta-carotene. Thus a plant with a *Del* gene would have high levels of delta-carotene and low levels of lycopene and would be more yellow than red. The *B* and *og* (named for high levels of *beta*-carotene and for the tomatoes *old-gold* color) lead to higher than normal conversion from lycopene into beta-carotene.

8. Using information from the QTL study, where would you predict you might find the *t* gene on the tomato genetic map? Why? (Hint: Tomatoes with the *t* phenotype would have <u>low</u> levels of what compound?)

9. Using information from the QTL study, where would you predict you might find the *Del* gene on the tomato genetic map? Why? (Hint: Tomatoes with the *Del* phenotype would have <u>low</u> levels of what compound?)

10. Using information from the QTL study, where would you predict you might find the *B* and *og* genes on the tomato genetic map? Why? (Hint: Tomatoes with the *B* or *og* phenotype would have <u>low</u> levels of what compound?)

11. Table 9.3 contains the chromosomal locations for the mutant genes in the pigment pathways. Fill in table with the QTLs associated with each bin where the gene is located.

Table 9.3. Chromosome locations for genes in the color pigment pathway in tomatoes.

Gene	Chromosomal bin	Associated QTL(s)
t	10E	
Del	12C	
B	6E	
og	4E	

12. Record the locations of the genes in Table 9.3 on the chromosomal map. Which of the mutant genes coincide with QTLs in the color pathway?

13. Make a hypothesis (an educated guess) about what is happening at one of these QTLs.

14. What would you need to do to TEST your hypothesis? (Hint: Look at the fw2.2 example in the text.)

15. Do any of the mutant genes NOT coincide with QTLs in the color pathway? If so, describe why there might not be a relationship between a mutant gene and QTL.

16. What can you conclude from this exercise about quantitative traits and QTL studies? (Are they useful? What can they tell you? Why do people do them?)